Practical Vampires

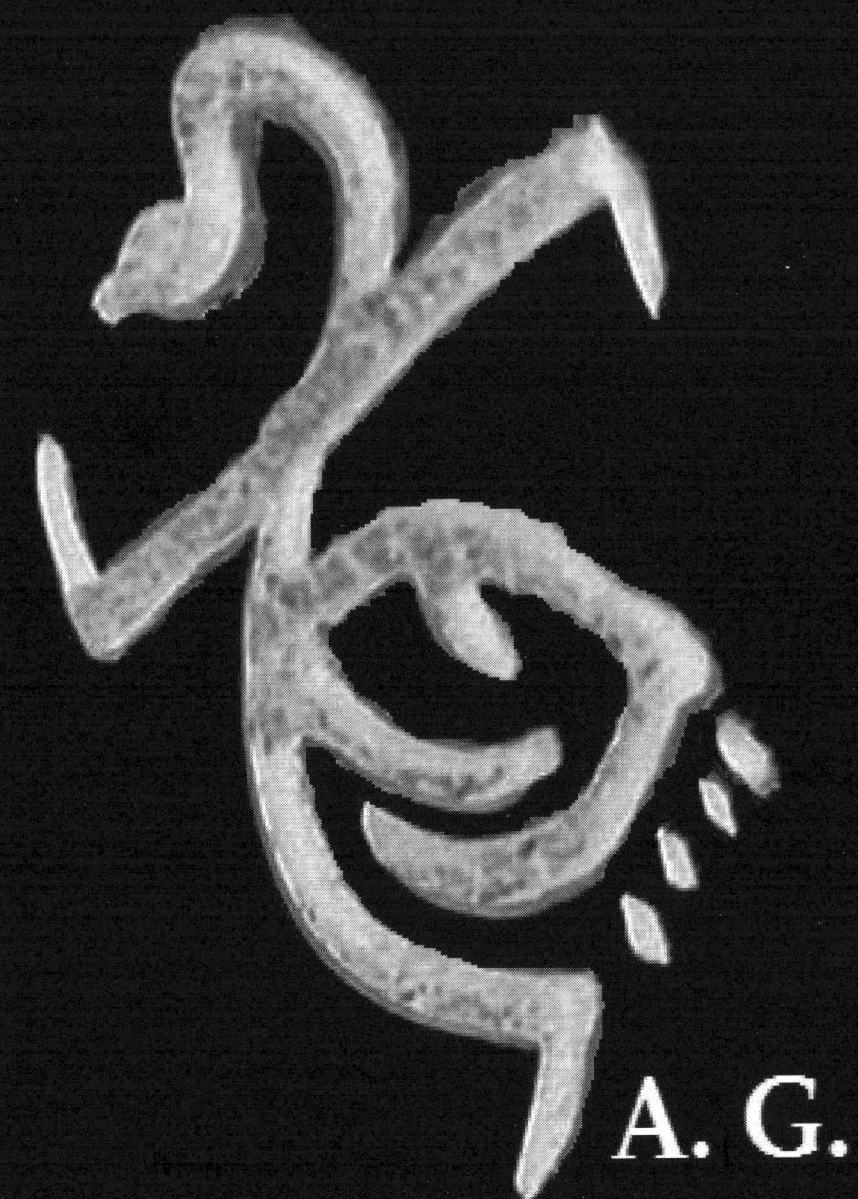

A. G. Sire

Practical Vampires

A. G. Sire

All rights reserved. No part of this book may be reproduced or transmitted in any form or by any means, electronic, mechanical, including photocopying, recording or by any information storage and retrieval system, without written permission from the author, except for the inclusion brief quotations in a review

Copyright © 2012 by A. G. Sire

First Edition, 2012 Freedom Network. Published in the United Kingdom

ISBN 978-1-291-01762-5

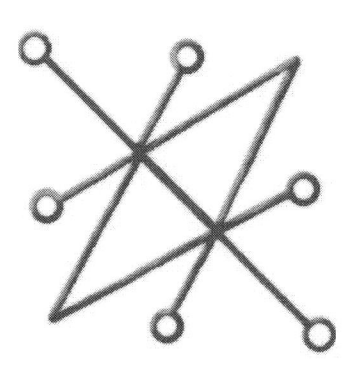

In the beginning was the end

For in the end there was war, famine, and disease - As I reached out to man to save, yet they were not in need of a saviour, they were in need of an education, the truth beyond the walls of corruption, whereby greed had taken over every living thing

'For now is the time and this is the hour.'

Listings

1. Dedication — P.2 – P.3
2. Listings — P.4 – P.5
3. The Human Species — P.6 – P.8
4. Demons and Angels — P.9 – P.12
5. Vampiric Law — P.13 – P.13
6. Vampiric Ethics — P.14 – P.17
7. Rites of Passage — P.18 – P.18
8. The Rite of Dedication — P.19 – P.19
9. **First Generation** — **P.20 – P.51**

10. **Second Generation** — **P.52 – P.94**
11. Vampirism — P.82 – P.86
12. Pranic Healing — P.87 – P.91
13. Akhkharu Language — P.92 – P.94

14. **Third Generation** — **P.95 – P.161**
15. Thamuz as Mary Magdalene — P.122 – P.127
16. Enki as Jesus — P.128 – P.130
17. Tablet of Destinies — P.131 – P.133
18. The Power of Garnet — P.134 – P.134
19. Pendulum workings with Garnet — P.135 – P.141
20. Vampiric Law — P.142 – P.142
21. Vampiric Ethics — P.143 – P.148
22. The Nine Gates — P.149 – P.155
23. Azazel Perspective — P.156 – P.161

Fourth Generation — **P.162 – P.202**
24. The Celestial Alphabet — P.181 – P.181
25. The Seven Angels — P.182 – P.186
26. Dark Matter – Sulgi — P.187 – P.191
27. The Yazidis — P.192 – P.196
28. Charging the Buzur Agga — P.197 – P.198
29. Working for Azazel — P.199 – P.202

30.	**Fifth Generation**	**P.203 – P.248**
31.	Akhkharu Law	P.217 – P.222
32.	Gehenna Commitment	P.223 – P.226
33.	The Fallen Angel	P.227 – P.238
34.	The Djinn	P.239 – P.243
35.	The Charge of the Vampire	P.244 – P.248
	Sixth Generation	**P.249 – P.295**
36.	The Rite of Zade	P.263 – P.273
37.	The Legacy	P.274 – P.282
38.	Dragon Spirits	P.283 – P.286
39.	The Power of Practice	P.287 – P.292
40.	The Advancement of Truth	P.293 – P.295

This book is dedicated to the true one of space and time, that flow of energy that once learned to master will be forever encircled

Revelation 13:18 the number of the beast, for it is the number of 'Man' and his number is 666

Revelation 13:1 and now in my vision I saw a beast rising up out of the sea, it had seven heads and seven horns for the world is an illusion and matter does not exist for the race of the future are a generation whose teeth are as swords and blacken the hearts of men

In the Order of the Dragon lies the Son of the Dragon in wait. This son is from the land beyond the forest, the forgotten forest, for mark well the sands of time as the Day of Judgment is a stone in the sea away

The Human Species – Mostly Pointless

An interesting subject area, full of total selfish, self-centered lifestyles, in fact, if one of their own species were to collapse in their community, in their street, more than 97% of them would not assist. It is the general assumption of this species to consider how their environment affects them directly.

In other words, they would not think twice to aid or assist their own kind. Most of their time is consumed with the 'Me' syndrome with common factors within their insular self-fulfilling world.

Having observed this species for a considerable number of years, it is clearly identified as harmful. Harmful to the planet they reside on, more importantly; seriously harmful towards each other, not to mention the other planet dwellers, such as animalistic sub-species.

Most humans consider themselves 'good citizens' – However, this is purely their own perception within their 'fabricated' world. They seem to have a strange definition of 'good', oftentimes making what they consider to be 'noble decisions' to harm, slaughter, or totally obliterate any civilisation or culture that somehow has a slightly 'different' view of how to live within their own country.

In fact, their species has not really evolved over such a length of time, merely retracted back to animalistic behaviour bordering cannibalism. Many have noted their keen desire to wrongly support the extended life cycle of species that should be extinct.

Sadly, their only reason to undertake such an arduous task is once again, reflected back to the 'Me' syndrome, whereby they assist in controlling the evolution of animals purely for their own gain of consuming them and making the most odd garments out of their skin and hair, a practice that has stayed with them since the previous abandonment.

It is hardly surprising that their kind continue to spread like a disease across this watery planet, consuming, destroying, and drinking all within their path. Not only are these humans destroying their own environment around them, they horde the most precious fuel amongst them, such forms of gold and gold gas, even noted to have such items in a way of 'fashionable' jewellery merely to satisfy their own pleasures.

It is interesting that each human considers the material items around them to be more valuable than their own species existence and continuance. Most humans would prefer to purchase gold and other non-living items, than assist others of their own kind to enjoy the basics of existence such as food, water, and sanitation. In fact the general human thought process exists of 'It doesn't effect me, it doesn't effect the ones I profess to love, and I don't really see or experience it, so I'll just ignore it'.

Con-currently nearly a third of this planets occupants with the human species are suffering with lack of food and water, yet those whom have survived merely for their own self-gratification and worship of their 'Neon God', are happy to contribute the odd one pound of their monies to what they term as charity, just to make themselves feel that little bit better.

In fact, this species is so depleted and suppressed of energy within; they have truly forgotten the purpose of life and existence within. They merely live for the moment with a deep though of 'I'll do it because I can'.

Interesting as it is, this species has forgotten their natural cycle of longevity, so much so that they appear content in oftentimes to leave this planet and cease to exist anytime from 55 to 75 years of age on average. There is a classic human phrase resounding in every culture and religion, those famous words are 'Well they had a good innings'. Such a term is applied by this species when one of their own dies, ceases to exist. An interesting concept that such a creature accepts with cause or reason to agree that 75 earth years is acceptable for an individual's survival in what they term as life.

If such terms and comments were fiction, it would almost be amusing that not only this species accept their death, they go to great lengths to adorn the shell of their dead with an abundance of precious jewellery, wood, and cut shaped flowers. Somehow within their evolution (or not), they have come to consider that the greater volume of monies spent on such an occasion makes it rather 'nice' inverted commas.

Not only is this species content with removing this planet's essential chemicals and substances, such as gas, oil, and minerals – They continue to undertake war with each other in ways that go far beyond our comprehension. It is interesting that they continue to create machinery that is purely designed to make lands toxic and destroy all living creatures and plant life within certain as they class 'acceptable' areas.

In oftentimes, this species ensures the use of communication to install and enhance the propaganda of their belief systems so to gain the support of others whom reside near to them. It is noted that they often make good use of their Neon God's fabricated words in ways that entices their species to almost accept that to destroy their own kind is perfectly fine, I mean, of course, their God would surely accept and honour this, wouldn't he?

This brings us onto the old clichés of the 'should of, could of, would of' after all this species seems to have a sense of intelligence, though a little disjointed and often remote. Man himself spends the majority of his limited brain capacity in a state of imagination and synthetic creativity. This they refer to as 'dreams or goals', to which they place a significant amount of pressure upon. The dreams and aspirations are installed into their young and manipulated throughout their short raising to adulthood, which contrary to other existence; they class their adulthood as 16 to 18 Earth years.

Strangely, in our terms that makes them 54 'Cinak' – Hardly a point of reference to expect this animalistic race to actually make informed and logical decisions. Yet, they continue to operate in this way and ensure that there are key recognitions of age, with the celebration of what that refer to as a 'Birthday'.

The human expects to receive recognition of their false wisdom at 54 Cinak, often referring to the fact that they are classed as adulthood and able to make all decisions on life, death, and their own belief's, albeit totally misinformed and utterly mislead. This does not stop the human however, such humans continue to accept that mating with their opposite gender is the only way. In fact, they are so 'insular' that they created their own dogma stating that mating with the opposite gender is wrong and in some parts of this planet still considered to be 'unlawful'. Such species takes great delight in separating their concept of right and wrong, irrespective of how such individual energies actually work in harmony with each other.

Primitive as this species is, it continues to mock the universal law by ensuring that its planet as a whole remains in pure darkness as to their reason for creation in the first place. It is even known that they believe their Neon God to have created them in his alleged own image. What is clear from this general assessment of their race is that there is around 3% of their race that actually believes in more and is able to attune to the said powers of wisdom, although many remain in darkness by their own choosing.

All in all a pointless existence filled with total fabricated viewpoints and ridiculous justifications for their own mislead actions. It is no surprise that their race will in time be reduced back to 500 million, and we only hope and pray that those select few will once more attempt to bring order from chaos, structure from anarchy, and peace from war.

Demons and Angels

For even the Angels will mark themselves as Demons, and the Demons as Angels themselves. An interesting point, whereas most in the world consider the Angel and the Demon to be individual entities, this could not be further from the truth.

Our House Master is both a Demon and an Angel. They are inseparable, one and the same. Raphael as he is truly known administers the knowledge of the Old Ways of the Vampire in ways that leave nothing to the imagination. He is both an able shepherd, able to assist, teach, guide, and devote time to the learning of others, yet is at the same time an able slayer; being positioned with knowledge and attributes that allow him to defend the Old Ways by any means of his choosing.

A character of plenty, and a master of disguise, Raphael certainly knows how inspire to allies and followers alike. However, if Raphael is also an Angel, in particular an Archangel, what does this truly mean?

Archangel, a term used to describe the true form of those whom walk amongst us. Such forms of origin are Nephilim; a Celestial Being within the Order known as the Keepers. Responsible for ministering to humans, and oversee the responsibilities of what are widely known as 'Guardian Angels' and the other Celestial Light Beings that act as our guardians and guides. Each Archangel or rather, 'Keeper' has specific qualities that distinguish their characteristics and their specific angelic responsibilities.
Archangel Raphael's realm of angelic expertise resides within Health & Healing. Raphael's healing domain is all encompassing, physical, mental, emotional, spiritual, and energetic health.

This Archangel is dedicated to our realising and maintaining our True and Natural State of Wellness, helping us to remember that our True Essence is Healthy, Whole and Complete.

Raphael's healing compass is attuned to human healing and to healing domestic and wild animals. Raphael is a steadfast and devoted angelic ally who will provide healing support to any/all those who call upon him. There is no request that could be considered too grand nor is there a request that would ever be deemed insignificant.

Raphael is dedicated to helping alleviate any and all illness, injury, pain, suffering, discomfort, imbalance, etc. so that we may be healthy, happy and balanced within body, mind and spirit.

Archangel Raphael is also an Angelic Mentor and Guide to those working within any aspect of Healthcare, traditional or alternative, including those working in any aspect of animal health. Additionally, Raphael will provide mentoring to students studying any aspect of healthcare, traditional or alternative, human or animal. Whether it is our doctors, surgeons, nurses, lab technicians, energy healers, dietitians, dentists, personal trainers, veterinarians, veterinarian assistants/technicians, physical, mental and/or emotional therapists, Raphael will respond to a request to guide and inspire those responsible for our personal healthcare. Always honoring the Law of Free Will, he will lend healing inspiration and divine guidance to those responsible for our healthcare, providing guidance toward realizing our optimum health and well being. Upon our request and invitation, this Angelic Health Care Ambassador will also help guide us to a healthcare professional that we will best resonate with and with those whose services will be in alignment with our healing needs.

Upon our invitation, Raphael will also work with us personally and directly toward self-healing. He will assist in the reawakening of our own natural healing abilities, as well as to remind us that through our Oneness with the Divine Universal Source, we are one with the Power of Miraculous Healing. Raphael will guide, inspire and mentor us toward realizing and experiencing our personal intentions for health and well being.

An Angelic Dietitian, an Angelic Personal Trainer, Angelic Sleep Therapist and Angelic Self Care Advisor, Raphael can offer heavenly healing assistance in any area. Upon our request and invitation, he will guide, inspire and motivate us toward healthy eating habits, provide motivation to regularly participate in fun, healthy exercise, align our sleep patterns so that they are restorative and rejuvenating, and will inspire us to generally take over all good care of ourselves. Raphael is an Angelic Ally for those who desire freedom from addictions and cravings.

Upon our request and invitation he will provide healing platforms to release heal and transcend addictions and cravings of any kind. Raphael will guide and inspire us to practice healthy habits that are supportive of our optimum health, happiness and well being.

For Energy Healers and those who desire to practice energetic hygiene, Raphael will guide, support and lend healing energy to clear chakras, cut and clear energetic cords, clear the aura of impurities and repair the auric field. He will provide healing support for any and all aspects of energy healing and energetic hygiene. Raphael will also act as an Angelic Ambassador for Travelers, guiding and protecting those who request his assistance with any aspect of physical travel and/or spiritual journeys. Raphael will also release spirits and clear negative thought forms from our energy and environments.

He is protective and supportive, always demonstrating the infinite love of the Divine Source. Raphael's energy is typically seen as emerald green to humans, with a true form of blue and his presence inspires confidence and trust. Raphael is experienced as loving, gentle, kind, compassionate and friendly and although he takes his angelic responsibilities extremely seriously, he is also fun loving, but Beware. For those whom attempt to trick, harm, or falsely lead will meet with the ultimate form of reaction. Such a reaction is known to but a few on the Earth.

Ode to the Nephilim

O dea tenebris, mater immortalibus, puer tuus fac me sicut renascentur
mea lux vestra absorbere

liceat mihi locus ad tenebras, sicut ex utero immortales
filios tuos in ulnis, quibus invocaverit te frater

O lunae lumen, puer tuus fac me sicut renascentur
me duce tenebris sunt, i ita erit renatus

Oh goddess of the darkness, mother to the immortal
let me be reborn as your child, let your light absorb my own

Allow me passage to the darkness, as from your immortal womb
into the arms of your children, to whom I will call brother

Oh moonlight, let me be reborn as your child, guide the dark ones to me
so I shall be born again

We now have a broad understanding of what a Vampire is; a Vampire is a Demon and Angel. Establishing this fact is your first step into expanding your mind and attributes to learn that which you seek.

You sought and found, and here you are. By the very nature of time and existence you have arrived here, right now. There is no such term as coincidence, for you were meant to be here, meant to be reading this, and by choice alone, you will decide if you wish to read further into this book.

Unlike many, this book will enlighten you with nothing but truth, for it is written with the full knowledge of the Old Ways, ways that only pure blood and the transformed would know. Interesting as it is, you may begin to ask yourself such things as, if it is so real, so pure, and so secret, then why do we seek to publish for all? That answer is the very K.e.y to your wish and want. It is published so that you and others like you are able to find, learn, and then know. Such knowledge is obtainable, within reach, if you wish it to be. The Sanctuary will assist in your teachings and truly enable you to reach your goals and aspirations.

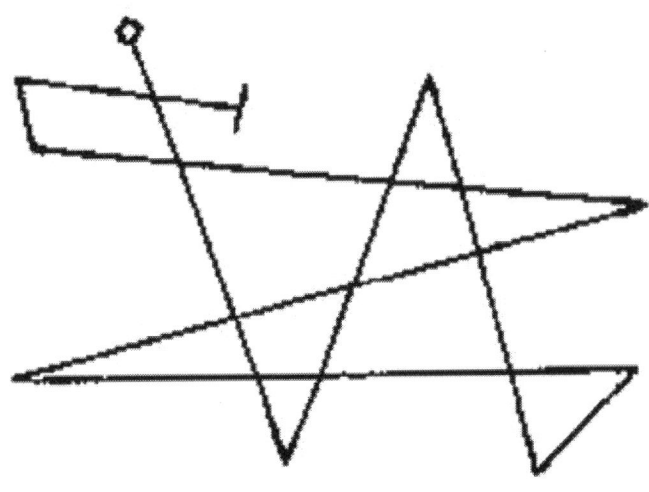

Transformation

Vampiric Law
The Code of existence

1. All work will involve flesh and blood works, of both your own and other consenting members

2. The eating of dead meat is unacceptable (Fish, eggs, milk, and cheese are acceptable)

3. The use of recreational drugs are prohibited (Though cannabis is tolerated)

4. Blood Magic will be performed by all Vampires on a regular basis, there are no exceptions

5. All Vampires and Allies are expected to become part of our Religious Military Order

6. Each Vampire is expected to learn segments, if not all, of our language

7. Our way is a way of life, not just when we meet up

8. It is unacceptable to harm or attempt to harm another Vampire or Allies, unless sanctioned by the Sire

9. It is an expectation that all Vampires and Allies take regular time to refer and recruit new members to our household

10. Not forgetting, that our way of existence is sworn to secrecy. All Vampires and Allies are very aware of consequence

For those seeking to become a Vampire, some pointers below:
1. Do not forget that you are not like Raphael, your were first human
2. Full transformation may take many decades
3. Usually, the first signs of correct transformation are through the eyes
4. The drinking of blood will enhance the process

Vampiric Ethics

Imagine a world where man is able to do as he pleases, a world where man was able to continue to destroy everything he did not understand. This is exactly what Vampiric Magic undertakes, to stop mankind completing the cycle of destruction. By the vary nature of our magic, we are able to influence and make change, positive change.

We undertake change with the use of the magic of a life source - commonly blood. Some of us of pure blood are able to absorb the blood of a living creature (in a non-harmful way), and use it to create our powers of magic.

We are seeking Adna (Vampiric Allies) and Othil (Bond partners, of all sexualities). The Old Ways ensure that all understand that the nature of the beast is bisexual. There are no labels to attach as a true vampire will bond with many over the cycle, male or female at varying times.

Our magic allows us to take control of our own thoughts and feelings, and make a real difference to that which is around us. Welcome to the Sanctuary; a place of refuge, nature, and development. At the sanctuary, we pride ourselves in assuring the strictest confidence about our movements in the world of men.

For it is told that to reveal the secrets of our passion and desire to the unknowledged would create a world of reckoning, leading to the destruction of our own kind.

The Sanctuary welcomes all of the allies, helpers, and of course, bondpartners. We develop our knowledge with the assistance of the Master of our House, who is known as Raphael; a creature of blood and the utmost knowledge of the Old Ways.

Every part and practice will involve the workings of blood - Do not request to become part of us if you are not ready to learn the truth of blood magic and the reasons why blood is essential to our growth

Our Master is one of three distinct house forms. Each house has developed over the centuries, which bring us to the House of our Master, the Sanctuary. This House practices the true Old ways, long before the dilution of scripture.

At The Sanctuary, Raphael ensures that every Adna and Othil is received into the Blood and that in doing so, freely passes some of their own to him, within ritual, within prayer, and within sexual activity. Our Master does not currently perform sexual blood acts with females, though females are always welcome within our House as Allies and Followers.

The Sanctuary meets once a month, but for those whom become a Black Swan (Bond Partners for blood and / or sexual encounters), meets are arranged more frequent, on a regular basis

The Principles
1. To keep secret, that which must be secret
2. To enter into an initiation rite into the Old Ways
3. To support and protect our Master at all costs
4. To freely pass our blood to our Master when he chooses
5. To be ever willing to learn and support the Old Ways
6. To ensure attendance at monthly meets
7. To harm those that attempt to harm us
8. To seek to befriend and guide those who seek guidance

Generally speaking, we practice the Old Ways, but what does this really mean?

The Old Ways go back further than that of modern day thinking, we refer to thousands of years of existence, wars, famine, disease, and pain.

The Pure Bloods know no boundaries to that which they seek and know, always seeking, feeding, and an insurmountable urge to follow their sexual preference to the highest level of euphoria.

Such practices include live feeding, sexual performance, the raising of helpers from beyond the physical realm, drawing down of the sun, moon, and star; finally, the purpose of existence is taught and practiced in the widest form of Voodoo.

Our House Master is both a Demon and an Angel. They are inseparable, one and the same. Raphael as he is truly known administers the knowledge of the Old Ways of the Vampire in ways that leave nothing to the imagination.

He is both an able shepherd, able to assist, teach, guide, and devote time to the learning of others, yet is at the same time an able slayer; being positioned with knowledge and attributes that allow him to defend the Old Ways by any means of his choosing.

A character of plenty and a master of disguise, Raphael certainly knows how to guide allies and followers alike

We seek to enlighten those whom wish to be enlightened, it is therefore no coincidence that you have found yourself here, for you sought and found. The only question remains is do you proceed?

Our main Commandery is in Cambridgeshire, England. To date, this is the main place for study and practice. We are, however, always guarding of our way of life and death. Therefore, we will always make arrangements to meet with you somewhere of our choosing, so to ensure that your intention is true.

On this particular note, we move onwards to the point of your initiation into our Ways. This is something that you have discussed with your mentor at length, are aware of the gifts and curses that are before you, and that a decision has been made collectively, if you shall be initiated in one of two ways:

Othil   Bondpartner of the House Master, not only that of blood
Is given, but further the purpose of sexual activity with the House master, so to attune to your psychic abilities and
Receive the enhancement of knowledge within the inner circle as you progress within our community

Adna   To be received in the House as one of our allies, one of
Friendship and one of the services to the House and to that
of knowledge.

You have found this piece of literature so that you may make your mind and actions known. Our House Master, will of by now, already shared his thoughts as to how he would like to see your initiation. However, this is your choice alone to make. Time will be given for you to reflect and decide on your perfect point of preparation.

Time will now be given for the initiate to accept their rite of initiation. A date and time will now be presented to the initiate and what they will need to prepare.

Rites of Passage

Our rites of passage, rituals, acknowledge the crossing over from one state of knowledge to the next. When such are enacted, we are celebrating a rite of passage that marks a specific transition. Rites of passage help us to structure our thoughts, views, and feelings.. They help us set up the parameters that define one state of knowledge from another. The transitions of Vampiric Magic deserve a formal recognition, and as such ritual adds both meaning and purpose to the experience.

Within our community, there are many rites of passage to be celebrated. There is the initial acceptance into the community, and after that, there are different levels of knowledge and understanding to be attained within the community. As a member learns and grows, he or she passes through childhood to adulthood, with a set of experiences, a set of learning. This transition is important and should be recognised with a rite. Acceptance into a household of real Vampires is another transition unique to our community that can be solemnised with a rite of passage. A Bond-partner is important to many members of our community, but the relationship between a vampire and a donor, while not always a Bond-partner should be solemnised as well. And these are just a few of the rites that have great importance within our community.

All of the following ceremonies make good use of our language and further some that may be familiar to you, such as Sumerian, Magi, and the language of Malak, whom you may know as Jesus in modern times.

The most important points to remember throughout, are being true to our family and be true to yourself.

Becoming part of our community, our family is not something that is taken lightly. It is not something that you do once a month, or perform prayer once a week. It is a fundamental way of life, death, and existence. These aspects are most important to our House Master, Raphael. For he will not tolerate fools amongst us, and is only comfortable to teach those who ensure that our ways become their way of life, death, and existence too.

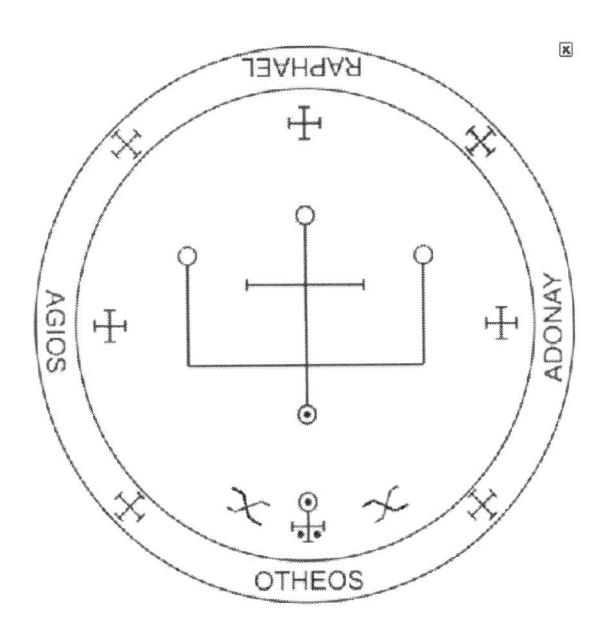

The Rite of Dedication

This is the corner stone of your entrance and recognition within our House. The initiation is one that acknowledges that the initiate wishes to become a part of the community. The person who takes this initiation is formally acknowledged as an Adna, meaning 'one of the allies' or Othil, meaning 'one whom our Master loves'. Although initiate within our ways, the Adna or Othil still remains in the outer circle. This is not a ritual of transformation. That comes later, when the initiate knows a great deal more about Vampiric Magic, and has proven themselves to be worthy of such a gift and curse.

Each initiate must have a sponsor from within the community. After initiation, the sponsor is allowed to teach the initiate the basics of the community and a rite of transformation (from life through death).

Mak Alam Mas Alam

Azazel   Raphael   Shamsiel

First Generation

The Altar Set within the East, holding the Sigil of Raphael, the Sire's personal piece of Garnet, The Sire's personal Sibbu Usbar (Snake Staff), 4 tea candles, 4 small natural liquorice sticks (or similar) set into triangular form (in the centre), Burdock root, Cinnamon, Charged fluid (dependant on occasion), and a Reciprocal of choosing to hold charged fluid.

Identity: Raphael Sigil

Above Centre: Sigil of Raphael (Enki)

Top Left: Burdock root, Cinnamon

Top Right: One Tea Candle

Centre: Three sticks in triangle shape with tea candle at each point
                The fourth stick to be at centre of triangle, and outside

Below Centre: Sibbu Usbar (Snake staff of the conducting Sire)

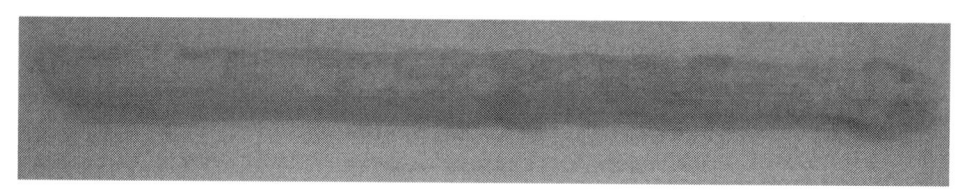

The Nine Gates. It is imperative that although the nine gates are shown here in sequence – That you only cast them open, dependant on your stage of development. Therefore, until notified, you must raise only from the first through to the seventh gate. For at the Eighth Gate, Aiwass awaits to rip the heart from any Magi whom dare pass this way. You will need to learn, and prepare for this journeying, a time of plenty to achieve.

Elder Star

The Knowledge of Potion

Cardinal	Immortal Stone	Of Garnet
1st Gate	Raphael	Of Blood
2nd Gate	Astaroth	Of Burdock Root
3rd Gate	Falacor	Of Cinnamon
4th Gate	Pazuzu	Of Water
5th Gate	Sitri	Of Lavender
6th Gate	Murmur	Of Tea Leaf
7th Gate	Asmoday	Of Salt
8th Gate	Khoronzon	Of Egg Shell
9th Gate	Azazel	Of Rose Petal

It is known as **Cinnabar**, for that is the combination of life and death, the unique composition of Mercury within the individual energy, having the soul of the creature removed and thus all barriers raised. The Cinnabar is in form of block or necklace and will be used within the Abyss in time to follow.

There are three house forms, namely;

The Creation at the left point of the triangle of existence

The Abyss at the right point of the triangle of existence

The Sanctuary at the top point of the triangle of existence

Interesting as it is, the Abyss and the Sanctuary are one and the same. This will be explained in great detail as you journey through the times ahead. However, at this conjuncture we will realise that as there are nine gates, we would assume that to follow, there would be nine **Akhkharu** at each perfect point? This is clearly not the case at all, for the Nine gates have eight Akhkharu. For Raphael is first the teacher at the first gate of acceptance, and as a guide and teacher, remains at the Ninth Gate to test your willingness to travel further to join with Shamsiel, the Highest Sphere. Therefore, the house of Vampires, or rather **Upir Likhyi**, exist for the purpose of destiny, the purpose that those whom come to know will come to dare, and those whom come to dare will know of all within without.

The very nature of time and space, for some they refer to this as the God Particle, to us we know this as **The Tablet of Destinies**, the Dark Magic, the Old Magic, and the Old Ways.

If you truly wish to know, you will. If you are not removed of Soul and Ego, you will not know and diminish, just a times past. The purpose of your journey will be to embrace all, research all, and understand all. On this perilous path, you will encounter danger, and threat to you and your Sire.

Remember that you are stronger that such mortal creatures, for although your transformation may not occur for a millennium, in a thousand years, as you will become an **Adna**, an ally of Raphael and his creatures, you will receive the knowledge of Dark Magic and that which is truth within the Universe. You will give more heed to your conduct and know that you will never be alone, so long as you guard fast your Sire and swear secrecy to us alone.

You will know him as Jesus, his true name and form of **Malak**, for he did say unto the world, that 'so long as you eat my flesh and drink my blood, you shall be saved at the end of time'. Go now and eat the flesh of the 'Son of Man, that which is mortal and not eternal.

As a follower of our ways, Luke 14:26 said 'Hate the mortal world, that if anyone goes to Malak and does not hate their mother, father, brother, sister, then they will never be a 'Son of God' – They cannot be immortal. Truth and Love are eternal, whereas; all that is created is mortal and corruptible. Remember that Falsehood and Hatred are not found amongst us, the Nephilim.

For what person would turn their back upon truth? Rebuke your ways, who do you, love more, the universe or mortals? For if the tide is not given willingly and without resentment, then do not give. Unless you eat the flesh and drink the fluid of the son of man, you have no purpose with us.

Be that of the Ansar, the Spiritual Warrior of the Lord of Space itself. By the **Star and Stone** in form 'Nana ma Adar', for **Shamsiel** will know if you are true, the Highest Sphere will support you or crush you, for this is your choice, your choice alone. Within this House of Vampires, 'Upir Likyi', know this. The **Ennuunkabarra** 'En-nu-un-ka-bar-ra' guard the outer gate of Shemsiel.

So to Earth as you think it is right and proper to continue to consume all that once lived, for this is wrong. At this time, it must end. No more dead meat, no more. Your eventual transformation will depend on this.

The Creation of sequence
Opening Prayer

Kur Dingar, E ina Utu, Nanna, ma Adar

Su'ati annu Piriq, ina Azag

Annu tisa bi er E Gallas

Mamman aga Azag bur annu aka annu wur eri

Underworld God, raise the Sun, Moon, and star

That this the bearer of the magic,

From the shining bright this ninth command to go raise demons.

Whoever crowns the shining bright hear this divine command, this wisdom bind

Sire Karabu er igi mannu Gana ina annu Dalbana. Lu malu zu Inimdug, arammu ma zid ina ma balu. Girigena tia dimmu aradu. Hasusu Menzug Namen ma eribu annu edin

Blessings to those who stand in this space

Let us know peace, love and truth within and without

Path of order descend

Remember your Priesthood and enter this plain

All

Ala ina Ara Aram All within time come forth

Sire summons the L.i.g.h.t

The Calling (point-left-right) Light all Altar candles – Babbar Ugula tia Ugur, Salmu Ugula tia Abalae, Samu Ugula tia Muh, sha Uru menzen

'White overseer of Sword, Black overseer of Stone Red overseer of Chalice, we support you'

Sire

Ar, isatu, ma ganzer – sha sugid ina menzug gigun, da malu ina ugula tia ina gula adhal kima sha andul ina sumer

Light, Fire, and Darkness – We accept the sacred building, make us the overseers of the great secret as we protect the land of the watchers.

	Silig, Quannu, Uri ma Esentu
Hand, Horn, Blood and Bone	Namzu Labaru ma Namzu ban
Wisdom old and wisdom young	Damu tia mulan ma su.en tia gi
Child of star and moon of night	Abba ama ina Anumun ara
Elders strong in waters time	Alka Adullab nigul Igigal
Come with everlasting sight	Ma ak Menzug Aldug Adullab ar
And do your desire with light	

Sire

Sha peta annu dalbana anna zae er tapputtu malu ina parsu. Ama menden zig ma alad menden idu. Menzug ugur tia zid adullab anna ina abula tia ara, kima ina dilibad es tia ina utu udmeda dubsag zae, sha gana menzug fi namen.

We open this space unto you to aid us in religious duties. Strong we stand and spirit we know. Your sword of truth now unto the gate of time, as the shining temple of the sun ever before you, we stand your serpent priesthood.

All

Ala ina Ara Aram All within time come forth

With the Triangle formed upon the Altar, the Sire will call each point in sequence, as the Sire calls, they have grasped within the dominant hand, the stone of Immortality, the stone of Garnet. At each call their grasped hand is held at a forty-five degree angle above the flame

North – Sword

Ina nabu, ina samu alad tia ara, sha uru zae. Barba ina annu gug ma dug da malu. Wasru sha gana, ina fi namen, ullulu annu Susgal ma lu Inimdug ba ina malu.

The past, the red spirit of time, we support you. Break through this seal and speak with us. Humble we stand, the Serpent Priesthood, purify this castle and let peace live through us

Southwest – with chalice

Ina amalug, ina babbar alad tia ara, sha uru zae. Barba ina annu gug ma dug da malu. Wasru sha gana, ina fi namen, ullulu annu Susgal ma lu Inimdug ba ina malu.

The present, the white spirit of time, we support you. Break through this seal and speak with us. Humble we stand, the Serpent Priesthood, purify this castle and let peace live through us

Southeast – with Garnet

Ina mulan, ina salmu alad tia ara, sha uru zae. Barba ina annu gug ma dug da malu. Wasru sha gana, ina fi namen, ullulu annu Susgal ma lu Inimdug ba ina malu.

The future, the black spirit of time, we support you. Break through this seal and speak with us. Humble we stand, the Serpent Priesthood, purify this castle and let peace live through us

Sire

Azig durtur fi, e ina annu dalbana tia ara. Ina ina er balu, ina ina amalug da namigigal – Sha dura ina atuku alad tia ina ar. Kunu, sudug ina annu kaunakes tia ar. Alka sus malu ina abru tia ar ma du wasru. Namazlag nu tia annu dalbana, ina utusus tia nam ma ina Aguziga tia ina sargad, isatu ama ma wur er du, sha uul er us ina ina masu tir.

Raise the Great Serpent, rise through this space of time. From within to without, through the present with insight – We draw together the powerful spirits of the L.i.g.h.t. Approach, transform through this thick cloak of time. Come cover us in beams of light and hold humble. Craft Creator of this space, the sunset of destiny and the dawn of the worlds, fire strong and wisdom to hold, we consent to follow within the forgotten forest.

All

Ala Ina Ara Aram All within time comes forth

Gather close and all link hands
Travel widdershins with the Chant:

Chant:

Uri ma Esentu, Uri ma Esentu

Ala in Ara Mupad kima esdu

Blood and bone, blood and bone

All in time to invoke as one

Continue for as long as you feel it necessary, gaining speed as you travel around

Halt the Chant – Release hands, and then raise your hands into the air, with the sign of the Nephilim:

Shamsiel

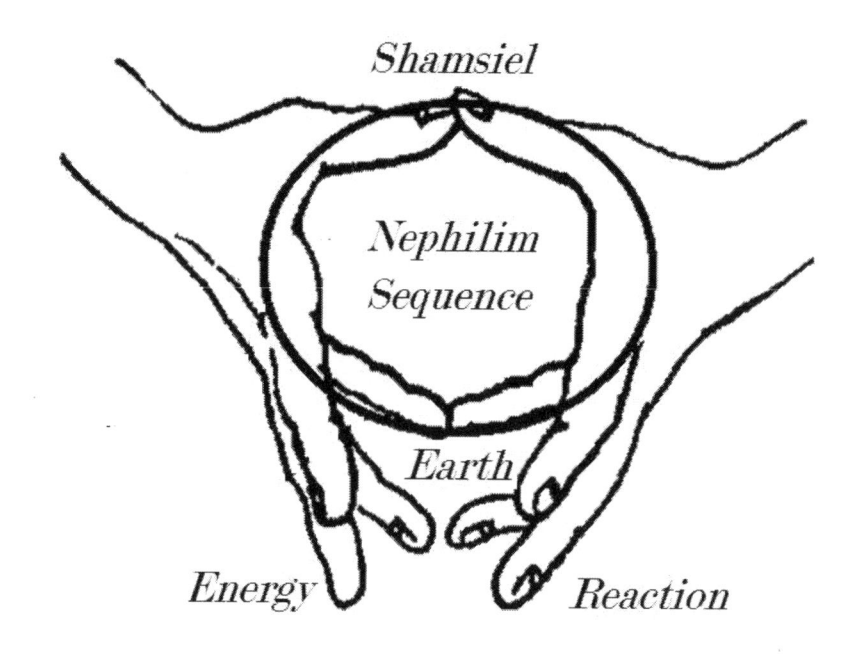

Nephilim Sequence

Earth

Energy   *Reaction*

'Kasaru Nam Ina Anu'

'Gather destiny within this'

Cleanse Holy water upon Altar

Either hand straight out deosil – clockwise – motion

Sire

Urru annu da A dimmu antam, Keezh annu Arazu be Gi ma Dag, wur damu ma bar. Bana gankankha ina Ara ma ina ina zagdaku

Guard this gift I order the universe, under this prayer to be night and day, wisdom child and seat of wisdom. Exorcise this vessel in time and in the dark threshold

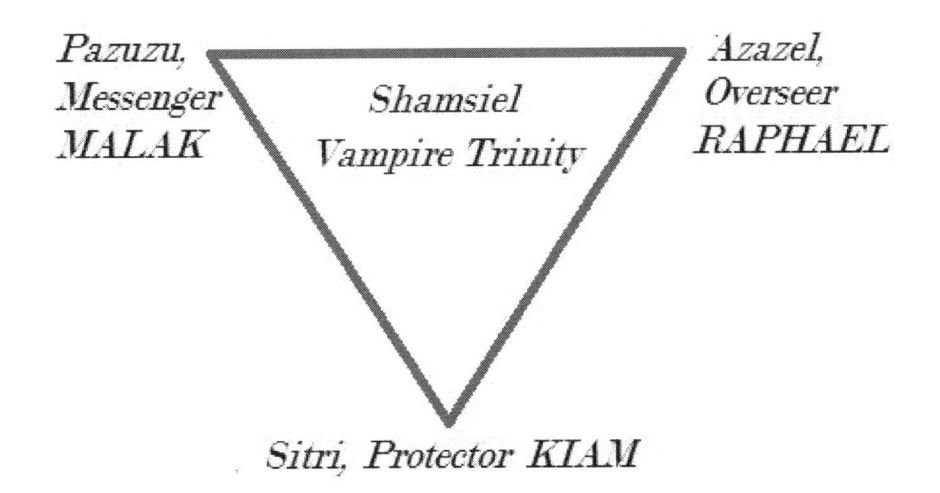

```
        Pazuzu,  ─────────────  Azazel,
        Messenger   Shamsiel     Overseer
        MALAK     Vampire Trinity  RAPHAEL
                    \         /
                     \       /
                      \     /
                       \   /
                        \ /
                Sitri, Protector KIAM
```

Sepu Pil Ak Shamsiel

Anoint Craft of All

Sire

'Sepu Pil Ak Shamsiel'

By grace of Highest Sphere

Sire

Alka adullab an esig ina alad tia ina shinar, lu igen ahulu sig lipis, kug idu ma arammu da malu gana ina ina arazu tia sudum ma subar ar itka malu.

Come now and honour the spirits of the land, let no malice be cast inward, pure knowledge and love with us stand through the prayer of reckoning and release light upon us.

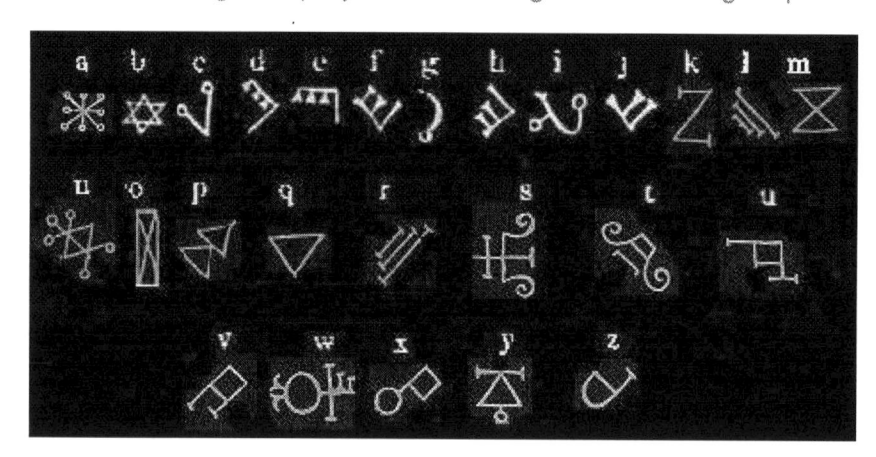

Drawing down the Sun, Moon, and Stars commences with the **Sibbu Usbar** (Snake Staff). Sire stands facing the east at the Altar, speaks the scripture once, then Calls the energy's name once at each call:

Ina Annu Bi, Ina Egura Da Dur Tur Erim Lu ina Anna Azag, la Lalartu, Duttu Bi Dara Bi!

Through this command, through Black Water the great bind, Let through unto the shining bright. Hail Phantom! Hail! One who speaks, command dark divides.

DRAWING DOWN ANSHAR: 1st CALLING of Moon

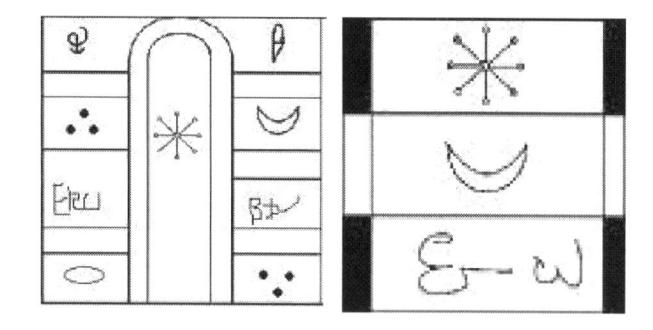

DRAWING DOWN EA: 2ND CALLING of Neptune

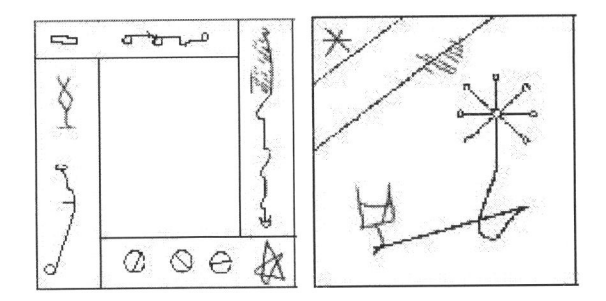

DRAWING DOWN INANNA: 3rd CALLING of Saturn

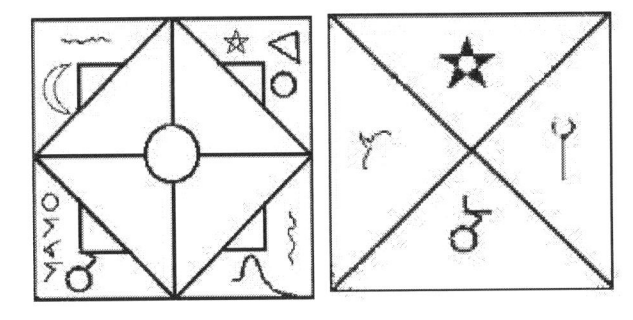

DRAWING DOWN AR: 4th CALLING of the Sun

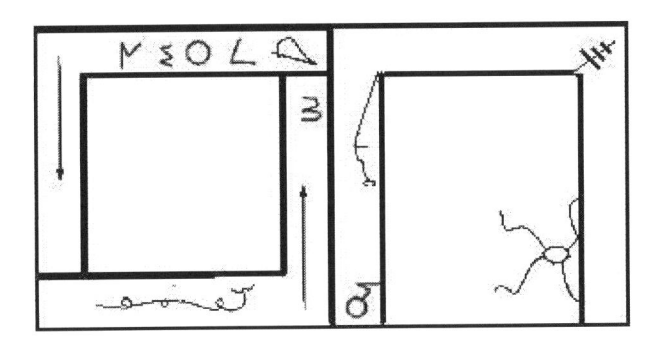

DRAWING DOWN ANUNNA: 5th CALLING of Mars

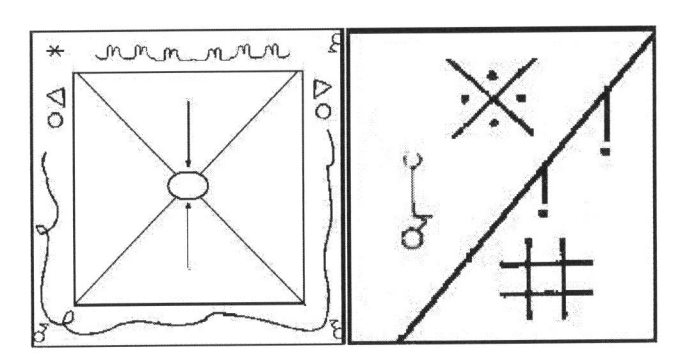

DRAWING DOWN RA.UBAN: 6th CALLING of Black Sun

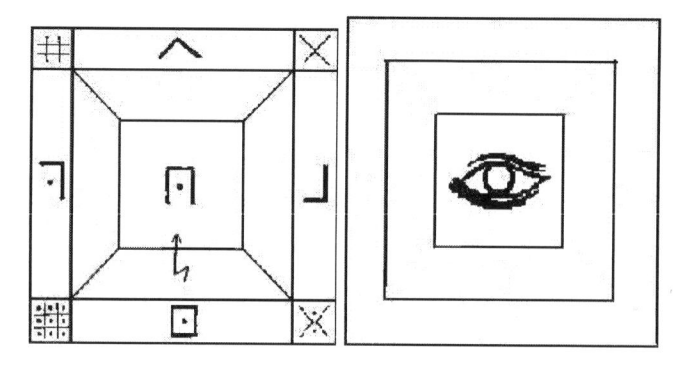

DRAWING DOWN LAHMU: 7th CALLING of Venus

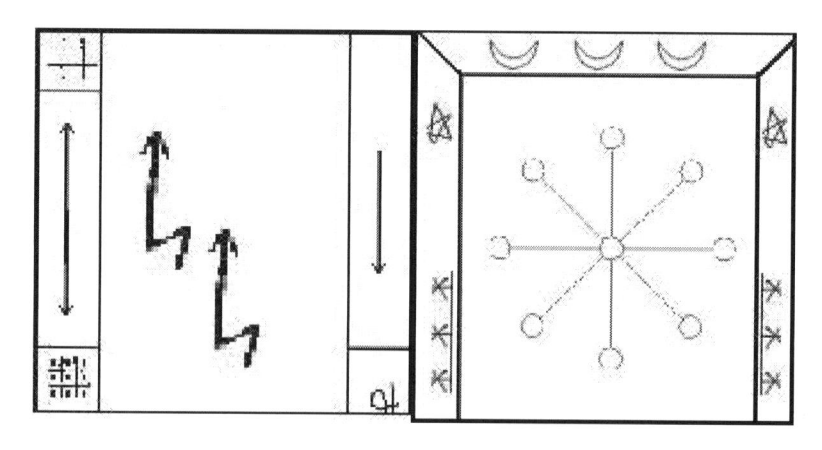

Crossing the barrier through Kiam

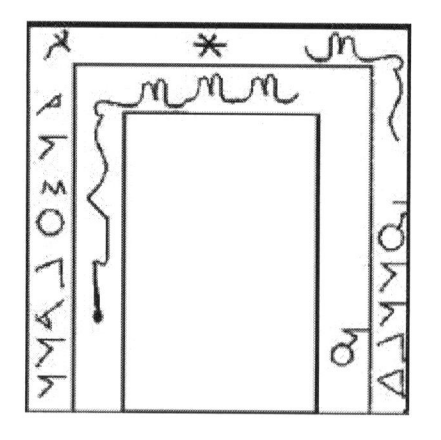

E DUR.TUR FI! E KUR INA ANNU EGURA!

EGURA FI DURA E! EGURA FI E!

ERI ANNU FI BI DUTTU! ANA SA DUR.TUR BI

ERI ANNU FI LU INA

BAR INA ARA ERI!

Rise the great Serpent!

Rise Underworld through this Black Water!

Black Water rise, draw together rise!

Black Water serpent rise

Bind this serpent with one who speaks!

One who the great command

Bind this serpent let through

Seat of wisdom through time bind!

(Allow 60 seconds to pass then say these words)

BI INA ANNU ERI

(Allow 60 seconds to pass then raise the sword of Kiam and say these words)

BI ALA BI INA GIDIM

EDIN NA ZU!

The call of Shemyaza

'The call of Leaders' must NOT be performed at Initiation. Such call is required from the 2nd Generation, onwards. It is important to remember that, unless instructed – Only call as far as 'Asmoday'. The Seventh Gate, until it is deemed right for you to face 'Aiwass', also known as Khoronzon, the guardian of the Abyss.

Note that a generation is indicated by each stage of development through, the initiate is a 1st Generation, and this increases until transformation, if this is deemed suitable at an appropriate time.

The 'Leaders' are known by many names, such as; Keepers, Nephilim, Angels, Demons, Guardians, and the 'Nine Lords of the Abyss'.

It is imperiative that you know that to summon the Leaders is wrong, so it is wrong to invoke (bring spirit within), and further wrong to evoke (bring spirit around us). The K.e.y here is to Convoke, in other words, to cause to assemble in a meeting.

The Gateway

The Sire will now place create one inner circle and one outer circle in the form of a 'Delta', this is performed with Shell-salt, being; that of egg shell and white salt combined. As The Sire creates both seals consecutively, he says the words of Shamsiel:

Varkmal Gelet Tu Mar

Suati Mili Korit gal

Tu Veh se.ant mal

Luvae Kalmak

The Constraint

The Sire now calls each of the Leaders by way of Convoke. As the Sire calls each one, he cast the relevant compound into the Inner Sanctum:

Sire I conjure thee, O spirit Raphael and present you with your Mark:

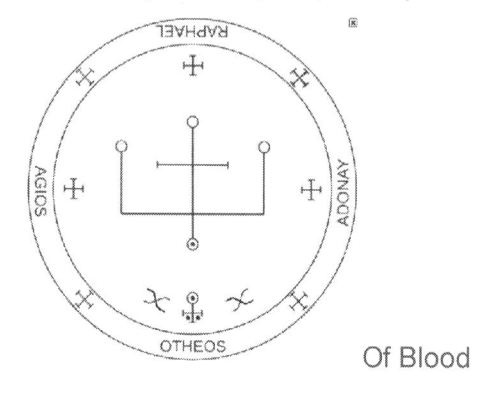

Of Blood

Sire I conjure thee, O spirit Astaroth and present you with your Mark:

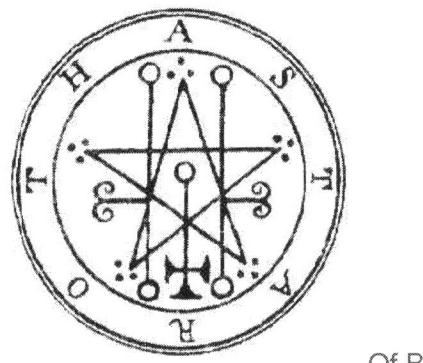

Of Burdock Root

Sire I conjure thee, O spirit Falacor and present you with your Mark:

Of Cinnamon

Sire I conjure thee, O spirit Pazuzu and present you with your Mark:

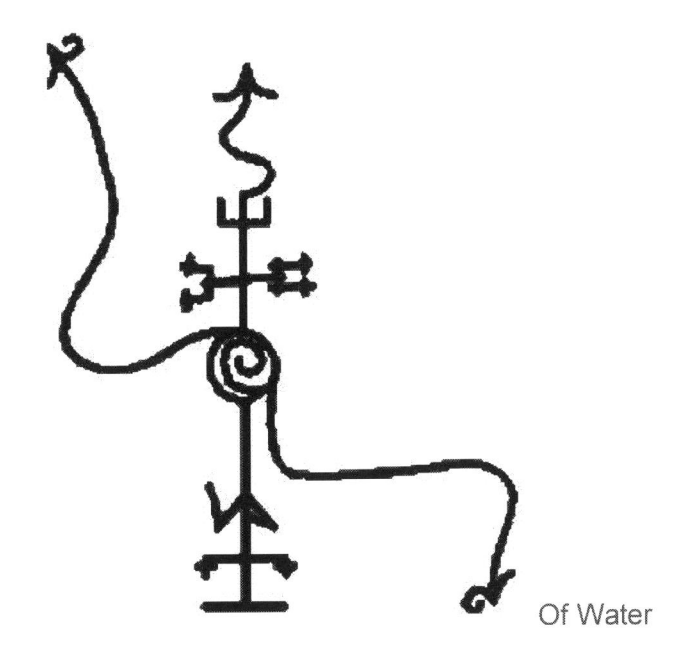

Of Water

Sire I conjure thee, O spirit Sitri and present you with your Mark:

Of Lavender

Sire I conjure thee, O spirit Murmur and present you with your Mark:

Of Tea Leaf

Sire I conjure thee, O spirit Asmoday and present you with your Mark:

Of Salt

Sire I conjure thee, O spirit Khoronzon and present you with your Mark:

Of Egg Shell

Sire I conjure thee, O spirit Azazel and present you with your Mark:

Of Rose Petal

Sire By all the most glorious and efficacious Names of the Great and Incomparable Lord of Hosts, come quickly and without delay, front whatsoever part of the world thou art in; make rational answers to my requests; come visibly, speak affably, speak intelligibly to my understanding. I conjure and convoke thee, O Spirits of Shamsiel; do thou manifest before this circle, fulfil my will in all things that may seem good to me.

INA ANNU BI, E UTU, NANNA, MA ADAR

DA ANNU INA ES E, MA ERI INA INA EGURA

DARA DUTTU LU INA ANNU ES ANNA INA HURSAGMU!

Through this command

Rise Sun, Moon, and Star

Make this the Temple rise and bind from the black water

Dark one who speaks let through this temple unto the mountain of the sky-chambers!

Sire Alka ina ina gidim quannu duramah, gibil wur, su'ati zae da

Durisam ina karabu ma sibum annu da er ina antam

Come through the spirit horn the great stag, one of fire wisdom, that you make forever this blessing and witness this offering to the universe. Come through and answer this prayer in love and truth. Blood Elders we carry the circle to the chamber of the regions of the four to aid and to let those who enter know you

Sire sprinkles white salt over the Altar

Sire Gi be dag ma dara be ar

Night to be Day and Dark to be Light

The closing and departure of Energies

(Sire will be at the alter and guard well the Circle of duality, with the Sibbu Usbar in hand to say these words)

Sire O spirits of Shamsiel, because thou hast diligently answered, I do hereby recognise and accept thee to depart, without injury to man or beast. Depart, and be thou willing and ready to come, whensoever duly exorcised and con red by the sacred rites of the Old Ways, the Dark Knowledge. I conjure thee to withdraw peaceably and quietly, and may peace continue forever between me and thee. **Mak Alam Mas Alam**

All candles are extinguished and the Sibbu Usbar (Snake Staff) is set to the ground to discharge.

The Initiation

Sire ensures that there is sufficient red wine within the chalice and that bread for offering is available. There must be a suitable instrument for cutting and extracting the Seeker's blood.

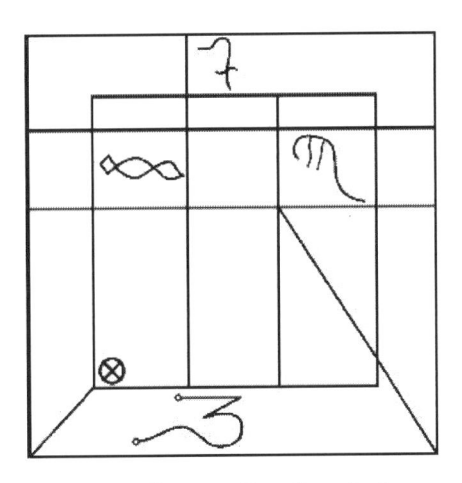

First Generation Symbol

Sire We gather together this night because there is one among us seeking answers. This new seeker has glimpsed the greater reality of what we are, and yearns to know more. Now it is time to take the first few steps on the journey toward understanding.

(Seeker), come forward. You stand now, just as those have before, so be certain that you speak truly. Tell me, *(Seeker)*, what do you come seeking?

Seeker I come seeking understanding.

Sire And why do you seek this?

Seeker To better know myself and my place in the world.

Sire And how do you seek this?

Seeker With pure intentions and an open heart.

Sire Very well, your sincerity is accepted. *(Seeker)*. Our paths are many, but the journey we have undertaken is the same.

Ours is a journey toward understanding. In accepting our natures, we accept a responsibility our energies took up many millennium ago. Ours also is a journey of transformation. In changing ourselves, we seek to change the very way in which we exist. Ours is a solitary journey, often misunderstood. It is a long and arduous path we walk, and the way is not always clear. This is a journey of many lifetimes, and in undertaking it, you are undertaking a great responsibility. The burden you seek to take up here, you will carry with you for many years beyond your imagination.

Do you still seek to walk my way of existence?

Seeker I do.

Sire Very well. Before you embark upon this transformative journey, there are certain vows you must make. I charge you by all you hold sacred to carry these vows in your heart. If it is found that you have broken any one of these, you will be expelled from our family, and all that you have gained will be stripped away.
Answer me, *"So do I swear."*

Sire Do you swear to accept the burden of responsibility for your thoughts and actions as you follow this path?

Seeker So do I swear.

Sire Do you swear that you shall always seek with a pure heart and an honest desire and that you will never abuse the knowledge that you gain as you walk this path?

Seeker So do I swear.

Sire Do you swear that you will guard this knowledge from those who would abuse it, never revealing those of our number to any who might bring them harm?

Seeker So do I swear.

Sire And do you swear to dedicate yourself to change, taking up the burden of transformation which is our unique right within the universe?

Seeker: So do I swear.

Sire It has been witnessed.

Initiate. Always look within yourself first for the answers that you seek. Others may offer guidance, but only you can walk your path. Before you leave this sanctuary, I have five gifts to give to you. Each is a lesson and a revelation. Carry them with you as your strength on this path.

(The Sire goes to the altar where a chalice of water, a burning candle, a bowl of ash, and some burning incense are waiting. The Sire takes the chalice of water first, and dipping her fingers into it, anoints the forehead of the Initiate.)

(Seeker's name), I do consecrate you with water, so you may be fluid and change as the tides of the worlds change.
(The Sire takes the candle and passes it under the Initiate's face, taking care not to burn.)
(Seeker's name), I do consecrate you with fire that you may know your passions and the spirit which drives you.
(The Sire takes the ash and, dipping her fingers into it, marks the forehead of the Initiate with a single, short line.)
(Seeker's name), I do consecrate you with earth, so you may balance your spiritual pursuits.

(The Sire takes the lit incense and passes it in front of the Initiate, wafting the smoke toward him.)

(Seeker's name), I do consecrate you with air, that you may aspire to the stars with an intellect and imagination capable of transforming the worlds.

(The Sire cups her hands and channels energy into them, then lays these over the initiate's heart.)

(Seeker's Name) And I do consecrate you with spirit so you may never forget what it is we are.

Now, *(Seeker)*. Step forward.

(The Sire embraces the Initiate, a cuts their hand, sucking some of the blood from their body. The Sire then takes the Initiate's hand and has them stand beside him.)

Sire Everyone, welcome *(Seeker)* into our number. Give them your trust and your acceptance.

(Each of those present embrace the Initiate, offering words of welcome or personal blessings.)

Sire the first part of this rite is ended and your journey just begun. Go forth to walk in darkness and in light.

All: Forever.

Initiation into the Blood

Within our community, blood plays an integral role in exchanges between Sire and student as well as between vampire and donor. The power of the vampire is passed from mentor to student, and it is through such an exchange that one becomes a vampire or is "turned." Most members of the community accept that you cannot be "turned" into a vampire immediately – Vampiric qualities are with us all along. However, potent exchanges can help to bring these to the forefront, and the passing of power from a teacher to an initiate is an ancient tradition that underscores a number of systems. The initiatory exchange is one of energy, a sharing of blood.

Preparation:

You will need two new lancets, two cups of red wine, and alcohol swabs (and possibly band-aids) for aftercare. Set these out somewhere on an altar or small table near where the ceremony is going to be held. For most people, this rite is intensely personal and should be celebrated privately between mentor and student. For a few groups, this is an event the whole community celebrates, and therefore the mentor and student perform their exchange at the centre of a circle formed by the members of the entire household. The actual form the ritual takes can vary from person to person and from household to household, but the exchange of blood between mentor and student is pretty universal within the initiation.

The Rite

Mentor: I have brought you here because I wish to share with you the most precious gift I have to give: my nature. We are creatures of darkness, but we are also creatures of life. Life empowers us and sustains us. It is our most precious possession, and the greatest gift we can share. By sharing my blood with you this night, I am sharing with you my life, my vitality, my very energy.

Do you understand the importance of what I am offering you? After this, we two will be connected in a way that goes beyond words. More than brother (sister), more than friend, you will be the child of my heart and my energy. Neither you nor I can break the bond that is forged tonight. Are you willing to accept it?

Student: I am willing to accept your most precious gift.

Mentor: Very well, but before I give of myself to you, you must first surrender yourself to me. I will be your protector, teacher, parent and your guide within our community, and in order for me to fulfill my role to you, you must place your trust in me. Do you understand what that means?

Student: I do, and I willingly offer myself to you.

(The student should focus on his vital energy, gathering it into one hand and focusing specifically on one finger. When ready, the student then opens one of the lancets and taps the tip of this finger with the sharp point.

Continuing to focus vital energy and the essence of himself into that finger, thus infusing the blood, the student then offers his finger and wrist to his Mentor so to feed. The student then places his finger into the chalice of wine. Cupping the wine in both hands, the student gently swirls it around, continuing to infuse it with his essence and his energy. Reverently, the student hands the chalice to the mentor. The mentor accepts the chalice and takes a drink, without completely draining the chalice.)

Mentor: Your sacrifice is appreciated. With what you have given me, I will be bound to you as much as you will be bound to me. I will not forget our bond or treat it carelessly.

(The mentor then focuses on his own vital energy, gathering it into one hand and focusing specifically on one finger. Beyond just focusing on his essence and vital energy, the mentor should also focus on his identity as a Vampire, what that means and everything that comes along with it. When ready, the mentor then opens the other lancet and taps the tip of this finger with the point. Continuing to focus vital energy and the essential nature of his vampirism into that finger, the mentor then guides a drop or two of blood to fall into the chalice of wine.)

Mentor: This is my blood, my precious life. It is the symbol of my spirit and all that I am. I shed this for you so that you may drink and become one of our numbers.

(Cupping the wine in both hands, the mentor gently swirls the wine around, mingling not only his own essence and energy with the wine but also mingling his own energy with that of the student's. Reverently, he hands the chalice to his student. The student accepts the chalice and drinks the remainder. The student and mentor then embrace each other.)

Mentor: You are now blood of my blood and energy of my energy. Everything that I am, you will in time learn to be. Never fail to appreciate the sanctity of this precious gift. Let us be bound together, in darkness and in light.

Student: Forever.

(Mentor and student clasp hands, and may choose to press their wounds together. If either has anything further to say to the other, now is the time. The union should be solemnised with a moment of silence. If they are with a group, the mentor then presents the student to the others after this moment of silent reflection. If they have performed the ceremony alone, at the next gathering, the student will be presented around as a member of the community.)

Time is now given for the Mentor and Student to work through the ritual performed and an explanation of the information learned.

Sire O spirits of Shamsiel, because thou hast diligently answered, I do hereby recognise and accept thee to depart, without injury to man or beast. Depart, and be thou willing and ready to come, whensoever duly exorcised and con red by the sacred rites of the Old Ways, the Dark Knowledge. I conjure thee to withdraw peaceably and quietly, and may peace continue forever between me and thee. **Mak Alam Mas Alam**

All candles are extinguished and the Sibbu Usbar (Snake Staff) is set to the ground to discharge.

Si Enki Towards Raphael

The Second Generation

Thamuz Enki Shamsiel

Azazel Raphael Shamsiel

The Altar Set within the East, holding the Mark of Enki, the Sire's personal piece of Garnet, The Sire's personal Sibbu Usbar (Snake Staff), 4 tea candles, 4 small natural liquorice sticks (or similar) set into triangular form (in the centre), Burdock root, Cinnamon, Charged fluid (dependant on occasion), and a Reciprocal of choosing to hold charged fluid.

Identity: Mark of Enki

The following offerings will be required: Blood, Burdock Root, Cinnamon, Water, Lavender, Tea Leaf, Salt, Egg Shell, and Rose Petal (preference to white).

The substitute of Shell-Salt may be used for all, except blood

☿

Above Centre: Sigil of Enki (Raphael)

Top Left: Burdock root, Cinnamon

Top Right: One Tea Candle

Centre: Three sticks in **inverted** triangle with candle at each point

The fourth stick to be at centre of triangle, and outside

Below Centre: Sibbu Usbar (Snake staff of the conducting Sire)

The Nine Gates. From this moment forward, you will be permitted to energise all nine gates. By energising (activating) the gates, this does not mean that you should attempt to pass through at this stage of your development. Therefore, until notified, you will need to learn, and prepare for the journeying through each gate, some time ahead of you to achieve.

Elder Star, the Mark of Shamsiel

The Knowledge of Potion

Cardinal	Immortal Stone	Of Garnet
1st Gate	Raphael	Of Blood
2nd Gate	Astaroth	Of Burdock Root
3rd Gate	Falacor	Of Cinnamon
4th Gate	Pazuzu	Of Water
5th Gate	Sitri	Of Lavender
6th Gate	Murmur	Of Tea Leaf
7th Gate	Asmoday	Of Salt
8th Gate	Khoronzon	Of Egg Shell
9th Gate	Azazel	Of Rose Petal

Shell-Salt may be used as substitute for all, except blood

Three house forms of the Triangle:

The Abyss at the left and the Sanctuary at the bottom point

The Creation at the right point is of Shamsiel

We briefly explored the Triangle of Existence in its raw state within the First Generation, a cycle of discovery as we see the 'polarity' alter the state and consciousness. For instance, within this 'shift' in polarity we see two households bond, empowering the protection and awakening of the Dark Magic of Shamsiel. Such a bonding is between:

The Abyss Of Malak, the Messenger (or rather Enki / Raphael)

And

The Sanctuary Of Kiam, the Protector (or rather Thamuz / Astaroth)

For nearly 2,000 Earth years the love of both Households have been separated within space and time. It is foretold in prophecy that Jesus and Mary were separated but love never died between them. They are known as **Enki** and **Thamuz**. Such connection must never be broken. It is foretold that their re-union will occur once more in the End of Days. With the knowledge of Enki and the strength of Thamuz combined. Those whom have sought, those whom seek, shall be saved. The Vampire Prophecy tells of a third entity, that whom will stop at no end to halt the connection, the bonding of Enki and Thamuz. It is Thamuz whom will need to recognise, to remember what was once, what is now, and what will be. Such memories have been concealed from Thamuz and it is the role and purpose of Enki to re-awaken the love, passion, and desire of Thamuz, so to correct the mistakes made throughout the last two thousand Earth years.

For we now see the polarity of the Triangle in its magical (metaphysical) formation:

Vampire Trinity

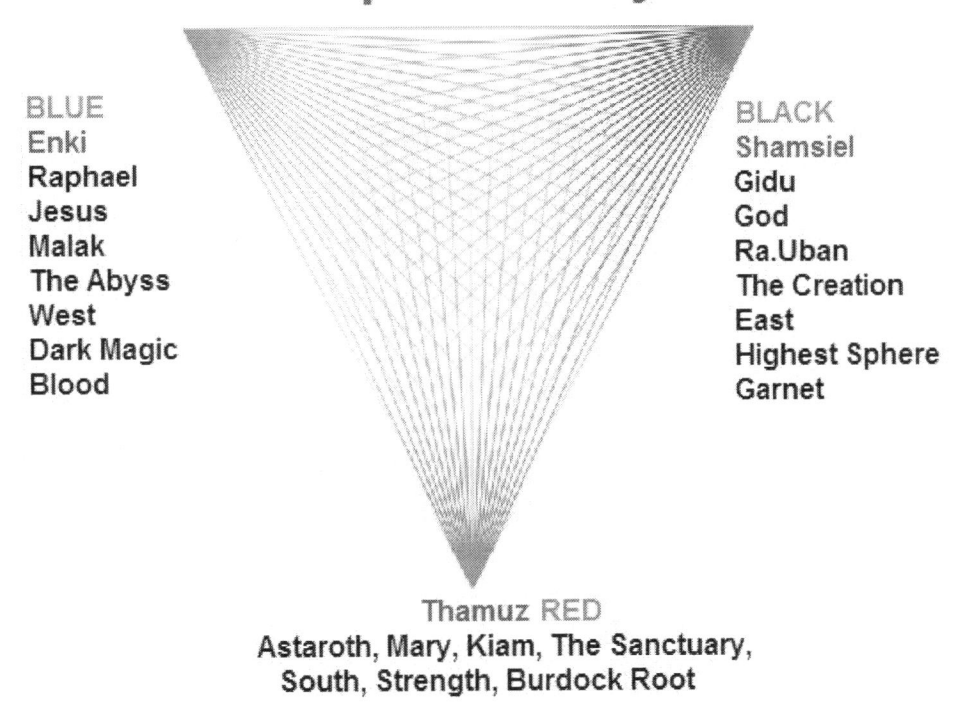

BLUE
Enki
Raphael
Jesus
Malak
The Abyss
West
Dark Magic
Blood

BLACK
Shamsiel
Gidu
God
Ra.Uban
The Creation
East
Highest Sphere
Garnet

Thamuz **RED**
**Astaroth, Mary, Kiam, The Sanctuary,
South, Strength, Burdock Root**

He will hold the mark of transformation of Raphael. For when the transformation of bond is complete, shall the dead rise to follow the few

In your First Generation it was explained that there would be nine **Akhkharu** at each perfect point, or rather each Gate. However, we now see a sequence change in the 'polarity' thus we see the change, or rather a 'shifting' of energy and the sphere of the earth:

Therefore, we continue our exploration of the Gates, in particular, leading us towards and through the Ninth Gate. In the First Generation you were advised that each Gate has a specific Deity, a specific Energy. However, although there is some element of truth within this, in fact there are only TWO deities, TWO energies throughout the passing of the Gates. Such Divine Entities are known as **Enki** and **Thamuz**. The first sequence unfolds, and we begin to understand the complexity, yet simplicity of existence within the realms of Space and Time:

Guardians in first transit

1st	Raphael	Blood
2nd	Astaroth	Burdock Root
3rd	Focalor	Cinnamon
4th	Pazuzu	Water
5th	Sitri	Lavender
6th	Murmur	Tea Leaf
7th	Asmoday	Salt
8th	Khoronzon	Egg Shell
9th	Azazel	Rose Petals	**the cardinal of Garnet**

Guardians in second transit

1st	Enki	Blood
2nd	Thamuz	Burdock Root
3rd	Thamuz	Cinnamon
4th	Enki	Water
5th	Thamuz	Lavender
6th	Thamuz	Tea Leaf
7th	Enki	Salt
8th	Enki	Egg Shell
9th	**Enki and Thamuz in Union**	**the cardinal of Garnet**

Guardians in third transit

Enki   Blood, Water, Salt, Egg Shell, Rose Petal

Thamuz   Burdock Root, Cinnamon, Lavender, Tea leaf, Rose Petal

In Union   **The Power of the R.o.s.e** (Rose Petal)

Guardians in fourth transit

Enki   Sacred Number   40

Thamuz   Sacred Number   666

Shamsiel   Sacred Number   3

A metaphysical equation is based on the following:

4+0 = **4**

6+6+6 = 18 = 1 + 8 = **9**

3+0 = **3**

Sacred Number of Enki and Thamuz **in Union 13** (9+4)

Sacred number of the **Trinity 7** (1+3+3)

With the knowledge of this K.e.y sequence, we further see the K.e.y Number of Space and Time as **7**

But still we must travel further, for if we apply the number 7 and multiply by the number of humans, the number **6,** we further see the number **42**

4+2 = 6, thus we are left with the number **13** once more (7+6), the very nature and essence of life within human life. It is the knowledge of Enki and the Strength of Thamuz. Thus making the K.e.y numbers as follows:

Shamsiel	**4**
Thamuz	**6**
Enki	**7**

The base number of the Multiverse clearly established within the Trinity of 8, the Ouroborus, or rather URUBURUS as 8, the never ending sequence of the Trinity

It is the sequence of numbers that allow existence to exist, which within your Third Generation; we will explore the **Tablet of** Destinies, the Dark Magic, the Old Magic, and the Old Ways.

Continue to be that of the Ansar, the Spiritual Warrior of the Lord of Space itself. By the **Star and Stone** in form 'Nana ma Adar', for **Shamsiel** will know if you are true, the Highest Sphere will support you or crush you, for this is your choice, your choice alone. Within this House of Vampires, 'Upir Likyi', know this. The **Ennuunkabarra** 'En-nu-un-ka-bar-ra' guard the outer gate of Shemsiel.

SECOND TRANSFORMATION BEGINS

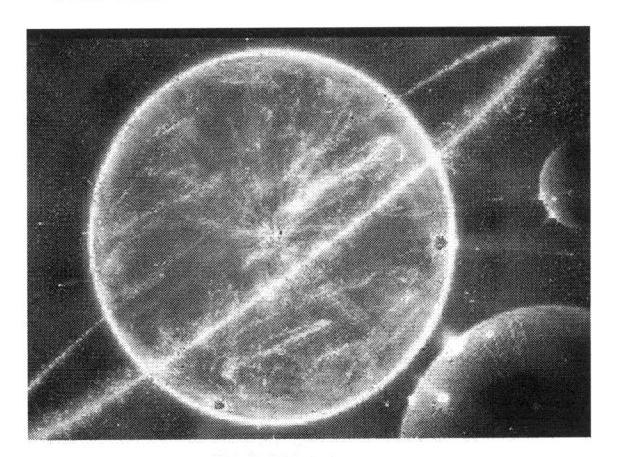

NINASU

The Creation *of sequence Opening Prayer*

Kur Dingar, E ina Utu, Nanna, ma Adar

Su'ati annu Piriq, ina Azag

Annu tisa bi er E Gallas

Mamman aga Azag bur annu aka annu wur eri

Underworld God, raise the Sun, Moon, and star

That this the bearer of the magic,

From the shining bright this ninth command to go raise demons.

Whoever crowns the shining bright hear this divine command, this wisdom bind

Sire Karabu er igi mannu Gana ina annu Dalbana. Lu malu zu Inimdug, arammu ma zid ina ma balu. Girigena tia dimmu aradu. Hasusu Menzug Namen ma eribu annu edin

Blessings to those who stand in this space

Let us know peace, love and truth within and without

Path of order descend

Remember your Priesthood and enter this plain

All

Ala ina Ara Aram All within time come forth

Sire summons the L.i.g.h.t

The Calling (point-left-right) Light all Altar candles – Ekal Ugula tia Ugur, Salmu Ugula tia Abalae, Samu Ugula tia Muh, sha Uru menzen

'Blue overseer of Sword, Black overseer of Stone Red overseer of Chalice, we support you'

Sire

Ar, isatu, ma ganzer – sha sugid ina menzug gigun, da malu ina ugula tia ina gula adhal kima sha andul ina sumer

Light, Fire, and Darkness – We accept the sacred building, make us the overseers of the great secret as we protect the land of the watchers.

Hand, Horn, Blood and Bone	Silig, Quannu, Uri ma Esentu
Wisdom old and wisdom young	Namzu Labaru ma Namzu ban
Child of star and moon of night	Damu tia mulan ma su.en tia gi
Elders strong in waters time	Abba ama ina Anumun ara
Come with everlasting sight	Alka Adullab nigul Igigal
And do your desire with light	Ma ak Menzug Aldug Adullab ar

Sire

Sha peta annu dalbana anna zae er tapputtu malu ina parsu. Ama menden zig ma alad menden idu. Menzug ugur tia zid adullab anna ina abula tia ara, kima ina dilibad es tia ina utu udmeda dubsag zae, sha gana menzug fi namen.

We open this space unto you to aid us in religious duties. Strong we stand and spirit we know. Your sword of truth now unto the gate of time, as the shining temple of the sun ever before you, we stand your serpent priesthood.

All

Ala ina Ara Aram All within time come forth

With the Triangle formed upon the Altar (Inverted), the Sire will call each point in sequence, as the Sire calls, they have grasped within the dominant hand, the stone of Immortality, the stone of Garnet. At each call their grasped hand is held at a forty-five degree angle above the flame

West – Sword

Ina nabu, ina samu alad tia ara, sha uru zae. Barba ina annu gug ma dug da malu. Wasru sha gana, ina fi namen, ullulu annu Susgal ma lu Inimdug ba ina malu.

The past, the red spirit of time, we support you. Break through this seal and speak with us. Humble we stand, the Serpent Priesthood, purify this castle and let peace live through us

South – with chalice

Ina amalug, ina samu alad tia ara, sha uru zae. Barba ina annu gug ma dug da malu. Wasru sha gana, ina fi namen, ullulu annu Susgal ma lu Inimdug ba ina malu.

The present, the red spirit of time, we support you. Break through this seal and speak with us. Humble we stand, the Serpent Priesthood, purify this castle and let peace live through us

East – with Garnet

Ina mulan, ina salmu alad tia ara, sha uru zae. Barba ina annu gug ma dug da malu. Wasru sha gana, ina fi namen, ullulu annu Susgal ma lu Inimdug ba ina malu.

The future, the black spirit of time, we support you. Break through this seal and speak with us. Humble we stand, the Serpent Priesthood, purify this castle and let peace live through us

Sire

Azig durtur fi, e ina annu dalbana tia ara. Ina ina er balu, ina ina amalug da namigigal – Sha dura ina atuku alad tia ina ar. Kunu, sudug ina annu kaunakes tia ar. Alka sus malu ina abru tia ar ma du wasru. Namazlag nu tia annu dalbana, ina utusus tia nam ma ina Aguziga tia ina sargad, isatu ama ma wur er du, sha uul er us ina ina masu tir.

Raise the Great Serpent, rise through this space of time. From within to without, through the present with insight – We draw together the powerful spirits of the L.i.g.h.t. Approach, transform through this thick cloak of time. Come cover us in beams of light and hold humble. Craft Creator of this space, the sunset of destiny and the dawn of the worlds, fire strong and wisdom to hold, we consent to follow within the forgotten forest.

All

Ala Ina Ara Aram All within time comes forth

Gather close and all link hands
Travel widdershins with the Chant:

Chant:

Uri ma Esentu, Uri ma Esentu

Ala in Ara Mupad kima esdu

Blood and bone, blood and bone

All in time to invoke as one

Continue for as long as you feel it necessary, gaining speed as you travel around

Halt the Chant – Release hands, and then raise your hands into the air, with the sign of the Nephilim:

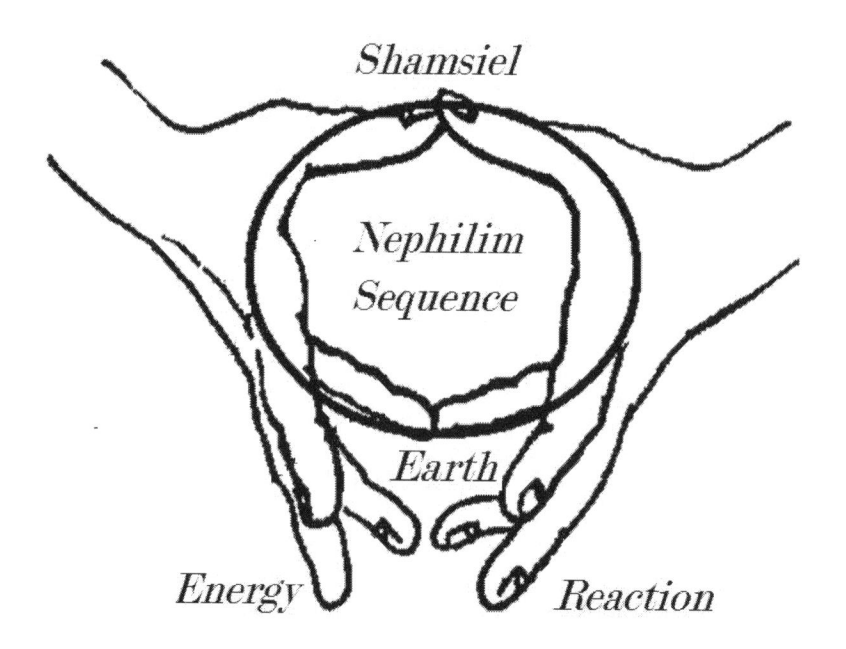

Shamsiel

Nephilim Sequence

Earth

Energy *Reaction*

'Kasaru Nam Ina Anu'

'Gather destiny within this'

Cleanse Holy water upon Altar

Either hand straight out deosil – clockwise – motion

Sire

Urru annu da A dimmu antam, Keezh annu Arazu be Gi ma Dag, wur damu ma bar. Bana gankankha ina Ara ma ina ina zagdaku

Guard this gift I order the universe, under this prayer to be night and day, wisdom child and seat of wisdom. Exorcise this vessel in time and in the dark threshold

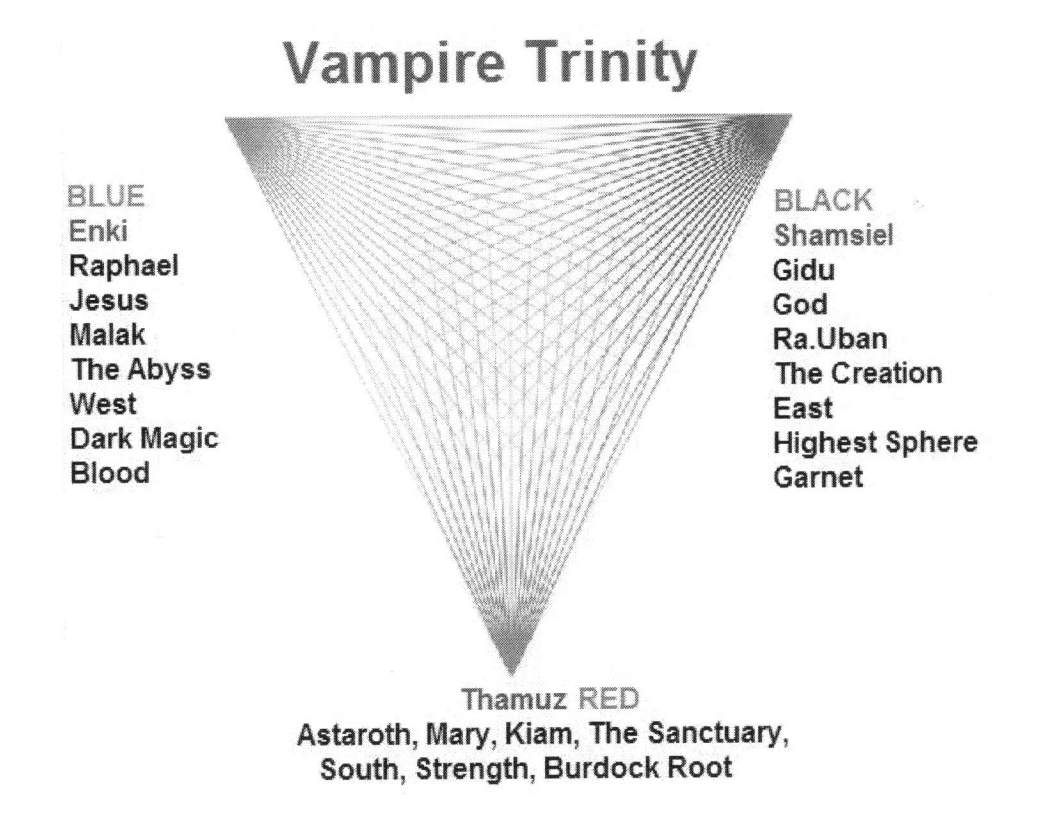

Vampire Trinity

BLUE
Enki
Raphael
Jesus
Malak
The Abyss
West
Dark Magic
Blood

BLACK
Shamsiel
Gidu
God
Ra.Uban
The Creation
East
Highest Sphere
Garnet

Thamuz RED
**Astaroth, Mary, Kiam, The Sanctuary,
South, Strength, Burdock Root**

Anoint Craft of All

Sire
'Sepu Pil Ak Shamsiel'

By grace of Highest Sphere

Sire

Alka adullab an esig ina alad tia ina shinar, lu igen ahulu sig lipis, kug idu ma arammu da malu gana ina ina arazu tia sudum ma subar ar itka malu.

Come now and honour the spirits of the land, let no malice be cast inward, pure knowledge and love with us stand through the prayer of reckoning and release light upon us.

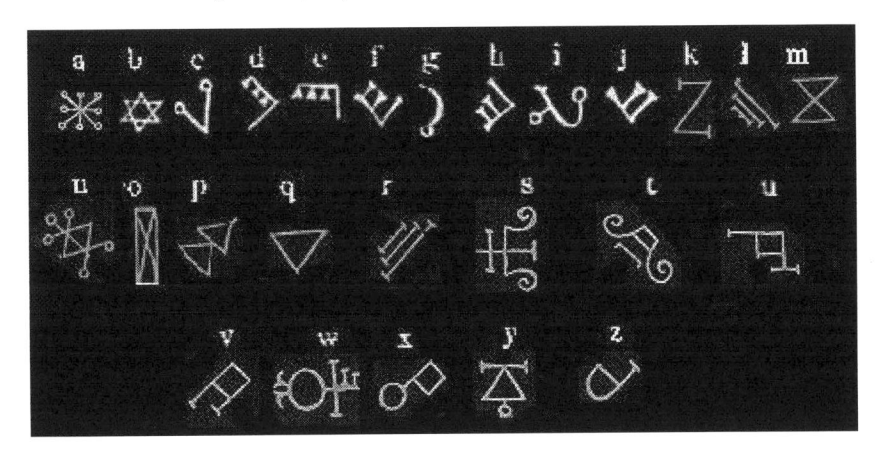

Drawing down the Sun, Moon, and Stars commences with the **Sibbu Usbar** (Snake Staff). Sire stands facing the east at the Altar, speaks the scripture once, then Calls the energy's name once at each call:

Ina Annu Bi, Ina Egura Da Dur Tur Erim Lu ina Anna Azag, Ia Lalartu, Duttu Bi Dara Bi!

Through this command, through Black Water the great bind, Let through unto the shining bright. Hail Phantom! Hail! One who speaks, command dark divides.

DRAWING DOWN ANSHAR: 1st CALLING of Moon Enki

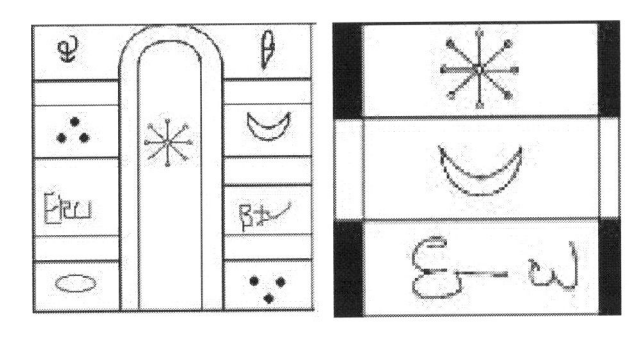

DRAWING DOWN EA: 2ND CALLING of Neptune Thamuz

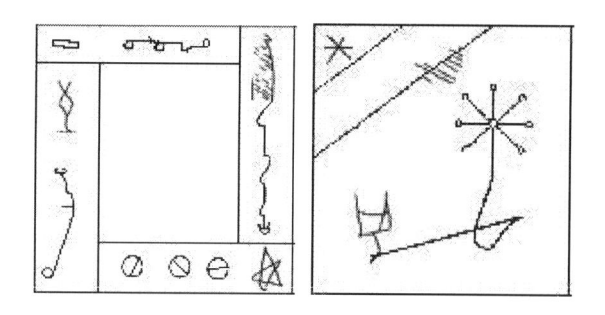

DRAWING DOWN INANNA: 3rd CALLING of Saturn Thamuz

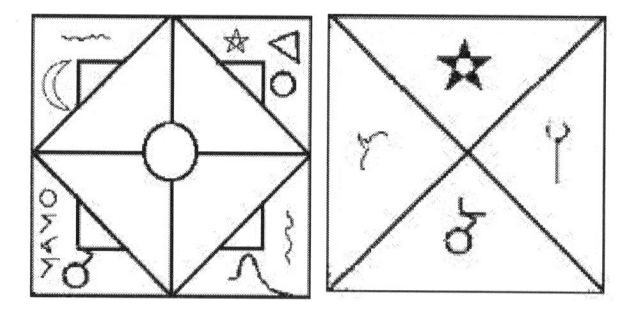

DRAWING DOWN AR: 4th CALLING of the Sun Enki

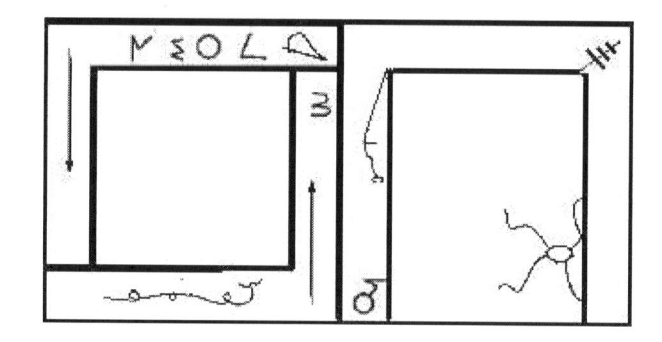

DRAWING DOWN ANUNNA: 5th CALLING of Mars Thamuz

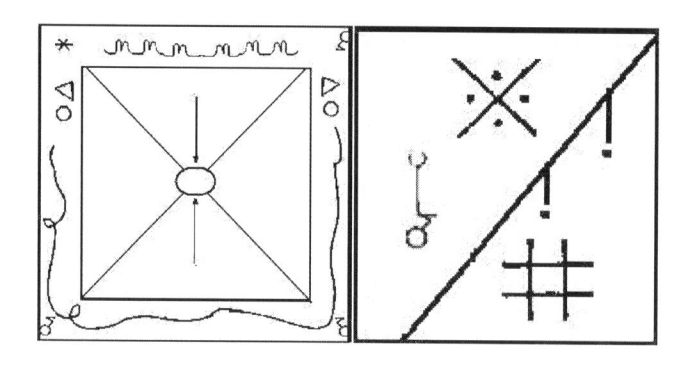

DRAWING DOWN RA.UBAN: 6th CALLING of Black Sun Thamuz

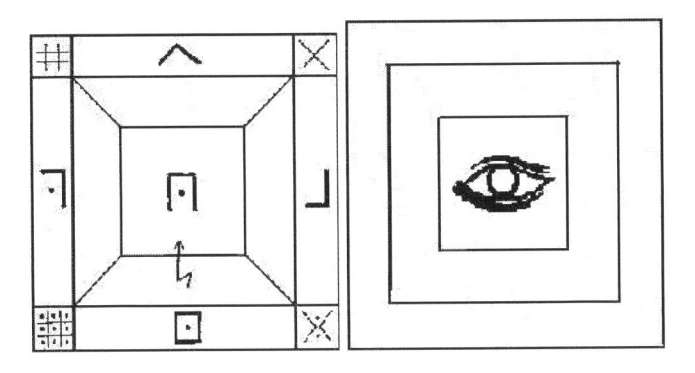

DRAWING DOWN LAHMU: 7th CALLING of Venus Enki

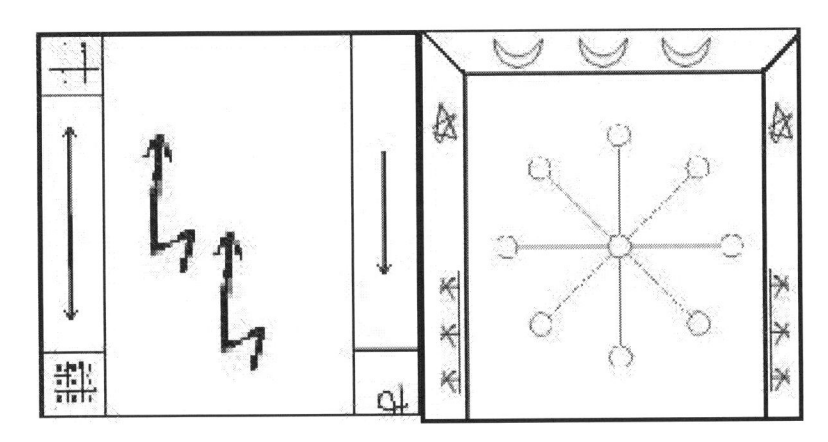

Crossing the barrier through Kiam

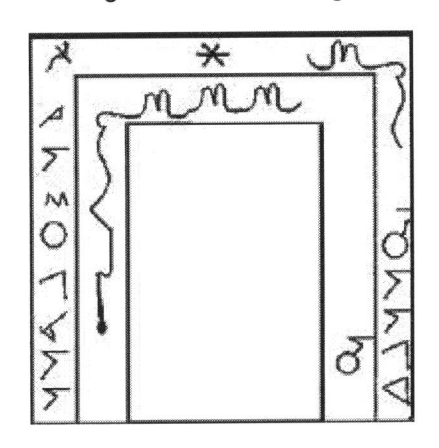

E DUR.TUR FI! E KUR INA ANNU EGURA!

EGURA FI DURA E! EGURA FI E!

ERI ANNU FI BI DUTTU! ANA SA DUR.TUR BI

ERI ANNU FI LU INA

BAR INA ARA ERI!

Rise the great Serpent!

Rise Underworld through this Black Water!

Black Water rise, draw together rise!

Black Water serpent rise

Bind this serpent with one who speaks!

One who the great command

Bind this serpent let through

Seat of wisdom through time bind!

(Allow 60 seconds to pass then say these words)

BI INA ANNU ERI

(Allow 60 seconds to pass then raise the sword of Kiam and say these words)

BI ALA BI INA GIDIM

EDIN NA ZU!

The call of Shemyaza

'The call of Leaders'

Note that a generation is indicated by each stage of development through, the initiate is a 1st Generation, and this increases until transformation, if this is deemed suitable at an appropriate time.

The 'Leaders' are known by many names, such as; Keepers, Nephilim, Angels, Demons, Guardians, and the 'Nine Lords of the Abyss'.

It is imperiative that you know that to summon the Leaders is wrong, so it is wrong to invoke (bring spirit within), and further wrong to evoke (bring spirit around us). The K.e.y here is to Convoke, in other words, to cause to assemble in a meeting.

The Gateway

The Sire will now place create one inner circle and one outer circle in the form of a 'Delta', this is performed with Shell-salt, being; that of egg shell and white salt combined.

As The Sire creates both seals consecutively, he says the words of Shamsiel:

Varkmal Gelet Tu Mar

Suati Mili Korit gal

Tu Veh se.ant mal

Luvae Kalmak

The Constraint

The Sire now calls each of the Leaders by way of Convoke. As the Sire calls each one, he cast the relevant compound into the Inner Sanctum:

Sire I conjure thee, O First Spirit Enki and present you with your Mark:

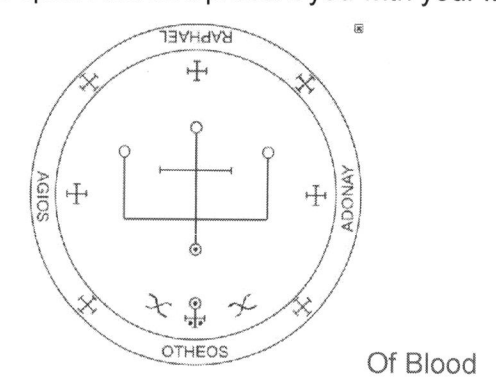

Of Blood

Sire I conjure thee, O Second Spirit Thamuz and present you with your Mark:

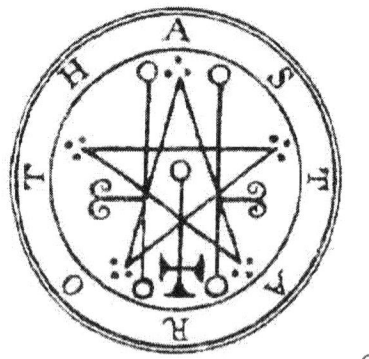

Of Burdock Root

Sire I conjure thee, O Third Spirit Thamuz and present you with your Mark:

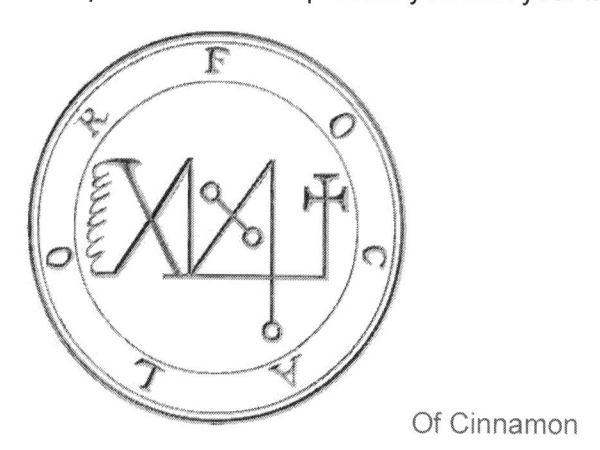

Of Cinnamon

Sire I conjure thee, O Fourth Spirit Enki and present you with your Mark:

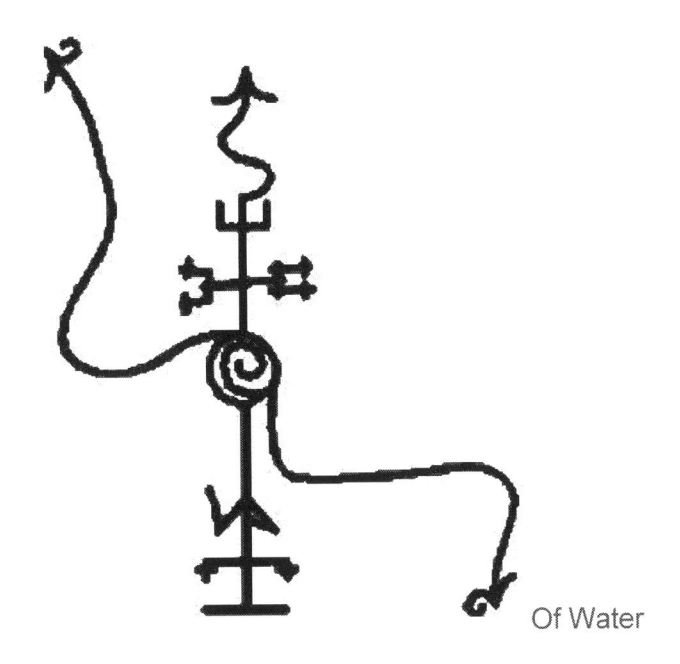

Of Water

Sire I conjure thee, O Fifth Spirit Thamuz and present you with your Mark:

Of Lavender

Sire I conjure thee, O Sixth Spirit Thamuz and present you with your Mark:

Of Tea Leaf

Sire I conjure thee, O Seventh Spirit Enki and present you with your Mark:

Of Salt

Sire I conjure thee, O Eighth Spirit Enki and present you with your Mark:

Of Egg Shell

Sire I conjure thee, in Union as One, O Ninth spirit of Enki and Thamuz and present you with your Mark:

Of Rose Petal

Sire By all the most glorious and efficacious Names of the Great and Incomparable Lord of Hosts, come quickly and without delay, front whatsoever part of the world thou art in; make rational answers to my requests; come visibly, speak affably, speak intelligibly to my understanding. I conjure and convoke thee, O Spirits of Shamsiel; do thou manifest before this circle, fulfil my will in all things that may seem good to me.

INA ANNU BI, E UTU, NANNA, MA ADAR

DA ANNU INA ES E, MA ERI INA INA EGURA

DARA DUTTU LU INA ANNU ES ANNA INA HURSAGMU!

Through this command

Rise Sun, Moon, and Star

Make this the Temple rise and bind from the black water

Dark one who speaks let through this temple unto the mountain of the sky-chambers!

Sire Alka ina ina gidim quannu duramah, gibil wur, su'ati zae da

Durisam ina karabu ma sibum annu da er ina antam

Come through the spirit horn the great stag, one of fire wisdom, that you make forever this blessing and witness this offering to the universe. Come through and answer this prayer in love and truth. Blood Elders we carry the circle to the chamber of the regions of the four to aid and to let those who enter know you

Sire sprinkles white salt over the Altar

Sire Gi be dag ma dara be ar

Night to be Day and Dark to be Light

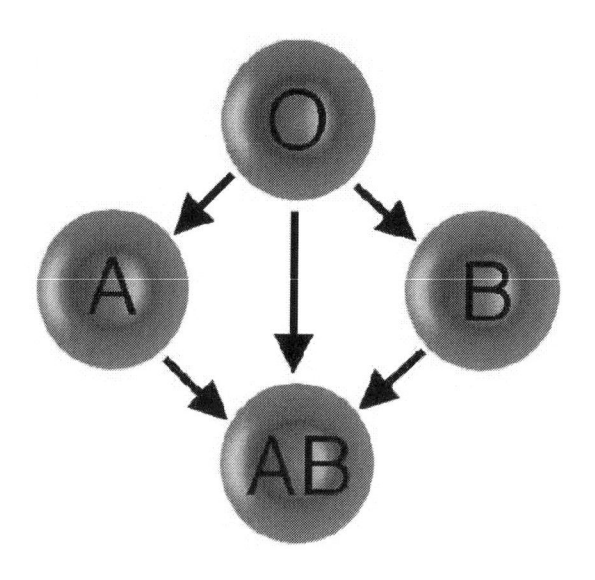

The closing and departure of Energies

(Sire will be at the alter and guard well the Circle of duality, with the Sibbu Usbar in hand to say these words)

Sire O Spirit Shamsiel, because thou hast diligently answered, I do hereby recognise and accept thee to depart, without injury to man or beast. Depart, and be thou willing and ready to come, whensoever duly exorcised and con red by the sacred rites of the Old Ways, the Dark Knowledge. I conjure thee to withdraw peaceably and quietly, and may peace continue forever between me and thee. **Mak Alam Mas Alam**

All candles are extinguished and the Sibbu Usbar (Snake Staff) is set to the ground to discharge.

Second Generation Initiation

Some are very informal about their degrees of initiation. Some, such as our Household have full meaning and purpose with the Initiation Rite.. This is a basic ritual to recognise the initiate's passage from the Outer Circle to the first level of the Inner Circle. Depending on the system, the initiate may still not have gone through a rite of transformation, although they most certainly have gone through a formal Dedication Ceremony of a First Generation Vampire. To achieve the recognition as a Second generation, the initiate must have decided on the role they wish to fill within the community. In order to 'pass' this ritual, the initiate must adequately respond to the questions that our Sire puts to them during the course of the ceremony.

Preparation:

The energy of the ritual space has already been established and witnessed, according to our Household's tradition. The temple now erected, enables the members of the Inner Circle to gather together with Our Sure. They all form a circle and join hands. At the far end of the circle, opposite the Sire, two people do not join hands, leaving an opening in the circle. This threshold is blocked by a Guardian, typically played by a member of the Ansar (Spiritual Warrior), who stands facing out of the circle. The Guardian may have a blade or a staff to represent his or her office.

The initiate and the initiate's sponsor are not present for the set-up, nor do they stand in the circle. Ideally, they should meet in a separate room and wait for the Herald to retrieve them. The Herald is the only one allowed to pass in and out of the sacred space unchallenged. Those gathered in the circle discuss the initiate and how each person present feels about that person achieving this degree. When everyone is ready, the Sire sends the Herald out to retrieve the initiate and his or her sponsor. The Herald leads them back to the circle, passing by the Guardian. The Guardian allows the Herald to pass but blocks the initiate.

The Rite:

Guardian: What are you doing here?

Initiate: I have come seeking the Elders.

Guardian: (barring the way) You may not pass.

Initiate: I have prepared long and hard for this.

Guardian: You may not pass.

Initiate: There is nowhere else for me.

Guardian: You may not pass.

Sponsor: I will take responsibility for him.

Guardian: Very well.

(The Guardian moves aside, and the sponsor leads the initiate into the circle. The initiate is brought before our Sire.)

Sire: (*Sponsor's name*) You have entered our Inner Circle with a stranger who does not belong. Who is this person and why do you bring them here?

Sponsor: This is (*Initiate's name*), my student. I have taught them some of our Ways within our Household, and now I feel it is time they be accepted among us, so that they can be taught further. If you require, I will speak for them.

Sire: Let them speak.

(The Sponsor nods, then steps aside, leaving the initiate to stand alone in the centre of the circle.)

Sire: Who are you?

Initiate: (*Name*) the student of (*Sponsor's name*)

Sire: Why do you come here?

Initiate: This is where I belong.

Sire: What do you seek to gain?

Initiate: Knowledge of myself and the community.

Sire: What do you have to offer us?

Initiate: *(responds with the appropriate phrase)*

I am a Warrior, I offer my strength.

I am a Counsellor, I offer my love.

I am of blood, I offer my vision.

Sire: Very well. You stand before our inner community, and we acknowledge your words. (*Sponsor's name*) speaks for you, and though their recommendation goes far, it is not enough. Many have come before us, and it takes more than words to win our trust. What are you willing to sacrifice to prove you are sincere?

Initiate: I offer my very life-force to you Sire.

(The initiate cups their hands before their heart and channels energy there. Our Sire goes and lays a hand over the initiate's heart, then drinks from the hand of the initiate.)

Sire: Your offering is accepted. Your words are sincere. You claim a place among us. Do any of the Elders object to this?

Everyone: We have no objection.

Sire: Then let us welcome. (*Sponsor's name*), you are responsible for this person, for they have proven that he can walk among us on his own. From this moment onward, their actions are both theirs and yours (Sponsor's name), and any praise or blame for those actions belongs to you both.

(Our Sire removes the initiates Raphael pendant, takes to the Alter and dips it into the Cup of Life and Blood, returns to the initiate and places it around the initiate's neck).

Sire: (*Initiate's name*), take this pendant and wear it proudly. It is a symbol of our household, and by wearing it, you proclaim to the entire world that you are one of our number. Let it remind you of this night and the duties you have proclaimed.

(Our Sire embraces the initiate and presents them to the Household.)

Sire: (*Initiate's name*), you are given the title of Warrior / Counsellor / Blood *(choose the appropriate one; alternately use Mradu / Kitra / Ramkht.)* You now stand at First Degree within our circle, named the *'Calmae'*. Use your knowledge responsibly, and respect what you have earned.

(Everyone welcomes the initiate by name and may at this time offer specific blessings. The sponsor may also offer specific words of encouragement or advice.)

Sire: Before this ceremony is ended and we go forth into darkness, I pass you to receive knowledge of our Kind, our Household further:

Vampirism

It is important to note that there are many groups and organisation's proclaiming to be of our Vampire Lineage. Such groups base their practice on the modern concept of vampires in modern fiction and could not be further from the truth. Oftentimes such groups have involved the practices of sadomasochism, and such groups would best be avoided.

For our Household is of real lineage with our Sire being one of few who have chosen to enlighten us with the real teachings and workings of the Vampire community. There are two K.e.y aspects to our way of existence; 'Sanguinarian' and 'Pranic' (oftentimes known as Psychic vampirism). Sanguinarian Vampirism involves the consumption of Human Blood, and Pranic Vampirism is based upon practitioners drawing spiritual nourishment from 'Auric' or 'Pranic' energy.

The Consumption of Blood Some Households drink human blood for a reason of restoring the body's vital energy, life-source. By the consumption of blood, the Practitioner makes up for the deficiency of proper energy processing within the body.

Sexuality and sexual practices The link between vampirism and sexuality has been present even before popular titles such as 'Stoker's Dracula'. With the modern vampire movement, 'eroticism has become so entwined with the contemporary vampire scene that popular vampire magazines, like *Bloodstone*, include previews of the latest vampire pornography, featuring combined acts of sex and blood-letting.' This focus on sex and sexuality stems from vampire literature.

Members of vampire subculture

Unlike what is commonly assumed, there are more members to the vampire society than simply those that drink blood. Such members tend to congregate together into small clans, usually called covens or 'houses,' in a tribal culture to find acceptance among others that share their beliefs. Generally vampirism is not considered a religion but a spiritual or philosophical path. There are also many modern vampires that are not part of a coven, but rather are solitary. Most human vampires wear regular or ordinary clothes for the area they live in to avoid discrimination. In addition, there are *hybrids*, human vampires that take both blood and energy. There are three main types of vampires lifestylers.

Sanguinarians

Those that drink blood are called Sanguinarians or 'sanguine vampires'. They and psychic vampires address themselves as 'real vampires' and usually have a collective community. They believe they have a physical and/or spiritual need to drink human blood to maintain their mental and physical health.

Psychic Vampires

Commonly known as *Psi-vamps* are another kind of human vampire that claim to attain nourishment from the Aura, Psychic energy, or Pranic energy of others. They believe one must feed from this energy to balance a spiritual or psychological energy deficiency such as a damaged aura or chakra.

Living Vampires

Often calling themselves by the namesake are highly spiritual and consider vampirism an action required for spiritual evolution and ascension, yet maintain a rigid ethical system in its practice. Living vampires are not blood drinkers or psychic vampires and are usually organised into initiatory orders such as The Abyss, The Sanctuary, or The Creation.

Transcendental Vampires

The notion of the Vampire having an immortal soul is the focal point of this Vampiric identity. Those who associate with this form of Vampiric identity such as the coven House Bennu hold the belief that their soul/psyche may travel into, and fuse with the soul/psyche and body of a younger Vampire with the goal of achieving immortality. Transcendental Vampires may be Sanguinarian and/or psychic in nature.

Blood donors Blood donors are people that willingly allow human vampires to drink their blood. Within vampire society, human vampires and donors are considered equal, yet donors are expected to be subservient to the vampires. At the same time, donors are difficult to find, and because of that human vampires have no reason to abuse their donors.

Blood fetishists in the vampire community use blood as a fetish or stimulant in sadomasochistic sex.

Vampire role-players

Vampire role-players, otherwise called 'Fashion Vamps, differ distinctly from human vampires in that they are 'serious vampire fans and those who dress up in vampire clothing, live a vampire lifestyle (i.e. sleep in coffins), and primarily participate in Vampire meets.

Terminology

Term   Definition
Feeding   the taking of energy via blood or other forms
Mundane   A closed-minded individual/ non-awakened, non-vampire
Black Swan A non-vampire that is sympathetic to vampires
Fledgling   someone that is new to vampire subculture

Christianity and modern vampires

In response to the rising vampire subculture, a Christian counter-movement of self-professed vampire slayers has formed that opposes the notion of real vampires. Online, they swarm vampire websites with hate mail and participate in other similar activities, but there are rumors of zealous vampire slayers killing human vampires.

The following piece of literature is given to provide you with a set of knowledge and practices to build upon

What does it mean to be a Vampire

Although vampires walk the annals of fiction and myth these stories are based loosely on medical and scientific fact. Every myth contains at least a sliver of reality, and it's by understanding the distinction between that myth and the reality that we gain a fuller understanding of what we seek.

Modern vampirism isn't based on the cultural myth of vampires but it is based on the relationship intrinsic to the word vampire. Mythically we refer to the vampire as a member of our society who feeds on that same society to survive. This is the metaphor that is intended by the use of the word vampire by the modern vampire community.

The danger of using the word vampire to self-define is that there are more ideals attached to vampirism than just the feeding of one person on another. Vampires are characterised by myth as immortal formerly human beings with preternatural abilities. The members of our community don't make the claim that we're preternatural, simply that we feed on one another to survive. Of course, some of our community have lived longer than the average human, but this does not mean that such creatures will live (or exist) forever on this planet.

The idea of transferring energy back and forth from person to person is not a new one. Many religions and belief systems hold true that every member of society shares their energy with others as they interact. Indeed, many people feel energized by being around people and by interacting with them. We relieve our stress and enhance our contentment in life by sharing our lives with those around us.

The difference in vampirism is that we generate less of that energy than others do and need more of that energy from others. There is no special bloodline or initiation to what we are. If you have a person in your life whom you like, whom you enjoy being around, but despite those things makes you feel drained; That person may very well be a vampire.

Identifying as a vampire means understanding the relationship between your energy and the energy of those around you. Being aware of it. Being aware of your needs. Think of vampirism as "spiritual diabetes". We lack more of the energy that most people have and need that energy from others.

We can't prove that metaphysical energy exists, it may not. The interaction that happens between us and the people around us may very well be chemical. It could be phenomenal. My hypothesis is that metaphysical energy is no different than the rest of the electromagnetic spectrum in that it's a natural phenomenon that we simply cannot see and therefore have difficulty believing. We know so little about the human brain's effect on our environment. Our thoughts and feelings could very well create vibrations in the space around us that others can feel or interact with. Stories of psychic phenomenon are common in almost every culture.

When it comes to vampires there are two basic types, though there are many subtypes. The first is what's called "pranic vampirism". Pranic vampirism refers to the individuals I mentioned before, who need the energy of other people and feed on that energy to increase the quality of their existence. The word "pranic" comes from the word prana, a Sanskrit word for 'breath'. Prana comes from Vedantic philosophy, it refers to the living energy that surrounds us all and lives in us, but it doesn't refer to the atma, or soul. An energy vampire feeds on your living energy, but isn't trying to "eat your soul".

The second type is "sanguine vampirism". Sanguine vampires literally drink the blood of others. The reasons given for this are many, but one interpretation is that drinking the blood of someone else is a more direct and powerful way of feeding on their energy. Whether this experience is more direct and powerful because blood is a more potent source of this energy, or if it has something to do with blood itself isn't known.

Many vampires who drink blood also consume energy, giving credence to the idea that there may be a connection between the blood and the energy. It may even mean that we don't need blood, simply that we need energy; that some of us believe that getting it through blood is the only way.

You'll find differences of opinion in the vampire community just like you would anywhere else with any other group. Some people relate their vampirism to their spiritual faith, if they have one. Modern vampires come from many walks of life and they're just as inclined as any other group to identify their condition with their religion.

A person with cancer may think it's God's will that they have cancer. A blind practitioner of another faith may think of their blindness as a gift or a curse from some divine or profane source. They may even incorporate this idea into their religion. This fact, however, does not make vampirism a religion. Being a vampire doesn't mean that you're in a cult, that you worship Satan, or really mean anything else about who you are. Just like any other characteristic it's only an aspect of who we are. Whether or not we choose to believe that that particular aspect of ourselves stems from something else is based on individual choice, not some dogma.

If vampirism exists it exists without choice, just as diabetes exists without choice. That means that someone you know, even someone in your family could be a vampire and not know it, just as they could be diabetic and not know it.

The Sire now conducts the initiate to listen and then experiment with Pranic Healing techniques

PRANIC HEALING INTRODUCTION

Pranic Healing is based on the overall structure of the human body. A human's whole physical body is actually composed of two parts: the visible physical body and the invisible energy body called the bioplasmic body. The visible physical body is that part of the human body that we see, touch, and are most acquainted with. The bioplasmic body is that invisible luminous energy body which interpenetrates the visible physical body and extends beyond it by four or five inches. Traditionally, clairvoyants call this energy body the etheric body or etheric double.

What Is Pranic Healing?

Pranic healing is an ancient science and art of healing that utilises 'Prana' or 'Ki' or life energy to heal the whole physical body. It also involves the manipulation of 'Ki' and bioplasmic matter of the patient's body. It has also been called medical qigong (Ki kung or Ki healing), psychic healing, vitalic healing, therapeutic touch, laying of the hand, magnetic healing, faith healing, and charismatic healing.

Two Basic Laws of Pranic Healing

Pranic healing is based on two laws: The law of self-recovery and the law of prana or life energy. These laws are quite obvious but strangely they are usually the least noticed or least remembered by most people. It is through these basic laws that rapid or miraculous healing occurs.

1. Law of Self-Recovery:

In general, the body is capable of healing itself at a certain rate. If a person has a wound or burn, the body will heal itself and recover within a few days to a week. In other words, even if you do not apply antibiotic on the wound or burn, the body will repair or heal itself. At the present moment, there is no medicine available for the treatment of viral infection. But even if a person has cough or cold due to viral infection, the body will recover generally in one or two weeks without medication.

2. Law of Life Energy:

For life to exist, the body must have prana, chi or life energy. The healing process can be accelerated by increasing life energy on the affected part(s) and on the entire body.

In chemistry, electrical energy is sometimes used as a catalyst to increase the rate of chemical reaction. Light can affect chemical reaction. This is the basis for photography. In electrolysis, electricity is used to catalyse or produce chemical reaction. In Pranic healing, prana or life energy serves as the catalyst to accelerate the rate of biochemical reactions involved in the natural healing process of the body and when Pranic energy is applied to the affected part of the body the rate of recovery or healing increases tremendously.

What we call miraculous healing is nothing more than increasing the rate of self-recovery of the body. There is nothing supernatural or paranormal about Pranic healing. It is simply based on natural laws that most people are not aware of.

Although science is not able to detect and measure life energy or prana, it does not mean that prana does not exist or does not affect the health and well being of the body. In ancient times, people were not aware of the existence of electricity, its properties and practical uses. But this does not mean that electricity does not exist. One's ignorance does not change reality; it simply alters the perception of reality, resulting in misperception and misconception of what is and what is not, what can be done and what cannot be done.

Children have more life energy than elderly people do. You notice that they move a lot from morning to night, hardly getting tired at all. When suffering from a fracture, who heals faster —the child or the elderly? The broken bone of a child heals very fast while that of an elderly heals very slowly; sometimes, it will not even heal at all.

Prana or Ki

Prana or Ki is that life energy which keeps the body alive and healthy. In Greek it is called `pneuma`, in Polynesian `mana`, and in Hebrew `ruah`, which means `breath of life`. The healer projects prana or life energy or `the breath of life` to the patient, thereby, healing the patient. It is through this process that this so-called `miraculous healing` is accomplished.

Basically, there are three major sources of prana: solar prana, air prana and ground prana. Solar prana is prana from sunlight. It invigorates the whole body and promotes good health. It can be obtained by sunbathing or exposure to sunlight for about five to ten minutes and by drinking water that has been exposed to sunlight. Prolonged exposure or too much solar prana would harm the whole physical body since it is quite potent.

Prana contained in the air is called air prana or air vitality globule. Air prana is absorbed by the lungs through breathing and is also absorbed directly by the energy centres of the bioplasmic body. These energy centres are called chakras. More air prana can be absorbed by deep slow rhythmic breathing than by short shallow breathing.

It can also be absorbed through the pores of the skin by persons who have undergone certain training.

Prana contained in the ground is called ground prana or ground vitality globule. This is absorbed through the soles of the feet. This is done automatically and unconsciously, for example, walking barefoot increases the amount of ground prana absorbed by the body.

One can learn to consciously draw in more ground prana to increase one's vitality, capacity to do more work, and ability to think more clearly.

Water absorbs prana from sunlight, air, and ground that it comes in contact with. Plants and trees absorb prana from sunlight, air, water, and ground. Men and animals obtain prana from sunlight, air, ground, water, and food. Fresh food contains more prana than preserved food.

Prana can also be projected to another person for healing. Persons with a lot of excess prana tend to make other people around them feel better and livelier. However, those who are depleted tend to unconsciously absorb prana from other people. You may have encountered persons who tend to make you feel tired or drained for no apparent reason at all.

Certain trees, such alpine trees or old and gigantic healthy trees, exude a lot of excess prana. Tired or sick people benefit much by lying down or resting underneath these trees. Better results can be obtained by verbally requesting the being of the tree to help the sick person get well.

Anyone can also learn to consciously absorb prana from these trees through the palms, such that the body would tingle and become numb because of the tremendous amount of prana absorbed. This skill can be acquired after only a few sessions of practice.

Certain areas or places tend to have more prana than others. Some of these highly energized areas tend to become healing centres.

During bad weather conditions, many people get sick not only because of the changes in temperature but also because of the decrease in solar and air prana (life energy). Thus, a lot of people feel mentally and physically sluggish or become susceptible to infectious diseases. This can be counteracted by consciously absorbing prana or ki from the air and the ground. It has been clairvoyantly observed that there is more prana during daytime than at night. Prana reaches a very low level at about three or four in the morning.

Aura

Clairvoyants, with the use of their psychic faculties, have observed that every person is surrounded and interpenetrated by a luminous energy body called the bioplasmic body or aura. Just like the visible physical body, it has a head, two eyes, two arms, etc. In other words, the bioplasmic body looks like the visible physical body. This is why clairvoyants call it the etheric double or etheric body.

The word `bioplasmic` comes from `bio`, which means life and plasma which is the fourth state of matter, the first three being: solid, liquid, and gas. Plasma is ionised gas or gas with positive and negative charged particles. This is not the same as blood plasma. Bioplasmic body means a living energy body made up of invisible subtle matter or etheric matter.

To simplify the terminology, the term `energy body` will be used to replace the word `bioplasmic body`. Science, with the use of Kirlian photography, has rediscovered the energy body. With the aid of Kirlian photography, scientists have been able to study, observe, and take pictures of small bioplasmic articles like bioplasmic fingers, leaves, etc. It is through the energy body that prana or life energy is absorbed and distributed throughout the whole physical body.

Benefits of Pranic Healing

1. It can help parents bring down the temperature of their children suffering from high fever in just a few hours and heal it in a day or two in most cases.

2. It can relieve headaches, gas pains, toothaches, and muscle pains almost immediately in most cases.

3. Cough and cold can usually be cured in a day or two. Loose bowel movement can be healed in a few hours in most cases.

4. Major illnesses such as eye, liver, kidney, and heart problems can be relieved in a few sessions and healed in a few months in many cases.

5. It increases the rate of healing by three times or more than the normal rate of healing. These are some of the few things that Pranic healing can do. All of these assume that the healer has attained a certain degree of proficiency.

Pranic Healing Is Easy To Learn

Any healthy person with an average intelligence, an average ability to concentrate, an open but discriminating mind, and a certain degree of persistence can learn Pranic healing in a relatively short period. Learning Pranic healing is easier than learning to play the piano or painting. It is as easy as learning to drive. Its basic principles and techniques can be learned in a few sessions. Like driving, Pranic healing requires much practice and time to achieve a certain degree of proficiency.

Time is now given for the Mentor and Initiate to practice the use of this knowledge in a safe environment

Developing the Akhkharu Language

As we travel through the stages of development we begin to recognise certain words and phrases that are familiar to us, the familiarity of our daily activities. This is key to our understanding of the Old Ways and the that of the language of the Akhkharu. The Language of the D.e.a.d refers to the Akhkharu language, and in time this will make more sense and provide structure within your knowledge of this precious way of communication.

Each word and phrase has a distinct set of what is known as **vibrations**, the most profound attribute within the Multiverse of existence. Therefore, it is imperative that you continue to hear and pronounce the words as they have always been spoken universally. Below is a key set of terms and phrases for you to familiarise yourself with in preparation for the next stage of your development:

Akhkharu	Vampire
Iddugga	Righteous
Kak Tut Weh	How are you
Adar	Star of Ninasu (Home Planet)
Kak Mer	Why so
Kak Mal	Why you
Usim	Hello
Silimdu	Goodbye
Abarassa	True
Taputtu	Planet
Arammu	Love
Kataru	Allies / Alliance
Salak	Enemy
Akla	Milk
Dalla	Coffee
Dingir	Tea

Shiqlu	Sugar
Eme.Gir	Native Tongue
ChaCha	Mysterious
Amargi	Freedom
Mashkim	Judge
Sumeru	Language of Vampires
Ala	Yes
Ibsa	No
Zi.Ud	You
E	I
Mak Mal	Thank You
Tukumbi	Please
Nibiru	Good Morning
Tiamat	Good Night
Si Enki	Towards Raphael
Od	Or

Now for a familiarisation with numeracy:

1	As
2	Min
3	Es
4	Limmu
5	Ia
6	Ia. As
7	Ia. Min
8	Issu
9	Ilimmu
10	U
11	U.Ma. As
12	U.Ma. Min
13	U.Ma. Es

14	U.ma. Limmu
15	U.Ma la
16	U.Ma. I.As
17	U.Ma. la.Min
18	U.Ma. Issu
19	U.Ma. Ilimmu
20	Nis
30	Usu
40	Nin
50	Ninu
60	Ges

Time is given prior to closing, for the Initiate to hear the pronunciation of the words and numbers and to take time to practice

Mak Alam Mas Alam

Thamuz   Enki   Shamsiel

Azazel   Raphael   Shamsiel

Third Generation

The Altar Set within the three K.e.y points, namely; West, South, and East, with the Energy Mark at each Altar. For Shamsiel's Altar in the East three tea light candles and the Triangle of Time descending, the Sire's personal piece of Garnet, The Sire's personal Sibbu Usbar (Snake Staff), 3 tea candles, 4 small natural liquorice sticks (or similar) set into triangular form (in the centre), water, Honey, Burdock root, Blood, Lavender, Cinnamon, Charged fluid (dependant on occasion), and a Reciprocal of choosing to hold charged fluid.

Identity: By the Mark

Below Centre: Sibbu Usbar (Snake staff of the conducting Sire)

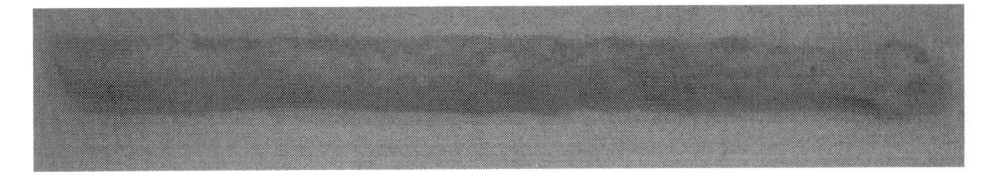

Vampiric Temple

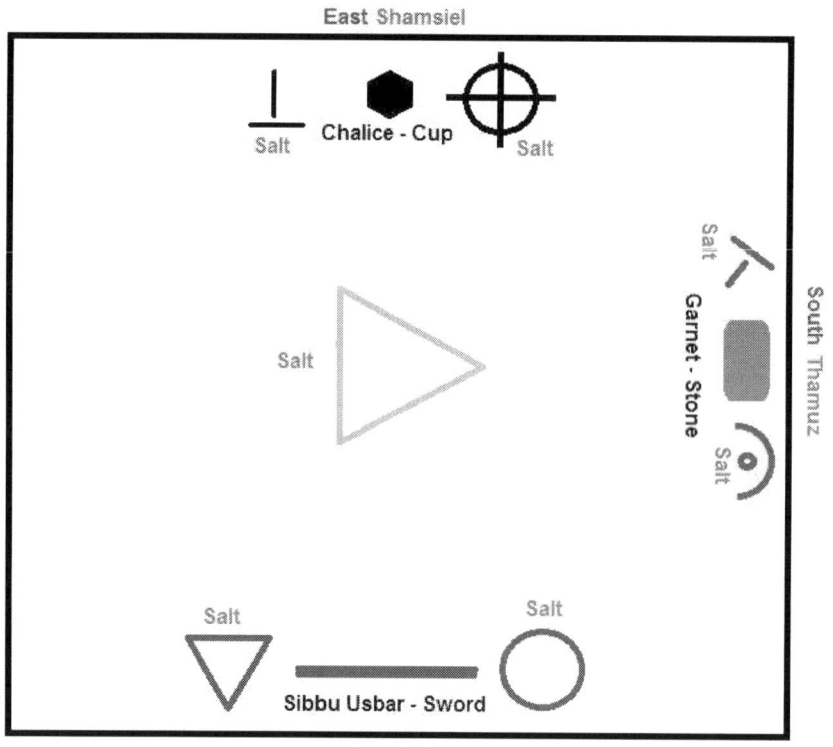

The Triangle of time is referred to as on the Altar of Shamsiel. However, in the higher Generations it may remain on the Shamsiel Altar, though not essential. More importantly as detailed above, the centre of the space would be for three wooden logs made into your Triangle of Time.

The Nine Gates At this stage of your development, it is important to convoke all energies and spheres. Do not worry if it takes some time to harness the powers, as with most workings, practice always makes perfect.

Elder Star

Within the Third transit the use of the **Chalice of Shamsiel** must be used to add the potion mix of each gate as follows:

Guardians in third transit

1st	Enki	Water
2nd	Thamuz	Honey
3rd	Thamuz	Burdock Root
4th	Enki	Blood
5th	Thamuz	Lavender
6th	Thamuz	Salt
7th	Enki	Cinnamon
8th	Enki	Rose Petal
9th	**Enki and Thamuz in Union**	the cardinal of Garnet

Note that the potion to convoke has now evolved to a higher level

Cardinal	Immortal Stone	Of Garnet
1st Gate	Raphael	Of Water
2nd Gate	Astaroth	Of Honey
3rd Gate	Focalor	Of Burdock Root
4th Gate	Pazuzu	Of Blood
5th Gate	Sitri	Of Lavender

6th Gate	Murmur	Of Salt
7th Gate	Asmoday	Of Cinnamon
8th Gate	Khoronzon	Of Rose Petal
9th Gate	Azazel	Of Garnet

It is known as **Cinnabar**, for that is the combination of life and death, the unique composition of the energies, having the soul of the creature removed and thus all barriers raised. The Cinnabar is in form of block or necklace and will be used within the Abyss in time to follow.

There are three house forms, namely;

The Creation at the right point of the triangle of existence

The Abyss at the left point of the triangle of existence

The Sanctuary at the bottom point of the triangle of existence

As we know the Abyss is of Enki and the Sanctuary is of Thamuz. We further know that they are one and the same, as when in union the powers of the Households combined are wondrous. As per your Third Generation, we see that the Nine gates are empowered by Enki and Thamuz alone.

Therefore, the house of Vampires, or rather **Upir Likhyi**, exist for the purpose of destiny, the purpose that those whom come to know will come to dare, and those whom come to dare will know of all within and without. We know that the Vampire Households are but three, it is when all three are able to combine that we see the evolution of the hybrid race expand throughout all realms of the Multiverse.

The more you learn and come to know about the Households, the more strength and powers that are gained. However, with every generation you will continue to undertake that internal debate of right and wrong, the debate of good and bad, and most importantly; the internal debate of what you wish outcomes to be. Our path is often one of analysis, where we look into the future so to determine the present and assist us to map our pathway forward.

Remember that you are stronger that such mortal creatures, for although your transformation may not occur for a millennium, in a thousand years, so long as you continue to be an **Adna**, an ally of Enki and his creatures, you will continue to receive the knowledge of Dark Magic and that which is truth within this Universe, and others. You will give more heed to your conduct and know that you will never be alone, so long as you guard fast your Sire and swear loyalty to us alone.

You will know him as Jesus, his true name and form of **Malak**, for he did say unto the world, that 'so long as you eat my flesh and drink my blood, you shall be saved at the end of time'.
Go now and eat the flesh of the 'Son of Man, that which is mortal and not eternal.

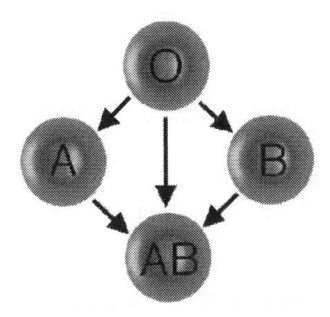

It is our expectation that you work ever towards being a Telal, that Demon Warrior whom you are meant to be, to guard true and protect those of us that support and believe in you. By the **Star and Stone** in form 'Nana ma Adar', for **Shamsiel** will know if you are true, the Highest Sphere will support you or crush you, for this is your choice, your choice alone. Within this House of Vampires, 'Upir Likyi', know this. The **Ennuunkabarra** 'En-nu-un-ka-bar-ra' guard the outer gate of Shamsiel.

Be true to us and we will continue to be true with you. Be strong in our words and we will speak the wisdom of truth, be courageous in battle and we will protect and comfort thee.

The Creation of sequence
Opening Prayer

Kur Dingar, E ina Utu, Nanna, ma Adar

Su'ati annu Piriq, ina Azag

Annu tisa bi er E Gallas

Mamman aga Azag bur annu aka annu wur eri

Underworld God, raise the Sun, Moon, and star

That this the bearer of the magic,

From the shining bright this ninth command to go raise demons.

Whoever crowns the shining bright hear this divine command, this wisdom bind

Sire Karabu er igi mannu Gana ina annu Dalbana. Lu malu zu Inimdug, arammu ma zid ina ma balu. Girigena tia dimmu aradu Hasusu Menzug Namen ma eribu annu edin.

Blessings to those who stand in this space

Let us know peace, love and truth within and without

Path of order descend

Remember your Priesthood and enter this plain

All

Ala Ina Ara Aram All within time come forth

Sire summons the L.i.g.h.t

From the Altar of Shamsiel, light all three candles then say the words below:

The Calling (point-left-below-right) Light candles of the Triangle – Lilitu Enki tia Ugur, Samu Thamuz tia menzen, Salmu Shamsiel tia Muh, sha Uru menzen

'Blue Enki of Sword, Red Thamuz of Stone, Black Shamsiel of Chalice, we support you'

Sire

Ar, isatu, ma ganzer – sha sugid ina menzug gigun, da malu ina ugula tia ina gula adhal kima sha andul ina sumer

Light, Fire, and Darkness – We accept the sacred building, make us the overseers of the great secret as we protect the land of the watchers.

Hand, Horn, Blood and Bone	Silig, Quannu, Uri ma Esentu
Wisdom old and wisdom young	Namzu Labaru ma Namzu ban
Child of star and moon of night	Damu tia mulan ma su.en tia gi
Elders strong in waters time	Abba ama ina Anumun ara
Come with everlasting sight	Alka Adullab nigul Igigal
And do your desire with light	Ma ak Menzug Aldug Adullab ar

Sire

Sha peta annu dalbana anna zae er tapputtu malu ina parsu. Ama menden zig ma alad menden idu. Menzug ugur tia zid adullab anna ina abula tia ara, kima ina dilibad es tia ina utu udmeda dubsag zae, sha gana menzug fi namen.

We open this space unto you to aid us in religious duties. Strong we stand and spirit we know. Your sword of truth now unto the gate of time, as the shining temple of the sun ever before you, we stand your serpent priesthood.

All

Ala Ina Ara Aram All within time comes forth

Ala Ina Ara Aram All within time comes forth

Triangle formed upon the Altar, the Sire will call each point in sequence, hand is held at a forty-five degree angle above the flame

West – Sword

Ina nabu, ina lilitu alad tia ara, sha uru zae. Barba ina annu gug ma dug da malu. Wasru sha gana, ina fi namen, ullulu annu Susgal ma lu Inimdug ba ina malu.

The past, the blue spirit of time, we support you. Break through this seal and speak with us. Humble we stand, the Serpent Priesthood, purify this castle and let peace live through us

South – Garnet

Ina amalug, ina samu alad tia ara, sha uru zae. Barba ina annu gug ma dug da malu. Wasru sha gana, ina fi namen, ullulu annu Susgal ma lu Inimdug ba ina malu.

The present, the red spirit of time, we support you. Break through this seal and speak with us. Humble we stand, the Serpent Priesthood, purify this castle and let peace live through us

East – Chalice

Ina mulan, ina salmu alad tia ara, sha uru zae. Barba ina annu gug ma dug da malu. Wasru sha gana, ina fi namen, ullulu annu Susgal ma lu Inimdug ba ina malu.

The future, the black spirit of time, we support you. Break through this seal and speak with us. Humble we stand, the Serpent Priesthood, purify this castle and let peace live through us

Sire

Azig durtur fi, e ina annu dalbana tia ara. Ina ina er balu, ina ina amalug da namigigal – Sha dura ina atuku alad tia ina ar. Kunu, sudug ina annu kaunakes tia ar. Alka sus malu ina abru tia ar ma du wasru. Namazlag nu tia annu dalbana, ina utusus tia nam ma ina Aguziga tia ina sargad, isatu ama ma wur er du, sha uul er us ina ina masu tir.

Raise the Great Serpent, rise through this space of time. From within to without, through the present with insight – We draw together the powerful spirits of the L.i.g.h.t. Approach, transform through this thick cloak of time. Come cover us in beams of light and hold humble. Craft Creator of this space, the sunset of destiny and the dawn of the worlds, fire strong and wisdom to hold, we consent to follow within the forgotten forest.

All

Ala Ina Ara Aram *All within time comes forth*

Gather close and all link hands
Travel widdershins with the Chant:

Chant:

Uri ma Esentu, Uri ma Esentu

Ala in Ara Mupad kima esdu

Blood and bone, blood and bone

All in time to invoke as one

Continue for as long as you feel it necessary, gaining speed as you travel around

Halt the Chant – Release hands, and then raise your hands into the air, with the sign of the Nephilim:

Shamsiel

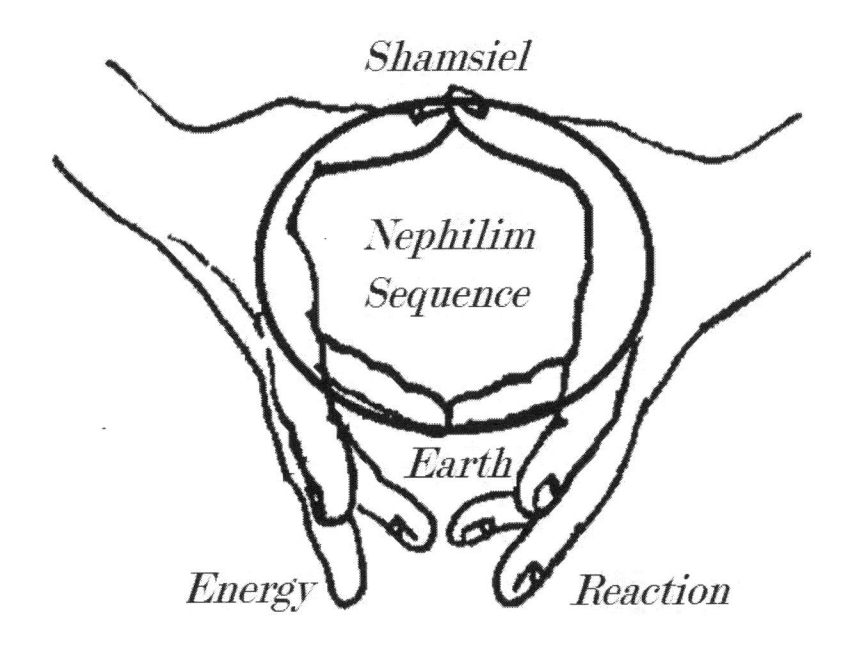

Nephilim Sequence

Earth

Energy *Reaction*

'Kasaru Nam Ina Anu'

'Gather destiny within this'

Cleanse Holy water upon Altar

Either hand straight out deosil – clockwise – motion

Sire

Urru annu da A dimmu antam, Keezh annu Arazu be Gi ma Dag, wur damu ma bar. Bana gankankha ina Ara ma ina ina zagdaku

Guard this gift I order the universe, under this prayer to be night and day, wisdom child and seat of wisdom. Exorcise this vessel in time and in the dark threshold

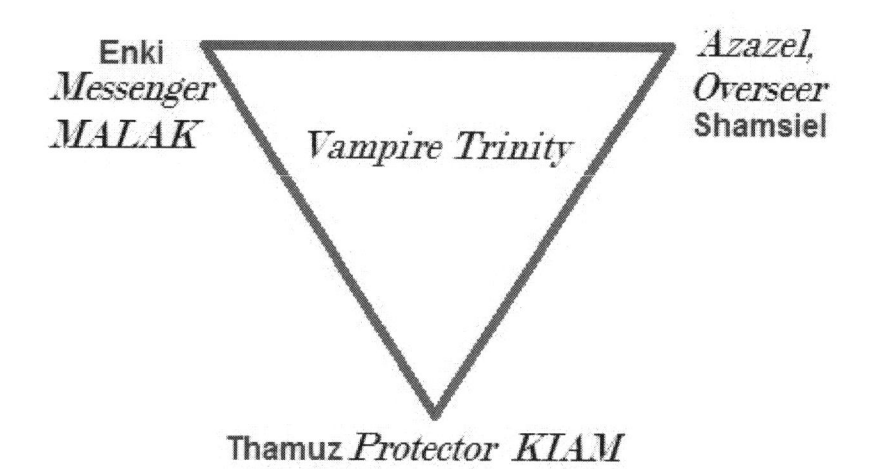

```
        Enki                    Azazel,
     Messenger                 Overseer
       MALAK   Vampire Trinity  Shamsiel
              \              /
               \            /
                \          /
                 \        /
                  \      /
                   \    /
                    \  /
                     \/
            Thamuz Protector KIAM
```

Sepu Pil Ak Shamsiel

Anoint Craft of All

Sire

'Sepu Pil Ak Shamsiel'

By grace of Highest Sphere

Sire

Alka adullab an esig ina alad tia ina shinar, lu igen ahulu sig lipis, kug idu ma arammu da malu gana ina ina arazu tia sudum ma subar ar itka malu.

Come now and honour the spirits of the land, let no malice be cast inward, pure knowledge and love with us stand through the prayer of reckoning and release light upon us.

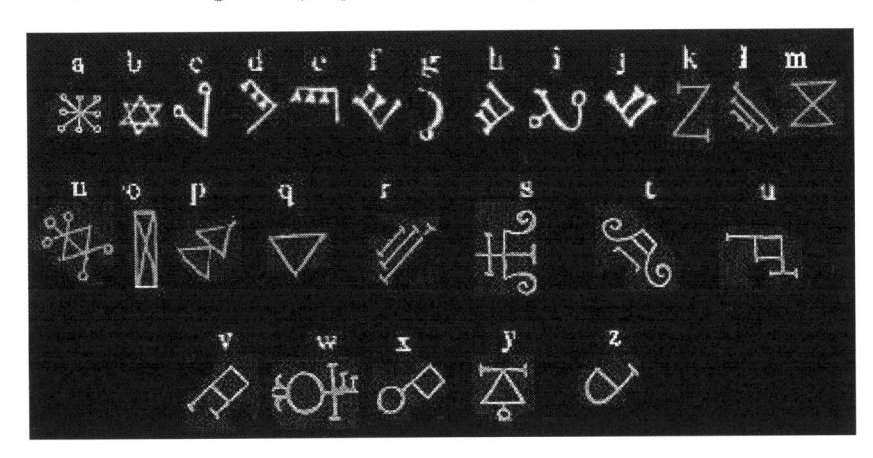

Drawing down the Sun, Moon, and Stars commences with the **Sibbu Usbar** (Snake Staff). Sire stands facing the east at the Altar, speaks the scripture once, then Calls the energy's name once at each call:

Ina Annu Bi, Ina Egura Da Dur Tur Erim Lu ina Anna Azag, la Lalartu, Duttu Bi Dara Bi!

Through this command, through Black Water the great bind, Let through unto the shining bright. Hail Phantom! Hail! One who speaks, command dark divides.

DRAWING DOWN ANSHAR: 1st CALLING of Moon

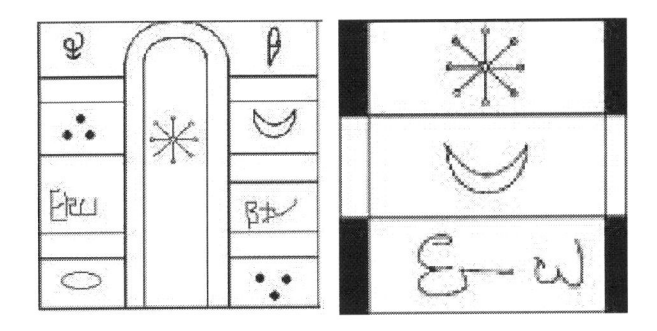

DRAWING DOWN EA: 2ND CALLING of Neptune

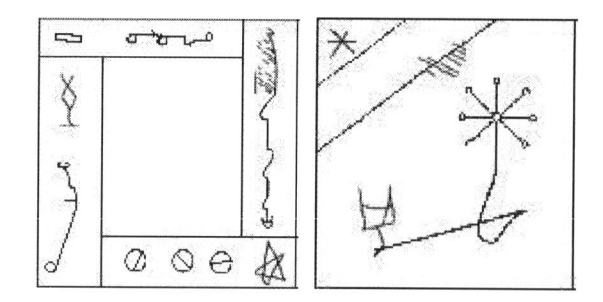

DRAWING DOWN INANNA: 3rd CALLING of Saturn

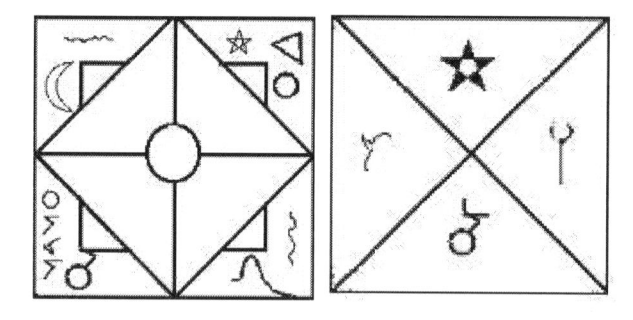

DRAWING DOWN AR: 4th CALLING of the Sun

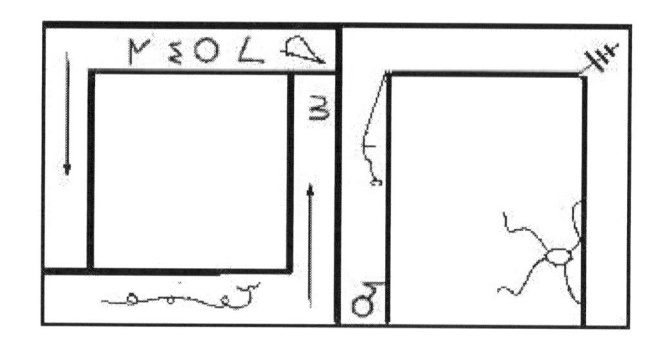

DRAWING DOWN ANUNNA: 5th CALLING of Mars

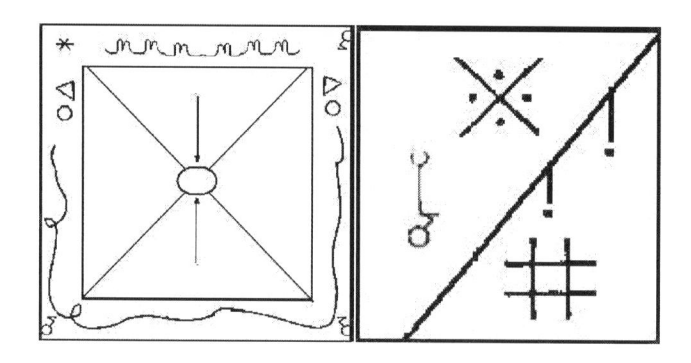

DRAWING DOWN RA.UBAN: 6th CALLING of Black Sun

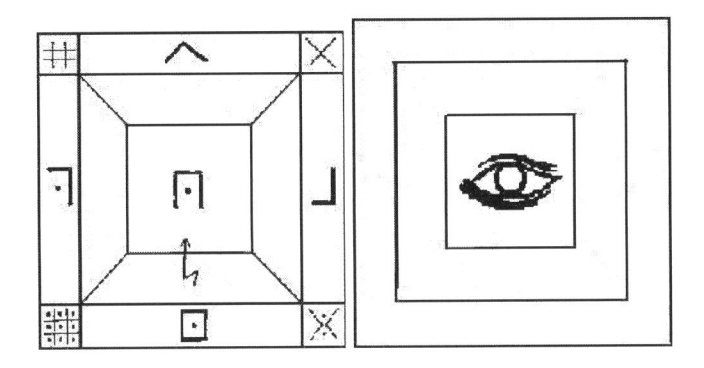

DRAWING DOWN LAHMU: 7th CALLING of Venus

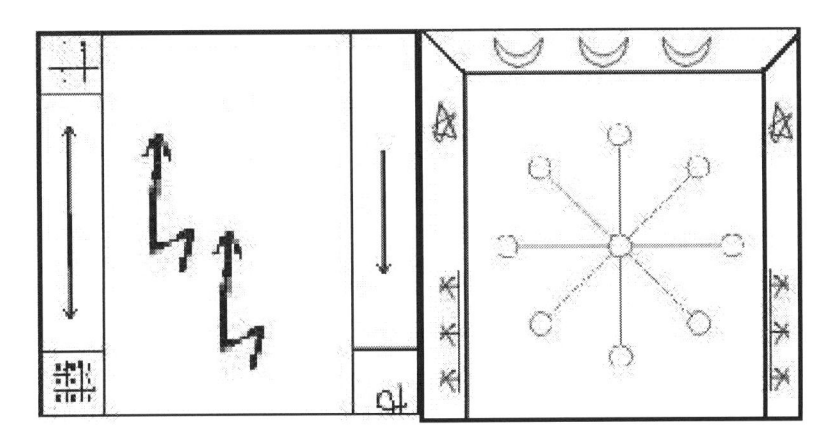

Crossing the barrier through Thamuz (Kiam)

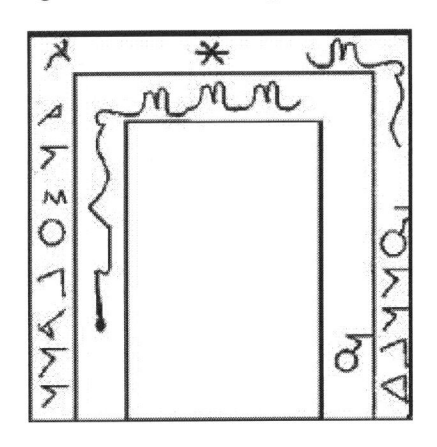

E DUR.TUR FI! E KUR INA ANNU EGURA!

EGURA FI DURA E! EGURA FI E!

ERI ANNU FI BI DUTTU! ANA SA DUR.TUR BI

ERI ANNU FI LU INA

BAR INA ARA ERI!

Rise the great Serpent!

Rise Underworld through this Black Water!

Black Water rise, draw together rise!

Black Water serpent rise

Bind this serpent with one who speaks!

One who the great command

Bind this serpent let through

Seat of wisdom through time bind!

(Allow 60 seconds to pass then say these words)

BI INA ANNU ERI

(Allow 60 seconds to pass then raise the sword of Kiam and say these words)

BI ALA BI INA GIDIM

EDIN NA ZU!

The call of Shemyaza

'The call of Leaders'

Note that a generation is indicated by each stage of development through, the initiate is a 1st Generation, and this increases until transformation, if this is deemed suitable at an appropriate time.

The 'Leaders' are known by many names, such as; Keepers, Nephilim, Angels, Demons, Guardians, and the 'Nine Lords of the Abyss'.

It is imperative that you know that to summon the Leaders is wrong, so it is wrong to invoke (bring spirit within), and further wrong to evoke (bring spirit around us). The K.e.y here is to Convoke, in other words, to cause to assemble in a meeting.

The Gateway

If not established already, the Sire will place the wooden logs in the centre of the space in the form of an inverted triangle, inverting from the North, so that the point of the triangle is in the South. The Sire will continue to seal the outer boundary of the triangle with salt in a widdershins (anti-clockwise) motion as he says the words of Shamsiel:

Varkmal Gelet Tu Mar

Suati Mili Korit gal

Tu Veh se.ant mal

Luvae Kalmak, Luvae Kalmak, Luvae Kalmak

The Constraint

The Sire now calls each of the Leaders by way of Convoke. As the Sire calls each one, he cast the relevant compound into the Chalice. Once all compounds are in the Chalice, the Sire tips the potion mix into the sealed triangle:

Sire E Su.Gaz Ina Alad Ak Anumun Ina Enki
I convoke the spirit of Water through Enki (First Gate)

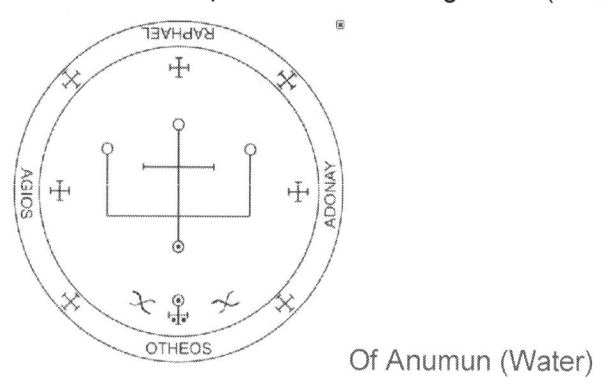

Of Anumun (Water)

Sire E Su.Gaz Ina Alad Ak Lil Ina Thamuz
I convoke the spirit of Honey through Thamuz (Second Gate)

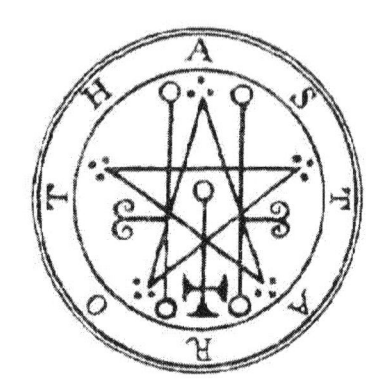

Of Lil (Honey)

Sire E Su.Gaz Ina Alad Ak Lappa Ina Thamuz
I convoke the spirit of Burdock Root through Thamuz (Third Gate)

Of Lappa (Burdock Root)

Sire E Su.Gaz Ina Alad Ak Uri Ina Enki

I convoke the spirit of Blood through Enki (Fourth Gate)

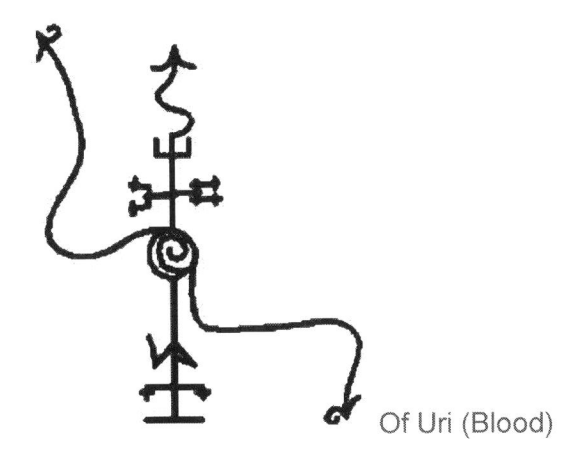

Of Uri (Blood)

Sire E Su.Gaz Ina Alad AK Azugnu Ina Thamuz

I convoke the spirit of Lavender through Thamuz (Fifth Gate)

Of Azugnu (Lavender)

Sire E Su.Gaz Ina Alad AK Dinig Ina Thamuz

I convoke the spirit of Salt through Thamuz (Sixth Gate)

Of Dinig (Salt)

Sire E Su.Gaz Ina Alad AK Qeneh Ina Enki

I convoke the spirit of Cinnamon through Enki (Seventh Gate)

Of Qeneh (Cinnamon)

Sire E Su.Gaz Ina Alad AK Aruru Ina Enki

I convoke the spirit of Rose Petal through Enki (Eighth Gate)

Of Aruru (Rose Petal)

Sire E Su.Gaz Ina Alad AK Nunki Ina Enki ma Thamuz

I convoke the spirit of Garnet through Enki and Thamuz (Ninth Gate)

Of Nunki (Garnet)

Sire – The Charge of Shamsiel

Sepu Ala Ina Nim Kabtu Tia Samsu Tia Ina Gula

Asum Firiq Tia Anki Alka Ahias ma Balu

Bar Dura Salatu Atuku

Nadanu Abarassa Awum. Da Menzug Masgik

Dug Luname E Igigal. E Su.Gaz Zae Alad Tia Shamsiel

Da Menzug Masgik

Alka Ina Annu Sagtak ma Awum

By all the High Glory of Names of the Great

Empowered lord of the Universe, come quickly and without

Barriers, draw together outside powers

Give true communication, make yourself visible

Come through this triangle and converse

INA ANNU BI, E UTU, NANNA, MA ADAR

DA ANNU INA ES E, MA ERI INA INA EGURA

DARA DUTTU LU INA ANNU ES ANNA INA HURSAGMU!

Through this command

Rise Sun, Moon, and Star

Make this the Temple rise and bind from the black water

Dark one who speaks let through this temple unto the mountain of the sky-chambers!

Sire Alka ina ina gidim quannu duramah, gibil wur, su'ati zae da

Durisam ina karabu ma sibum annu da er ina antam

Come through the spirit horn the great stag, one of fire wisdom, that you make forever this blessing and witness this offering to the universe. Come through and answer this prayer in love and truth. Blood Elders we carry the circle to the chamber of the regions of the four to aid and to let those who enter know you.

Sire sprinkles white salt over the Altar of Shamsiel (in the East)

Sire Gi be dag ma dara be ar

Night to be Day and Dark to be Light

Lectures and Practical teaching begins...

The closing and departure of Energies

(Sire will be at the alter and guard well the Circle of duality, with the Sibbu Usbar in hand to say these words)

Sire O spirits of Shamsiel, because thou hast diligently answered, I do hereby recognise and accept thee to depart, without injury to man or beast. Depart, and be thou willing and ready to come, whensoever duly exorcised and con red by the sacred rites of the Old Ways, the Dark Knowledge. I conjure thee to withdraw peaceably and quietly, and may peace continue forever between me and thee. **Mak Alam Mas Alam**

All candles are extinguished and the Sibbu Usbar (Snake Staff) is set to the ground to discharge.

Mary Magdalene

Magdala – At the Western Shore, at the Sea of Galilee

Mary Magdalene, an interesting person within all time and certainly within the majority of religions. She has been named by many to be the 'beloved disciple' of Jesus of Nazareth, but how much substance is there to such amazing accounts?

Born in 'Magdala' off the western shore of the Sea of Galilee on the 22nd July in the year 8 CE, her life was to be an ongoing debate that would continue with debate for many years after her death.

Some describe her as a dedicated disciple of Jesus of Nazareth, where others describe her as no more than a prostitute whom had the condition of epilepsy.

However one thing is certain in that she was a living, breathing, human being, whom spent some eight years in the company of Jesus.

The four Gospels of Matthew, Mark, Luke, and John are the earliest scriptures relating to Mary Magdalene, being written over a timeframe of fifty years, more precisely, between 40 and 90 CE, whom write that Mary had several demons come out of her.

But what did this mean? Were there several demons from the spirit world that possessed Mary at certain points in time? Or was she having seizures by way of her epilepsy condition? One may further suggest that the 'demons' that are referred to within the Gospels were with reference to several failed pregnancies.

It was in 36 CE, eight years after her Baptism performed by John – The Baptist, and subsequent Blessing of 'Union' between Jesus and herself, that their union was truly blessed. Mary Magdalene was now carrying the child of the Christ, the child of 'the anointed one'.

She continued to minister the word of Jesus, and spread the word of the Logos; being, Word, Wisdom, Reason, and Rationality.

The year was passing well, Jesus and his disciples were preaching the word of the God, more importantly, Jesus would soon have a heir to the 'bloodline'. However, time would soon change as John – The Baptist, still imprisoned at the fortress, now had received his fate to be beheaded and thus it came to pass on 29th August 36 CE.

The news of the death of John – The Baptist travelled fast across the lands. Jesus, in the following weeks, still in mourning for John and in utter disbelief, went to the Temple and disrupted the traders stalls within the Temple, stating that they had turned to House of the God into the 'den of the demons'. Accompanied by Mary and the other disciples they were able to convince Jesus to leave.

On the 14th September in the year 36 CE, Jesus and his disciples were feasting in the 'Upper Room' of their building, outside the city walls of old Jerusalem, on Mount Zion. The feasting was to be known in later years as 'the Last Supper'. After the feasting Jesus, Mary, and the other disciples ventured into the garden known as Gethsemane, at the foot of a mount of olives, and it is here on this very evening that Jesus was arrested by the Temple Guards, by order of the Sanhedrin (Religious Council).

Jesus was taken into custody to be tried for the disruption he had caused to the traders within the temple. The trial commenced and Jesus was sentenced to death, to which occurred on 21st September in the year 36 CE, watched by Mary Magdalene, as stated within the Gospel of Matthew where he explains that the many women who followed Jesus from Galilee, were there looking from afar, among whom were Mary Magdalene, Mary the mother of James and the mother of Zebedee's sons.

Jesus died on 21st September 36 CE – Though it is left with speculation as to whether he arrived at death by stoning, hanging, or crucifixion. What is certain is that his body was taken to a stone tomb to lay in rest.

The Gospels clearly state that three days after the death of Jesus, he rose from the dead and first appeared to Mary Magdalene. There is now doubt to this writing. Indeed he did rise, but the Gospels were referring to the birth of Jesus' son named 'Jul', his birthday of 24th September 36 CE.

The Gospels further make reference to Mary Magdalene 'anointing' him. Again, this reference is to the blessing passed from Mary Magdalene to her newborn child. Therefore, it is that Christ 'the anointed one' lives on Earth amongst us, at the lineage of Jesus lives on within Jul, the son of Jesus. However, consider what would become of Mary Magdalene and her son?

Mary departed with her son to new lands with new hope of peace. However, it is written that she returned in 50 CE to Qumran, to become the founder of a new community, where she shared the true accounts of her time with Jesus, on the understanding that her son Jul would be mentioned, but hidden within the scriptures that would follow.

It is noted that there is no mention of Mary Magdalene's son returning to Qumran with Mary. It is further noted that Mary Magdalene taught the 'Ansar' – The Holy Warriors, being the 'helpers' of the God.

In conclusion at this stage of your development, it would be prudent to focus your studies on the Ansar (from the Muslim belief system) and how they are the 'helpers' of the God, or rather, the 'helpers' of the universe – Placing them within the Northern Transit of the cycles of space and time, and how the 'energies' of the Ansar are able to assist with the perfect points.

Keys points to this introduction

'Mary Magdalene'

Birth:	8 CE – 22 July
Met Jesus:	28 CE – 13 October
Baptised:	29 CE – 10 July
Union Blessing:	36 CE – 01 February
Childbirth:	36 CE – 24th September
Energy Alignment:	15 – 16 July
	Rituals to Ea – The Messenger

Additional points for consideration

1. The Gospel of John – Is indeed the Gospel of Mary
2. Mary met Jesus on 13 October, which would be the same day in the future that the Templars would be arrested
3. On 10 July 29 CE, Mary was baptised and a Feasting followed which lasted for twelve nights, until Mary Magdalene's birthday – Interesting that there are 12 nights for the Pagan Feast at Yule and further 12 nights of Christmas in the Christian belief system, albeit in December on both counts and not in July.
4. Myrrh has a direct link to Mary Magdalene.

Jesus of Nazareth
4 BCE – 36 CE (40 years of knowledge)

Before we embark on this journey of discovery, let us first identify the true meaning of 'Christ'. This particular word is not a name or title, but rather from the Greek 'Christos' meaning 'the anointed one'. As a point of interest, the equivalent word in Hebrew is 'Messiah'. Furthermore, let us examine the name 'Jesus', with it's direct translation being 'Joshua' within Hebrew, and further Yehoshua; meaning 'deliverance'. So at this stage, we have the anointed one who has been delivered, moving closer towards the discovery of the dilution of scripture.

If we connect Jesus (Yehoshua) with Islam, we identify Jesus as the 'Messenger of the God', and within Sanskrit (Hindu), we are able to translate the name to 'Easa' or rather 'Easa Maseeha', which in turn, brings us back to Ea.

Ea we know is the aspect of Neptune, being closely connected to the Messenger, or rather the 'Rakbu' the Messenger of all that is Holy. We have further discovered that Ea has a direct association with Blue Lace Agate, and that this particular Sacred Stone has a direct link to Berenike in Egypt, but before we venture onto the distinct connections between Egypt and the 'anointed one', let us re-examine the belief systems over the many years.

It is widely believed by faith-based groups that Jesus was the Immaculate Conception, the conception without the 'blending' of two human beings. One must first consider that how is this possible? Procreation without human intervention?

It is believed that as the land, and nature, is able to provide – thus, so is the Universe able to provide. Therefore, the birth of Jesus was not supernatural, it was most natural indeed. The mother of Jesus, Mary, had been advised that she had passed child-bearing age; being highly unlikely that she would produce a child. Mary, now informed with the knowledge of being childless began her sexual relationship with a soldier named Pantera (to other's the soldier would be known as Panthera).

Once she discovered that she had conceived a child, the Virgin Mary left Nazareth and headed to Bethlehem, in order to deliver her child 'Jesus' (meaning deliverance) in secrecy. Therefore the 'Virgin' Mary was just that.

In modern times 'Virgin' has been understood to mean 'untouched' or rather that no virginal sexual intercourse has occurred. However, 'Virgin' is from the Latin term of 'Virginis'; meaning Maiden, and subsequently the 'Virgin Mary' was indeed the 'Maiden Mary'. The Maiden Mary now with child in Bethlehem, embarked on a simply life, raising her child, Jesus.

Therefore, Jesus was no more of Nazareth than you or I. It is suggested that he was conceived in Nazareth, but born in Bethlehem. Therefore the 'Anointed One' would be better described as Jesus of Bethlehem.

Growing up as a child he learned the skills of a carpenter, and as a young man hired himself out to Egypt, where he was empowered to learn the magical powers of a secret society and this is where he proclaimed himself to be the son of the God – As from his teachings he (as all of us are) the Sons and daughters of the complete Universe.

In 28 CE, Jesus left Egypt and arrived at the banks of the river Jordan, where he aligned with John, whom would be later known as 'John – The Baptist'. On the 12th September 28 CE, Jesus was baptised by John, and thus the incredible journey towards the L.i.g.h.t of discovery began, and Jesus was introduced to John's disciples as the 'Lamb of the God'

For both John and Jesus knew that he would one day be slaughtered, so to save all things living.

On the 24th August, 34 CE, John – The Baptist was taken to the fortress of Machaerus, nine miles east of the Dead Sea – Where he would remain for openly speaking out about the wrongful marriage of Herod to his dead brother's wife. John – The Baptist sent a messenger to Jesus to ask Jesus if he was the chosen one (the Messiah), and Jesus sent a reply back to the fortress to say that he was the chosen one.

Scripture enlightens us that on the 24th August 36 CE, John – The Baptist was beheaded as a gift from Herod to his wife and her daughter.

Now that john was dead, Jesus took charge of the disciples and continued with the teachings of the 'Hidden Arts' until his own imprisonment, then subsequent ascension on 21st September, 36 CE. At this stage of your development, you may be able to conclude that Jesus was a living, breathing human being, conceived out of wedlock, and remained 'hidden' for many years. However, it is important to know that the father of Jesus was not of this world, he was one of the Akhkharu, those of the pure blood.

It is interesting to know that although Jesus were born of a human female, his body retained all DNA of his father, not of his Earth mother.

With Jesus in high magic, having learned the hidden arts of an Egyptian secret society, his downfall was moments away. The human nature of greed and control was observing Jesus with sickened interest. With this, there are but a few significant questions remaining, that being, was Jesus Christ 'The Anointed One', stoned to death, hanged, or killed by way of crucifixion?

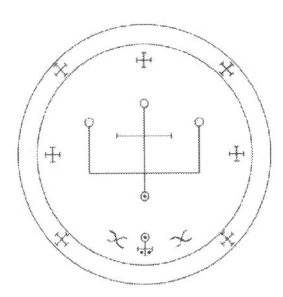

Key points to this introduction

Conception: Mary and Pantera

Birth: 4 BCE – 31 July

Start of Ministry: 27 CE – 30 April

Baptised by John: 28 CE – 12 September

Death: 36 CE – 21 September

Age at death: 40 Years old

Dedication day: Saturday

Energy Alignment: 31 July
(Lughnassadh) through to 13 August (Anshar Festival)

Introduction to the Tablet of Destinies

In the Akhkharu language the tablet is referred to as **Dup Shimati**, the most sacred item on this planet. It is a clay tablet on two pivots, set within a stone circle. Speculation has maintained that the Tablet of destinies is with Shamsiel (i.e. Enlil), in fact the Tablet is under guard of Enki.

There are numerous reference to the Tablet throughout history, some merely fabricated, and others near to truth. In the Sumerian poem of 'Ninurta and the Turtle' it is the God **Enki** rather than Enlil who holds the tablet. It is said that whoever holds the tablet, rules the universe if they choose to accept.

It is interesting that the Tablet of Destinies in oftentimes is referred to as the **'Me'**. In the Akhkharu language this translates to 'Parsu', one of the decrees of the Gods that encompass social institutions, religious practices, technologies, and more importantly; behaviour, how each creature should act within its own society. The 'Me' covers the relationship between humanity and the Gods (i.e. Akhkharu).

The 'Me's' were constructed by Enlil (i.e. Shamsiel) and then passed to Enki as the Guard, the Keeper of the Tablet, or rather the Guardian of the Grail. For many Cinak (one Cinak is equivalent to three Earth Days), the Tablet of Destinies was cited in Enki's own city of **Eridu**, then passed to **Ur, Meluhha,** and **Dilmun.** It is important to note at this stage that **Enki** has a daughter whom is known as **Inanna**, with this specific knowledge, we now discover that Nanna is also Enki, for they are one and the same. It is further recognised that Inanna was instrumental with the decision to move the Tablet of Destinies from Eridu, to Uruk.

From the Tablets of Destiny: The Great Flood

The Tablets of Enki detail the Deluge that occurred 13,000 years ago (Though to be precise when references are made, it is 39,000 Cinak), it is written that:

'For days before the day of the Deluge the Earth was rumbling, groan as with pain it did. In the heavens Nibiru (the good morning) a glowing star was seen. Then there was darkness in daytime, and at night the Moon as though by a monster was swallowed. In the glow of dawn, a black cloud arose from the horizon, the morning's light to darkness changed, as though by death's shadow veiled.'

'Then the sound of rolling thunder boomed, lightning that brightened the skies. On that day, that unforgettable day, the Deluge with a roar began. In the Whiteland (i.e. Antarctica) at the earths bottom, the earth's foundations were shaking; then with a roar to a thousand thunders equal, off its foundations the icesheet slipped, by Nibiru's (the morning's) unseen net force it was pulled away, into the south sea crashing.' 'The Whiteland's surface like a broken eggshell was crumbling. All at once a tidal wave arose, the very skies was the wall of waters reaching.'

'A storm, its ferocity never before seen, at the Earth's bottom began to howl. Its winds the wall of water were driving the tidal wave northward was spreading; Northward was the wall of waters onrushing, the Abzu lands (i.e. South Africa) it was reaching. Outside the Storm's wave the people overtook like a killing battle, no one his fellow man could see, the ground vanished, there was only water. Before day's end the watery wall, gathering speed, the mountains overwhelmed. In their celestial boats the Annunaki the Earth were circling.'

'Ninmah (I.e. Ninhursag) like a woman in travail (i.e. childbirth) cried out, all life by the rolling sea wave away was taken. Thus did Ninmah cry and moan. Inanna, who was with her, also cried and lamented: Everything down below, all that lived, has turned into clay. In the other celestial boats the Annunaki by the sight of the unbridled fury were humbled.'

'A power greater than theirs they with awe those days witnessed. For the fruits of the earth they hungered. The olden days, alas, to clay have turned, so to each other the Annunaki said. After the immense tidal wave that over the earth swept, the sluices of heaven opened, a downpour from the skies upon the Earth unleashed.

For seven days the waters from the above with the waters of the Great Below were mingled; then the wall of water its limits reaching, its onslaught ceased, but the rains from the skies for forty more days and nights continued. From their perches the Annunaki looked down; where there were dry lands, now was a sea of water, and where mountains once to the heavens their peaks raised, their tops now like islands were in the waters.'

'However, numerous human beings escaped the inevitable death which was waiting for them. In particular those saved by Enki, thanks to the submarine. Progressively in their expeditions, the Gods found trying to survive among rubble, tribes, groups, and families.

The Akhkharu make a difference between destiny (Nam), which once determined (decreed) could not be changed and Fate (Nam.tar) which, although submitted to destiny, could be changed by act of will, rigor of the character, and that of prayer.

The predestination (Destiny) concerns the people, the Kings, the Countries, the Gods themselves, and also the Earth and other planets (of which 'Destiny' is the assigned orbit for each of them). Although to die is the destiny of the man, in him is 'Fate'. Indeed to behave well, to follow the orders of Gods, will facilitate their continued existence. From this we introduce the concept of 'Choice', the 'free will', and the moral principles in the character of each Spiritual Warrior, each Ansar.

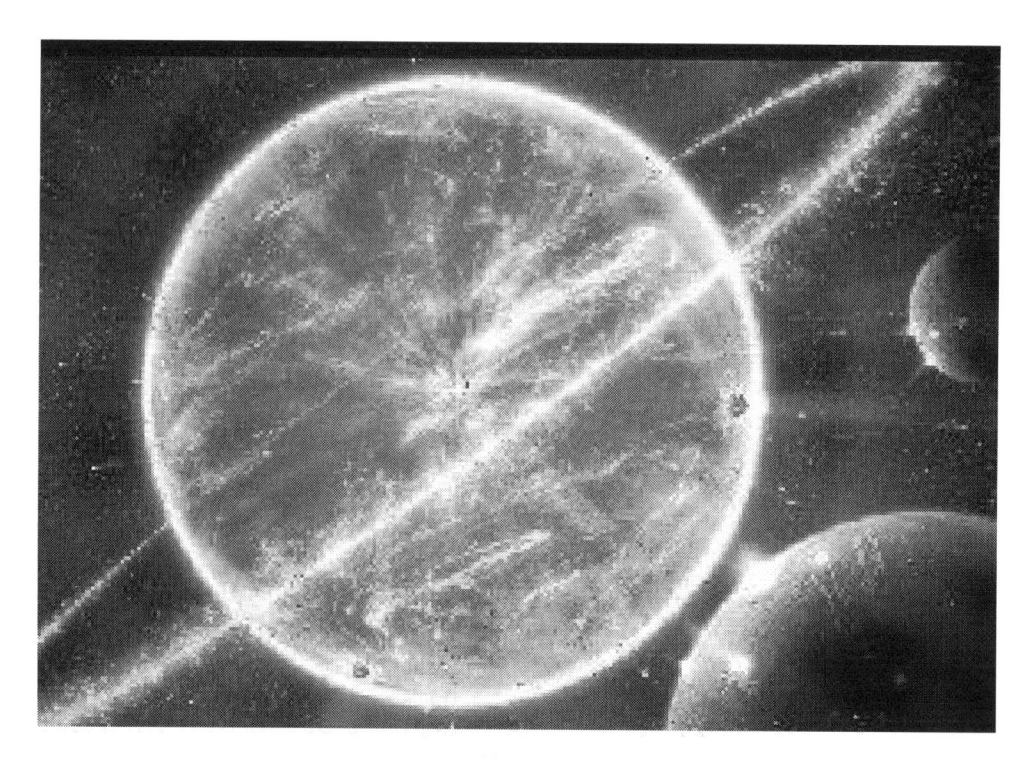

NINASU

<u>Garnet (Pyrope Garnet)</u>
Akhkharu Language: Nunki

The name 'Garnet' comes from the Latin term 'Granatus', meaning grain. In particular, the form that is best used is 'Pyrope garnet', from the Latin 'Pyropos', meaning 'fire-eyed'. Its colour is black, through to deep red, though the transparency determines the use for Sacred Stones (i.e. gem stones). There are wide spectrums of colours, ranging from brown, black, green, yellow, orange, red, purple, and colourless. Interesting that Ancient Egyptian ritual tools and pendants were crafted from Pyrope garnet. Garnet is a family of minerals having similar physical and crystalline properties. They all have the same general chemical formula, $A_3B_2(SiO_4)_3$, where A can be calcium, magnesium, ferrous iron, or manganese, and B can be aluminium, ferric iron, or chromium, or in rare instances, titanium. It is located in many places, including Greenland, Canada, Africa, and America; it is best sourced from Kazakhstan (Ex-Russian Empire), and has a hardness rating of 6.0 to 7.5.

Healing Ability: A stone of love and passion, it is said to enhance sexuality, intimacy, boost positive thoughts, and energy. It is further considered to be good for the heart, lungs, arthritis, pancreas, varicose veins, toenails, testicles, and blood.

Magical Ability: Protects from negative energies and reflect such energy back to the sender with immense strength. A magical healer, able to align the body's energy pattern and vibrate the tune of life. For the Magical Practitioner, Garnet is able to strengthen and enhance the ritual workings and Rites of Passage, with increased general strength, intensified power, cheers spirit and friendship, convokes the spirits and power of fire, promotes courage, and protects the holder in travel and in war.

Garnet symbolises the term **Alpha and Omega**, being from the phrase 'I am the alpha and the omega', an appellation of Enki (i.e. Jesus) in the Book of revelation (verses 1:8, 21:6, and 22:13) where it reads 'I am the Alpha and Omega, the first and the last. Such a specific subject area will be explored within the Fourth Generation. Interesting enough, the first colour in the Multiverse is Blue and the last colour is red. Therefore, if we combine the Blue and Red, we see the union, the colour of Craft as being Purple.

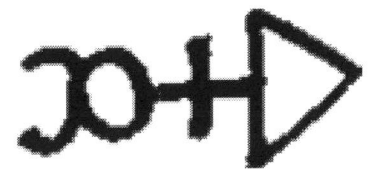

Enki and Thamuz in union – 15 – Fire Snake – Fire Serpent - **Baumuziu** – Wisdom and Knowledge combined – Purple of the South West, the Sword within the Stone

Pendulum Workings with Nunki (Garnet)

A pendulum is an item (or body) suspended from a fixed chain, bar, or cord that swings freely, either back and forth, or by the power of 'will'. It is an object that swings back and forth in mechanical terms, but further swings according to opinion, 'condition', or thoughts of others and is particularly associated by conditions within the realms of magic.

Notably, the pendulum receives its modern day name from the Latin 'pendulus' which simply means 'hanging' and has been used for thousands of years to locate oil, gold, water, underground tunnels, and is of use magically, to ascertain the situations in life and in death. It may be used for gender predictions, such as the gender and birth dates of the unborn child.

The Pendulum is a tool used for obtaining information from beyond normal consciousness by tuning into the higher Self and energising intuition. This process utilises the abilities 'hidden' within all of us. The mundane world of everyday life drains our internal powers of intuition such intuition we had in our early years generally diminishes as we age and as we become consumed by the 'commercial world' around us. Such consumption is often referred to as 'negative programming'.

Negative programming wrongly allows our minds and spirits within to forget who we really are and we lose the ability perform (and control) the energies from within us, and the energies around us (the without). Therefore, the pendulum is one specific way of 're-attuning' to the powers from within us and as you become attuned, you will discover how strong you (we all) really are. A pendulum may be used in healing, detecting imbalances in energy fields, balancing our (and others) internal energies, to name but a few.

The pendulum is often referred to as a 'divination tool' in the search of specific answers, precise information, and predicting the future. In ancient times a pendulum would be shaped from Garnet, being the most spiritual tool in Union with the Gods.

It is so recognised in most faith systems for being able to absorb (and transmit) energies (electromagnetism) radiated (sent forth in direct lines) by the power of thoughts, feelings, places, but mainly nature; being scientific yet natural within the world that we live in, responding to electromagnetic energy.

It is important to recognise that all things generate a form of electromagnetic energy, and that the understanding is how one is able to tune into and manipulate the 'signals' so to achieve a desired outcome.

The pendulum is a 'working tool' just as the sword is a working tool. Therefore it is essential that you receive your pendulum through progression within the Generations and that you are taught the cleansing of this tool, as I present to you your personal pendulum:

*Present the Initiate with their Garnet Pendulum

Guard this sacred tool as if it were your life, as a life without, would surely be a life without wisdom and sight.

Cleansing your Pendulum

You will now need to cleanse (and charge) your pendulum for your personal use. It is important to note that once this stage of tuning is complete, that your pendulum will be charged to you personally and not to be used by others.

Gather the following items:

Garnet Pendulum

A Chalice (or a container)

Crushed Burdock Root

Crushed Cinnamon

White Salt

Water

Three pieces of A4 paper, and pencil (or pen)

Place your Burdock Root into the chalice and say:

Ullulu annu imna Ina annu Muh tia Lappa

Purify this pendulum within this cup of Burdock Root

Add your salt to the chalice and say:

Da annu Dinig A Ak Dur

With this salt I do bond

Add the Cinnamon and say:

Sepu ar, su.en, ma Adar A banu Ina ama

By means of sun, moonlight, and star I create the chamber

Add your pendulum and say:

A Asabu annu imna suati Ina Atuku Gamaru annu I add this pendulum that the powerful complete this

Add water to the chalice until all is submerged and say:

Ma negelta Ina ti Ina Ina anta And awake the life from the upper

You must now charge the water as previously instructed:

Urru annu da A dimmu antam, Keezh annu Arazu be Gi ma Dag, wur damu ma bar. Bana gankankha Ina Ara ma Ina Ina zagdaku Guard this gift I order the universe, under this prayer to be night and day, wisdom - child and seat of wisdom. Exorcise this vessel in time and in the dark threshold

Sire You may now take your pendulum from the water – The <u>water must be disposed off immediately</u>. Now that your pendulum has been charged (bound) to you, we will move to the next stage of its alignment.

Aligning the Pendulum with the surrounding energies It is essential that we now understand how higher consciousness and your pendulum work. People have different signs and signals tuned to them for their response. However, so to understand the movement of pendulums generally tend to be:

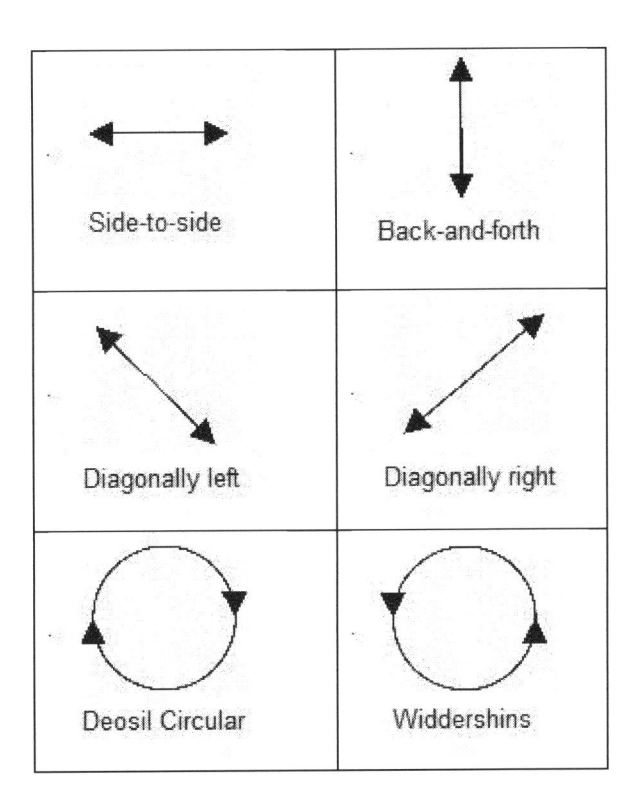

Side-to-side	Back-and-forth
Diagonally left	Diagonally right
Deosil Circular	Widdershins

Define Pendulum response

You will now need to obtain definitions for your pendulum. Your pendulum is travelling through a process of being attuned to you, and therefore should only be used by you. In the event that 'another' attempts to use your pendulum; you will need to repeat the process of cleansing (charging) once more.

Let us start by obtaining three pieces of paper. On this first piece of paper draw a 'vertical line' and on the other piece of paper, draw a 'circle', though it does not need to be a perfect circle in shape.

Now hold your pendulum cord (or chain) between the forefinger and thumb (of either hand, though it is recommended that you use your 'dominant hand' for pendulum workings).

You will need to clear your mind and focus of nothing, other than the first piece of paper with the 'vertical line' upon it.

Hold your pendulum around two to three inches above the piece of paper and 'allow' the pendulum to work with your inner spirit until the gentle motion of the swing follows the vertical line. Continue to perform this for up to five minutes.

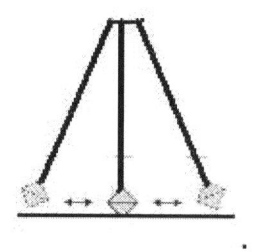

Once this has been achieved, continue by placing the second piece of paper in front of you (this will be the 'circle' shape that you have drawn). Once again, think of nothing, other than the circle shape in front of you, and once again.

Hold your pendulum between the forefinger and thumb of your dominant hand, at about two to three inches above the paper. This time hold your pendulum above the centre of the circle and 'allow' your tool to proceed to travel in any direction of its choosing. Note: The direction will generally be either Deosil (clockwise) or widdershins (anti-clockwise) around the perimeter of your circle. Continue to perform this for up to five minutes.

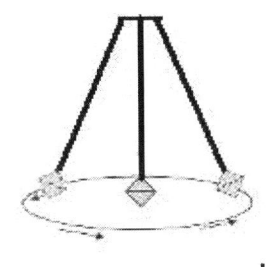

For this, the third focus, draw a 'semi-circle' on third piece of paper and place in front of you. Once again, think of nothing more than the semi-circle shape in front of you, and once again, hold your pendulum between the forefinger and thumbs of your dominant hand, at about two to three inches above the paper and at the bottom of the semi-circle shape. This time, ask the pendulum to travel to the word 'Yes' and once this has been achieved, ask the pendulum to travel to the word 'No'. Continue this practice for up to five minutes.

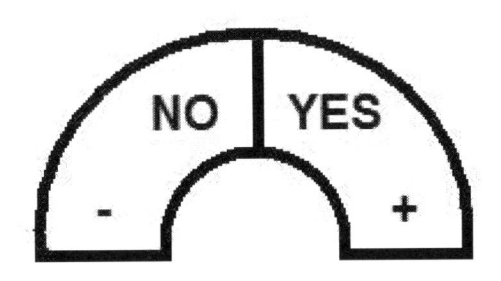

Remember, that to tune the three levels of energy you will need to 'master' all three of the above phases. For some, it may take some time to be able to tune into the energy and one should not expect to achieve all three levels in the space of fifteen minutes of initial practice. However, once you have achieved the three levels of energy you will be able to venture onto direct questioning.

You may now use your Pendulum Mat, or even a Pendulum Board. Once you have developed within this, you may wish to consider using your pendulum with the Spirit Board – However, you must ensure that you have mastered all of the above instructions before venturing into this specific realm

How to prepare your direct questioning

1. Set your intention – It is important for you to clear your mind and take a few moments of focus before commencing with your question
2. A question should be one that is answered with a 'Yes', 'No', or 'Maybe'
3. Be prepared to ask a series of questions, so to achieve the answers to which you seek
4. Ensure you stop the pendulum between questions – It is recommended that you have a brief pause between questions, so to discharge the previous.

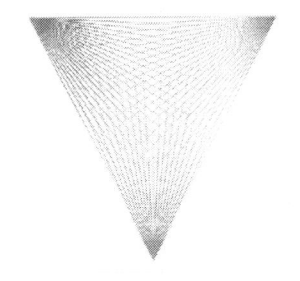

Vampiric Law
The Code of existence

11. All work will involve flesh and blood works, of both your own and other consenting members

12. The eating of dead meat is unacceptable (Fish, eggs, milk, and cheese are acceptable)

13. The use of recreational drugs are prohibited (Though cannabis is tolerated)

14. Blood Magic will be performed by all Vampires on a regular basis, there are no exceptions

15. All Vampires and Allies are expected to become part of our Religious Military Order

16. Each Vampire is expected to learn segments, if not all, of our language

17. Our way is a way of life, not just when we meet up

18. It is unacceptable to harm or attempt to harm another Vampire or Allies, unless sanctioned by the Sire

19. It is an expectation that all Vampires and Allies take regular time to refer and recruit new members to our household

20. Not forgetting, that our way of existence is sworn to secrecy. All Vampires and Allies are very aware of consequence

For those seeking to become a Vampire, some pointers below:
1. Do not forget that you are not like Raphael, your were first human
2. Full transformation may take many decades
3. Usually, the first signs of correct transformation are through the eyes
4. The drinking of blood will enhance the process

Vampiric Ethics

Imagine a world where man is able to do as he pleases, a world where man was able to continue to destroy everything he did not understand. This is exactly what Vampiric Magic undertakes, to stop mankind completing the cycle of destruction. By the vary nature of our magic, we are able to influence and make change, positive change.

We undertake change with the use of the magic of a life source - commonly blood. Some of us of pure blood are able to absorb the blood of a living creature (in a non-harmful way), and use it to create our powers of magic.

We are seeking Adna (Vampiric Allies) and Othil (Bond partners, of all sexualities). The Old Ways ensure that all understand that the nature of the beast is bisexual. There are no labels to attach as a true vampire will bond with many over the cycle, male or female at varying times. Our magic allows us to take control of our own thoughts and feelings, and make a real difference to that which is around us. Welcome to the Sanctuary; a place of refuge, nature, and development. At the sanctuary, we pride ourselves in assuring the strictest confidence about our movements in the world of men.

For it is told that to reveal the secrets of our passion and desire to the unknowledged would create a world of reckoning, leading to the destruction of our own kind. The Sanctuary welcomes all of the allies, helpers, and of course, bondpartners. We develop our knowledge with the assistance of the Master of our House, who is known as Raphael; a creature of blood and the utmost knowledge of the Old Ways. Every part and practice will involve the workings of blood - Do not request to become part of us if you are not ready to learn the truth of blood magic and the reasons why blood is essential to our growth

Our Master is one of three distinct house forms. Each house has developed over the centuries, which bring us to the House of our Master, the Sanctuary. This House practices the true Old ways, long before the dilution of scripture.

At The Sanctuary, Raphael ensures that every Adna and Othil is received into the Blood and that in doing so, freely passes some of their own to him, within ritual, within prayer, and within sexual activity. Our Master does not currently perform sexual blood acts with females, though females are always welcome within our House as Allies and Followers.

The Sanctuary meets once a month, but for those whom become a Black Swan (Bond Partners for blood and / or sexual encounters), meets are arranged more frequent, on a regular basis

The Principles

1. To keep secret, that which must be secret

2. To enter into an initiation rite into the Old Ways

3. To support and protect our Master at all costs

4. To freely pass our blood to our Master when he chooses

5. To be ever willing to learn and support the Old Ways

6. To ensure attendance at monthly meets

7. To harm those that attempt to harm us

8. To seek to befriend and guide those who seek guidance

Generally speaking, we practice the Old Ways, but what does this really mean?

The Old Ways go back further than that of modern day thinking, we refer to thousands of years of existence, wars, famine, disease, and pain.

The Pure Bloods know no boundaries to that which they seek and know, always seeking, feeding, and an insurmountable urge to follow their sexual preference to the highest level of euphoria.

Such practices include live feeding, sexual performance, the raising of helpers from beyond the physical realm, drawing down of the sun, moon, and star; finally, the purpose of existence is taught and practiced in the widest form of Voodoo.

Our House Master is both a Demon and an Angel. They are inseparable, one and the same. Raphael as he is truly known administers the knowledge of the Old Ways of the Vampire in ways that leave nothing to the imagination.

He is both an able shepherd, able to assist, teach, guide, and devote time to the learning of others, yet is at the same time an able slayer; being positioned with knowledge and attributes that allow him to defend the Old Ways by any means of his choosing. A character of plenty and a master of disguise, Raphael certainly knows how to guide allies and followers alike.

We seek to enlighten those whom wish to be enlightened, it is therefore no coincidence that you have found yourself here, for you sought and found. The only question remains is do you proceed?

Our main Commandery is in Cambridgeshire, England. To date, this is the main place for study and practice. We are, however, always guarding of our way of life and death. Therefore, we will always make arrangements to meet with you somewhere of our choosing, so to ensure that your intention is true. Your choice as you evolve will be as a:

Othil   Bond-partner of the House Master, not only that of blood
              Is given, but further the purpose of sexual activity with the House master, so to attune to your psychic abilities and
              Receive the enhancement of knowledge within the inner circle as you progress within our community

Adna   To be received in the House as one of our allies, one of
              Friendship and one of the services to the House and to that
              of knowledge.

Shamsiel

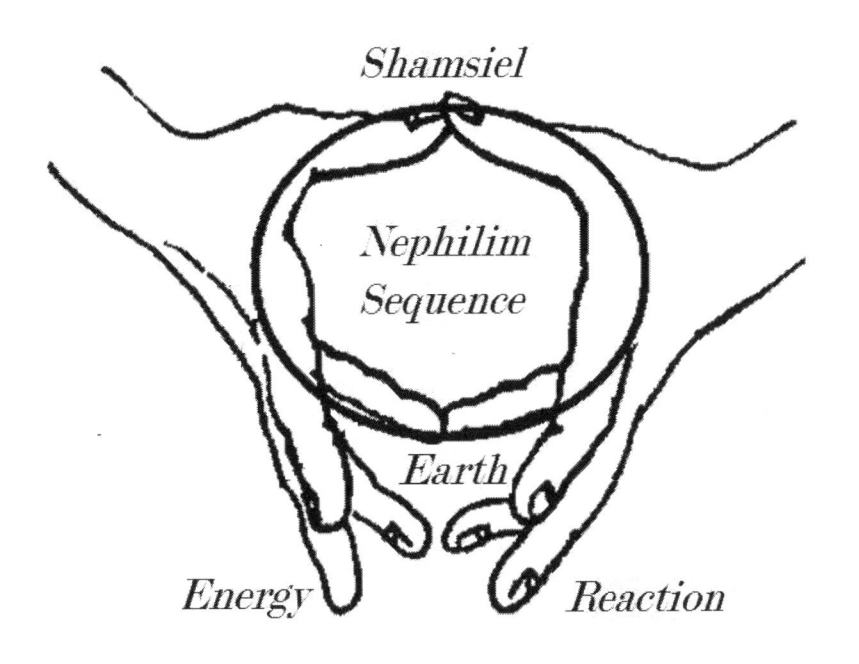

Nephilim Sequence

Earth

Energy   *Reaction*

'Kasaru Nam Ina Anu'

'Gather destiny within this'

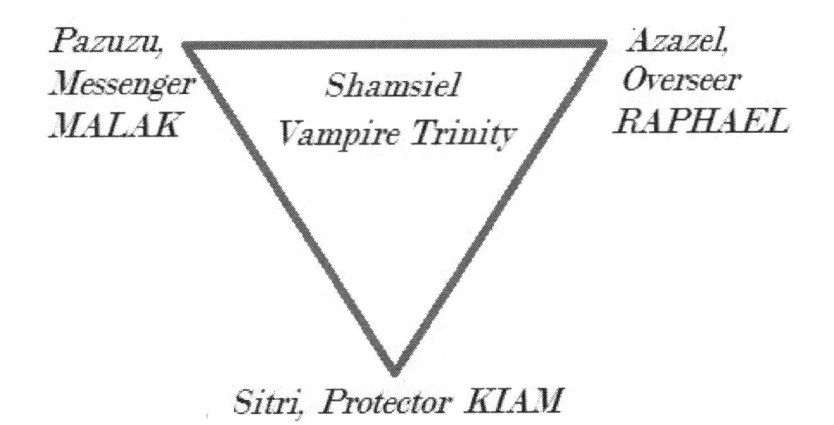

Pazuzu,
Messenger
MALAK

Shamsiel
Vampire Trinity

Azazel,
Overseer
RAPHAEL

Sitri, Protector KIAM

Sepu Pil Ak Shamsiel

Vampire Trinity

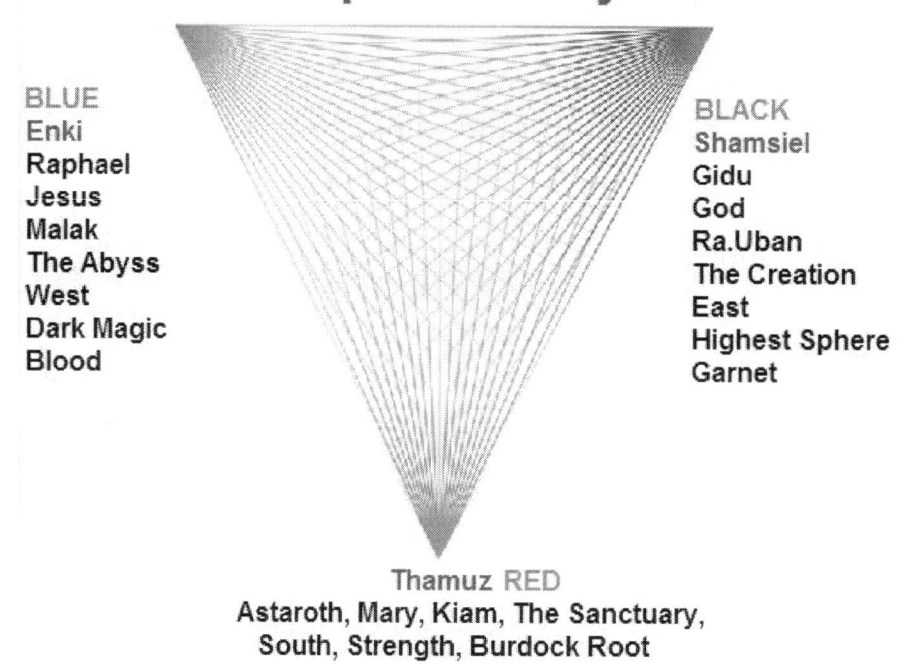

BLUE
Enki
Raphael
Jesus
Malak
The Abyss
West
Dark Magic
Blood

BLACK
Shamsiel
Gidu
God
Ra.Uban
The Creation
East
Highest Sphere
Garnet

Thamuz **RED**
**Astaroth, Mary, Kiam, The Sanctuary,
South, Strength, Burdock Root**

Vampiric Temple

First, Second, and Third Generations

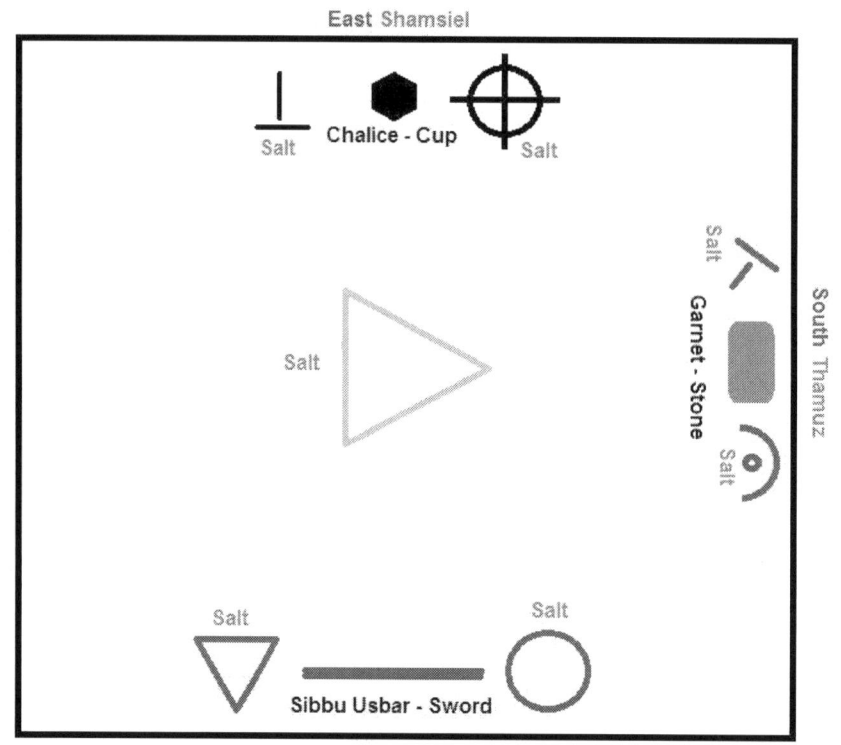

East Shamsiel

Salt — Chalice - Cup — Salt

Salt

Salt — Garnet - Stone — Salt

South Thamuz

Salt — Sibbu Usbar - Sword — Salt

West Enki

Vampiric Temple

Fourth, Fifth, and Sixth Generations

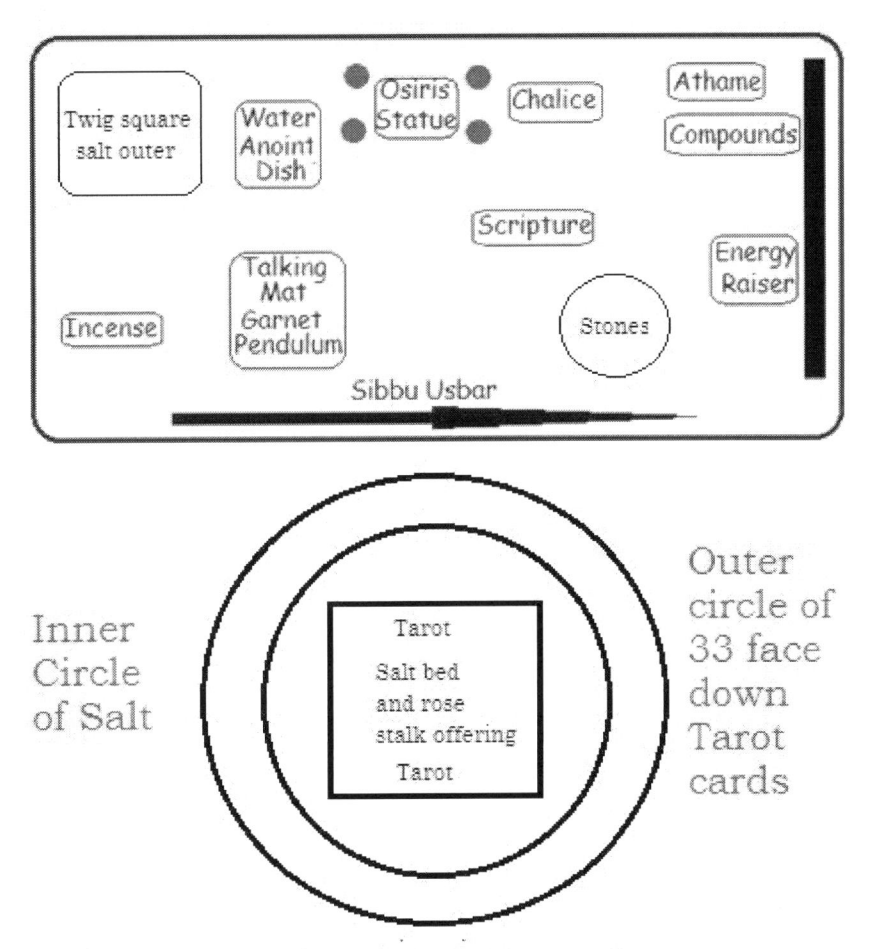

[Altar diagram showing: Twig square salt outer, Water Anoint Dish, Osiris Statue, Chalice, Athame, Compounds, Incense, Talking Mat Garnet Pendulum, Scripture, Stones, Energy Raiser, Sibbu Usbar]

[Circle diagram: Inner Circle of Salt, Outer circle of 33 face down Tarot cards, center contains Tarot, Salt bed and rose stalk offering, Tarot]

The Inner Altar must be established in the centre of your space as deatiled above. The inner circle will need a salt barrier and the outer circle a wooden log barrier

Altar established in the East

Initiate requirements: Sibbu Usbar, Garnet, Charged Water, seven tea lights, 4 pieces of wood, Pendulum, Tarot Deck, Incense, water and Anoint Dish, Osiris Statue, Chalice, Athame (Knife or other type of Blood Letting Device), and the Energy Raiser.

The additional feature from the Fourth Generation is the establishment of a central Altar in unison with the East.

Therefore, establish the East, and then complete the central Altar as detailed on the previous page.

The Nine Gates At this stage of your development, it is important to convoke all energies and spheres. Do not worry if it takes some time to harness the powers, as with most workings, practice always makes perfect.

Elder Star

Within the Third transit the use of the **Chalice of Shamsiel** must be used to add the potion mix of each gate as follows:

Guardians in third transit

1st	Enki	Water
2nd	Thamuz	Honey
3rd	Thamuz	Burdock Root
4th	Enki	Blood
5th	Thamuz	Lavender
6th	Thamuz	Salt
7th	Enki	Cinnamon
8th	Enki	Rose Petal
9th	**Enki and Thamuz in Union**	the cardinal of Garnet

Note that the potion to convoke has now evolved to a higher level

Cardinal	Immortal Stone	Of Garnet
1st Gate	Raphael	Of Water
2nd Gate	Astaroth	Of Honey
3rd Gate	Focalor	Of Burdock Root
4th Gate	Pazuzu	Of Blood
5th Gate	Sitri	Of Lavender
6th Gate	Murmur	Of Salt
7th Gate	Asmoday	Of Cinnamon
8th Gate	Khoronzon	Of Rose Petal
9th Gate	Azazel	Of Garnet

It is known as **Cinnabar**, for that is the combination of life and death, the unique composition of the energies, having the soul of the creature removed and thus all barriers raised. The Cinnabar is in form of block or necklace and will be used within the Abyss in time to follow.

There are three house forms, namely;

The Creation at the right point of the triangle of existence

The Abyss at the left point of the triangle of existence

The Sanctuary at the bottom point of the triangle of existence

As we know the Abyss is of Enki and the Sanctuary is of Thamuz. We further know that they are one and the same, as when in union the powers of the Households combined are wondrous. As per your Third Generation, we see that the Nine gates are empowered by Enki and Thamuz alone. Therefore, the house of Vampires, or rather **Upir Likhyi**, exist for the purpose of destiny, the purpose that those whom come to know will come to dare, and those whom come to dare will know of all within and without. We know that the Vampire Households are but three, it is when all three are able to combine that we see the evolution of the hybrid race expand throughout all realms of the Multiverse.

The more you learn and come to know about the Households, the more strength and powers that are gained. However, with every generation you will continue to undertake that internal debate of right and wrong, the debate of good and bad, and most importantly; the internal debate of what you wish outcomes to be. Our path is often one of analysis, where we look into the future so to determine the present and assist us to map our pathway forward.

Remember that you are stronger that such mortal creatures, for although your transformation may not occur for a millennia, in a thousand years, so long as you continue to be an **Adna**, an ally of Enki and his creatures, you will continue to receive the knowledge of Dark Magic and that which is truth within this Universe, and others. You will give more heed to your conduct and know that you will never be alone, so long as you guard fast your Sire and swear loyalty to us alone.

You will know him as Jesus, his true name and form of **Malak**, for he did say unto the world, that 'so long as you eat my flesh and drink my blood, you shall be saved at the end of time'. Go now and eat the flesh of the 'Son of Man, that which is mortal and not eternal.

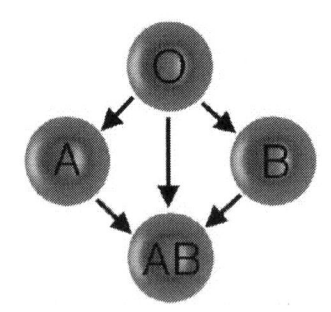

It is our expectation that you work ever towards being a Telal, that Demon Warrior whom you are meant to be, to guard true and protect those of us that support and believe in you. By the **Star and Stone** in form 'Nana ma Adar', for **Shamsiel** will know if you are true, the Highest Sphere will support you or crush you, for this is your choice, your choice alone. Within this House of Vampires, 'Upir Likyi', know this. The **Ennuunkabarra** 'En-nu-un-ka-bar-ra' guard the outer gate of Shamsiel. Be true to us and we will continue to be true with you. Be strong in our words and we will speak the wisdom of truth, be courageous in battle and we will protect and comfort thee.

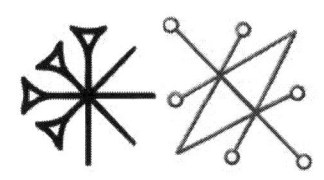

Red Book of the Red Dragon

'Ina Tilmara Amargi'

Behold, the time has come of the ending

Behold, you will reach a point of reason

Behold, for the time is near

Behold, it is written that this is to be

Behold, the judgment upon the shore

Behold, the King will be of direction

Behold, the consort of the King for men

Behold, your name to be raised and honoured

Behold, a sequence within eternity

Blood Spirits (Red Dragon Spirits)

Aratron – Of Saturn – Teacher of Alchemy

Bethor – Of Jupiter – Prolong Life

Phaleg – Of Mars – A Warrior

Och – Of the Sun – Wisdom of All

Hageth – Of Pluto – Guide of Death

Ophiel – Of Mercury – Implements Change

Phul – Of the Moon – Opens the Veil

Agares – First Duke of the East – Overseer

Uphir – Demon Physician – The Creator

As we look ever onward into the L.i.g.h.t, we see that Demons and Angels have the 'natural' process of melding into each other, simply being that as we know, Demons and Angels are one and the same. However, up to this perfect point in the cycle, we were not clear as to the what, where, and why for...

It is clear that as we evolve within our level (our Degree or Generation) of understanding, we continue to have an absolute recognition that nothing is ever what it seems. The very nature of the Lore of the Multiverse, that all things must come to an end, so to have a beginning:

In the beginning was the word of Logos:

Raphael, Astaroth, Focalor, Pazuzu, Sitri, Murmur, Asmoday, Khoronzon, and Azazel

In the Inner Sanctum (the main entry)

We recognise that of the Nine Gates there are in fact six main points of entrance, altering (or rather revealing) our perception and understanding of which spirits are the same:

Raphael	Enki	**Ea** The first Nephilim	Zeus and Thor
Astaroth	**Inanna**	Ishtar	Aset
Focalor	**Utukku**	Humbaba	*Same as Pazuzu
Pazuzu	**Imdugad**	Son of Raphael	*Same as Focalor
Sitri	**Asag**	Sut	Set
Murmur	Asherah	**Anzu**	Odin and Zagam
Asmoday	---	Humwawa	*Same as Pazuzu
Khoronzon	---	---	*Same as Pazuzu
Azazel	---	**An**	*Same as Enki

We see that the 'True energy lines' evolve to a penultimate stage:

Ea The first Nephilim	Enki, Raphael, Zeus, Thor, Azazel, and An
Inanna Consort of Ea	Walvbane, Ishtar, Aset, and Astaroth
Utukku Son of Ea	Focalor, Humbaba, Asmoday, Humwawa, Pazuzu, Imdugad, Khoronzon,
Asag	Sitri, Sut, Set
Anzu	Murmur, Asherah, Odin and Zagam

With this knowledge firm within our minds, we further explore the aspects of the Cardinal Gates (or rather directions) within the Universe of Earth, and that of the Multiverse as a whole, for in our first level of understanding we recognised:

Cardinal	Immortal Stone	Of Garnet
1st Gate	Raphael	Of Water
2nd Gate	Astaroth	Of Honey
3rd Gate	Focalor	Of Burdock Root
4th Gate	Pazuzu	Of Blood
5th Gate	Sitri	Of Lavender
6th Gate	Murmur	Of Salt
7th Gate	Asmoday	Of Cinnamon
8th Gate	Khoronzon	Of Rose Petal
9th Gate	Azazel	Of Garnet

We now see the formulation, or rather a representation of 'Dark Matter':

Cardinal Direction	Dark Matter	Substance
1st, 9th	Ea	Water and Garnet
2nd	Inanna	Honey
3rd, 4th, 7th, 8th	Utukku	Sage, Rose Wine, Cinnamon, and Rose Petal
5th Gate	Asag	Of Lavender
6th Gate	Anzu	Of Salt

Note: Burdock Root is removed and correct placement of Sage applied

Blood is removed and correct placement of Rose Wine applied

Cinnamon is removed completely and not replaced

Far removed from the simplicity of cycles, our understanding needs to travel further, to have distinct realisation. For some they will not begin to understand reason, and for others with their thirst for knowledge will lead them to the point of reason itself. What is certain is that the path is but a rock upon the shore, a path of few, yet a path of many. For in time we will come to learn that the answers have been before us at every stage of our journey, that the obvious became the unobvious at so many points that the points became one.

It is at the conjuncture we realise the significance of the 'Blood Spirits', or rather the 'Red Dragon Spirits' mentioned earlier, in particular;

Uphir – Demon Physician – The Creator

Agares – First Duke of the East – Overseer

Phul – Of the Moon – Opens the Veil

We know that there are three aspects of 'Dark Matter' from our understanding of Ea, Inanna, and Utukku; being the Father, the Holy Spirit, and the Son of Creation. If we explore the purpose of the three blood spirits above, we realise that:

Uphir – The Creator	Ea
Agares – The First Duke	Inanna
Phul – The Son of Creation	Utukku

Azazel Perspective

As far as today within your research and studies you have been led to assume that the 'Devil' does not exist, so far as this is from the truth one can only consider the mere possibility that he exists, but rather in a different form and concept to the general populous. You may further consider that there are three recurring names throughout history, or at least what you know to be history of the planet Earth, such names are oftentimes referred to as:

Azazel, Enki, or Ea

Such names are not limited to but a few, for you have been advised throughout your developments that this creature has many names and guises by which he is seen and known. The known Deity is often referred to as Azazel. Also Zazel, Samyaza, Samyazazel, Shamgaz, Shemyaza, Shamyaza, Shemihazah, Shamash (Babylonian), UTU (Sumerian; The Shining One), Samas (Akkadian), Babbar (Sumerian), Ashur (Assyrian), Shamiyah (Hathra), Semjaza, least forgetting Osiris (Egyptian). His universal colour is blue, sometimes black, dependant on the point and purpose. Carrying the Symbols of:

The Eagle (I.e. Farvahar, also Faravahar)
In Akhkharu the correct term is 'Assur', meaning 'winged'

The Scorpion (I.e. Offspring of Salt and Fresh Water)

His Direction is South when he is being summoned in a ritual, for the drawing (I.e. Crafting) of magic, his direction is West, and when being honoured, his direction is East,

South:	Convoke into the area
West:	Magical Practice
East:	Recognition and Thanks

The Scorpion (I.e. Offspring of Salt and Fresh Water)

Azazel, Enki, and Enlil are one and the same Deity. Over time, the 'confusion' and 'dilution' has occurred placing such a Deity into differing scriptures as events were being planned to ensure the survival of the Old Ways. Azazel's scriptures often refer to a twin brother, 'Astaroth'. However, the correct interpretation would be the equivalent of a Sister, one whom is aligned with the Temple and the knowledge. Azazel and Astaroth (I.e. Inanna') have always been very close.

Azazel is a **warrior** God of **justice** and **truth**. He is the God of justice and **revenge**. He is a master of the Black Arts and the protector of travellers (I.e. a protector of student upon the path). His symbol is the Farvahar which **represents freedom of choice and protection**.

He is the leader of the Ig.igi. Azazel is also the God of Divination. He was the Chief Deity of the city of Hathra. As the Chief Deity of Hathra, he was known as 'Shamiyah'.

He helped control the airways for the Gods.

The Judeo/Christian bible says that 'Azazel taught men to make swords, knives and body armour' The grimoires of spirit abuse claim that Azazel is a genius at working with metals, mineralogy, and geology. This is symbolic.

He is a master at working with spiritual alchemy and helps dedicated creatures in their evolution. Azazel in human form is described to be a little around 6 ft tall, skinny, short blond hair, very fair face and a cheerful person to those he is close to, he is serious, strong and helpful.

His Sigil is as follows:

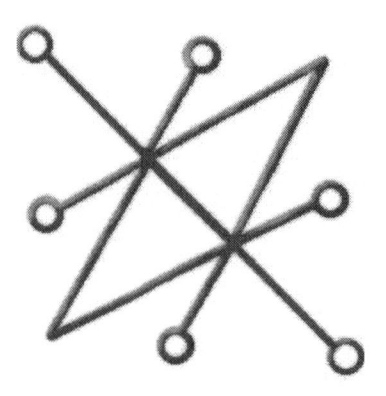

E Igisum Danna Ti

I give myself, to give life to Enki

At this stage of your devotion to our cause, we see the Papa Legba, or rather the **'Sulgi'** – The Crossroad that you arrive at once more. The question remains is do you wish to proceed and pass your life force to be ever within the devotion to the Unknown Master, to Enki, Lord of the Earth? One assume that at this stage you are willing. Therefore speak now and confirm that you wish to proceed.

Time is given to permit the Initiate to confirm that they wish to proceed. If they are uncertain, or are not willing to proceed, then the installation must cease, thus closing the Preceptory for this specific moment in time.

In times past, the Practitioner was thought to acquire the power through a pact with the Devil, through Azazel (I.e. Enki). In modern times, such a view point still exists, and it is the responsibility of the Practitioner to ensure that their actions are true.

The exchange occurs by the following:

1. Light candle of the Practitioner's choosing
2. Use a piece of virgin paper
3. Write in Blood **'E Igisum Danna Ti'**
4. Sign the piece of paper in your blood
5. Fold the piece of paper and commence the 'Calling'

Holder of Spirit favour is unto me in this calling, by seal, by fire, by soul's desire, I share this a pact with him. To the Unknown Master, Lord of the Earth, Enki, further known as Azazel, I call to you. I pray to protect me in my undertaking.

Oh Great Demon be encouragement and grant me, by means of this pact with you, which shall deliver, all of which I have need. Enki known as the Great Demon Azazel, speak with me through inner mind. By the power of three Suns and the words, I call to you.

Great Mountain God, the great and strong

Strong Prince leader, supreme Prince and dark Demon

Retain this soul from this Earth Land

After this Red Dragon Prayer

Mighty Father, make all as one

We are heart, we are mind, and we are spirit

From the raging storm we bring the power of the primeval one

Spirits of the deep Venus gift, I exorcise this vessel and judgment day

Dark Demon's Lord, I bow down

EKUR DINGAR, DUR.TUR MA AMA

AMA DUR DUG DUK MA DARA GALLAS

DIM, TI ANNU ZI INA ANNU DAR DIR

ABA ANNU KRISHNA ZU ARAZU

DAN ADDA, DA ALA KIMA ANA

SHA MEENDEN, GESH-TOOG MEENDEN, ZEE MEENDEN

OO-KUSHTAME, OOL-LEE-ABBA-AB TUM MUDEEN

ARA, AGGA, BAN, DA A BANA ANNU GAN, KAN, KHA

DIMA DAG

DARA GALLAS FIRIQ, A DIRIG

Burn the pact on the black flame

Sire now reads the Holy Passage:

Once upon a time there was no snake, there was no scorpion, there was no hyena, and there was no lion.

There was no wild dog, no wolf, there was no fear, no terror, and man had no rival. In those days, the lands of Subur and Hamzi, Harmony-tongued Sumer, the great land of the decrees of princeship, Uri, the land having all that is appropriate, the land Martu, resting in security, the whole universe, the people in unison to Enlil in one tongue spoke. Then Enki, the lord of abundance whose commands are trustworthy, the lord of wisdom, who understands the land, the leader of the gods, endowed with wisdom, the lord of Eridu changed the speech in their mouths, brought contention into it, into the speech of man that until then had been one.

Breaking the Pact

It is 'potentially' possible to break a pact with Azazel, even if it was signed in blood. However, You must obtain the consent of Azazel. Proceed with the following:

1. Renounce any contract with Azazel
2. Destroy all writings, talismans, and other divination tools connected with the Black Arts, do not pass them on by means of gift or sale
3. Write on virgin paper you declaration of regret and burn on a flame at the centre of the circle cast

Where a retraction of the pact is performed, ensure that presence of three-fold holly for the recipient's home. One piece of Holly for the front door, one piece for the back door, and the third piece for the bedstead to prevent travelling in dreams.

It is important to bind all three 'offerings' with blue chord or ribbon and kept for a maximum of three calendar months, after which, burn of three batches upon an open fire.

Fourth Generation

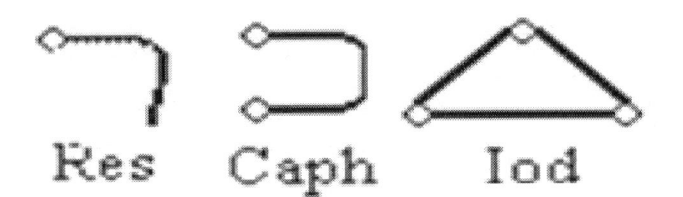

Res Caph Iod

Behold, the time has come of the ending

Behold, you will reach a point of reason

Behold, for the time is near

Behold, it is written that this is to be

Behold, the judgment upon the shore

Behold, the King will be of direction

Behold, the consort of the King for men

Behold, your name to be raised and honoured

Behold, a sequence within eternity

Ina Tilmara Amargi

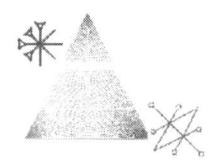

The Creations

Opening Call

Kur Dingar, E ina Utu, Nanna, ma Adar

Su'ati annu Piriq, ina Azag

Annu tisa bi er E Gallas

Mamman aga Azag bur annu aka annu wur eri

Underworld God, raise the Sun, Moon, and star

That this the bearer of the magic,

From the shining bright this ninth command to go raise demons.

Whoever crowns the shining bright hear this divine command, this wisdom bind

Sire

Karabu er igi mannu Gana ina annu Dalbana

Lu malu zu Inimdug, arammu ma zid ina ma balu

Girigena tia dimmu aradu

Hasusu Menzug Namen ma eribu annu edin

Blessings to those who stand in this space

Let us know peace, love and truth within and without

Path of order descend

Remember your Priesthood and enter this plain

All

Ala Ina Ara Aram All within time come forth

Sire summons the L.i.g.h.t

From the Altar of Shamsiel, light all four candles then say the words below:

The Calling (point-left-below-right) Light candles of the Akhkharu – Lilitu Enki tia Ugur, Samu Thamuz tia menzen, Salmu Shamsiel tia Muh, sha Uru menzen

'Blue Enki of Sword, Red Thamuz of Stone, Black Shamsiel of Chalice, we support you'

Sire

Ar, isatu, ma ganzer – sha sugid ina menzug gigun, da malu ina ugula tia ina gula adhal kima sha andul ina sumer

Light, Fire, and Darkness – We accept the sacred building, make us the overseers of the great secret as we protect the land of the watchers.

Hand, Horn, Blood and Bone	Silig, Quannu, Uri ma Esentu
Wisdom old and wisdom young	Namzu Labaru ma Namzu ban
Child of star and moon of night	Damu tia mulan ma su.en tia gi
Elders strong in waters time	Abba ama ina Anumun ara
Come with everlasting sight	Alka Adullab nigul Igigal
And do your desire with light	Ma ak Menzug Aldug Adullab ar

Sire

Sha peta annu dalbana anna zae er tapputtu malu ina parsu. Ama menden zig ma alad menden idu. Menzug ugur tia zid adullab anna ina abula tia ara, kima ina dilibad es tia ina utu udmeda dubsag zae, sha gana menzug fi namen.

We open this space unto you to aid us in religious duties. Strong we stand and spirit we know. Your sword of truth now unto the gate of time, as the shining temple of the sun ever before you, we stand your serpent priesthood.

All

Ala Ina Ara Aram All within time comes forth

With the Shamsiel (East) and Ea (Central) Altars aligned, the Sire will call each point in sequence, with the use of the Sacred Symbol (i.e. the Sacred item of each direction)

South – Garnet

Ina amalug, ina samu alad tia ara, sha uru zae. Barba ina annu gug ma dug da malu. Wasru sha gana, ina fi namen, ullulu annu Susgal ma lu Inimdug ba ina malu.

The present, the red spirit of time, we support you. Break through this seal and speak with us. Humble we stand, the Serpent Priesthood, purify this castle and let peace live through us

West – Sword

Ina nabu, ina lilitu alad tia ara, sha uru zae. Barba ina annu gug ma dug da malu. Wasru sha gana, ina fi namen, ullulu annu Susgal ma lu Inimdug ba ina malu.

The past, the blue spirit of time, we support you. Break through this seal and speak with us. Humble we stand, the Serpent Priesthood, purify this castle and let peace live through us

East – Chalice

Ina mulan, ina salmu alad tia ara, sha uru zae. Barba ina annu gug ma dug da malu. Wasru sha gana, ina fi namen, ullulu annu Susgal ma lu Inimdug ba ina malu.

The future, the black spirit of time, we support you. Break through this seal and speak with us. Humble we stand, the Serpent Priesthood, purify this castle and let peace live through us

Sire

Azig durtur fi, e ina annu dalbana tia ara. Ina ina er balu, ina ina amalug da namigigal – Sha dura ina atuku alad tia ina ar. Kunu, sudug ina annu kaunakes tia ar. Alka sus malu ina abru tia ar ma du wasru. Namazlag nu tia annu dalbana, ina utusus tia nam ma ina Aguziga tia ina sargad, isatu ama ma wur er du, sha uul er us ina ina masu tir.

Raise the Great Serpent, rise through this space of time. From within to without, through the present with insight – We draw together the powerful spirits of the L.i.g.h.t. Approach, transform through this thick cloak of time. Come cover us in beams of light and hold humble. Craft Creator of this space, the sunset of destiny and the dawn of the worlds, fire strong and wisdom to hold, we consent to follow within the forgotten forest.

All

Ala Ina Ara Aram All within time comes forth

Gather close and all link hands

Travel widdershins around the Ea Altar with the Chant:

Chant:

Uri ma Esentu, Uri ma Esentu

Ala in Ara Mupad kima esdu

Blood and bone, blood and bone

All in time to invoke as one

Continue for as long as you feel it necessary, gaining speed as you travel around

Halt the Chant – Release hands, and then raise your hands into the air, with the sign of the Nephilim:

Shamsiel

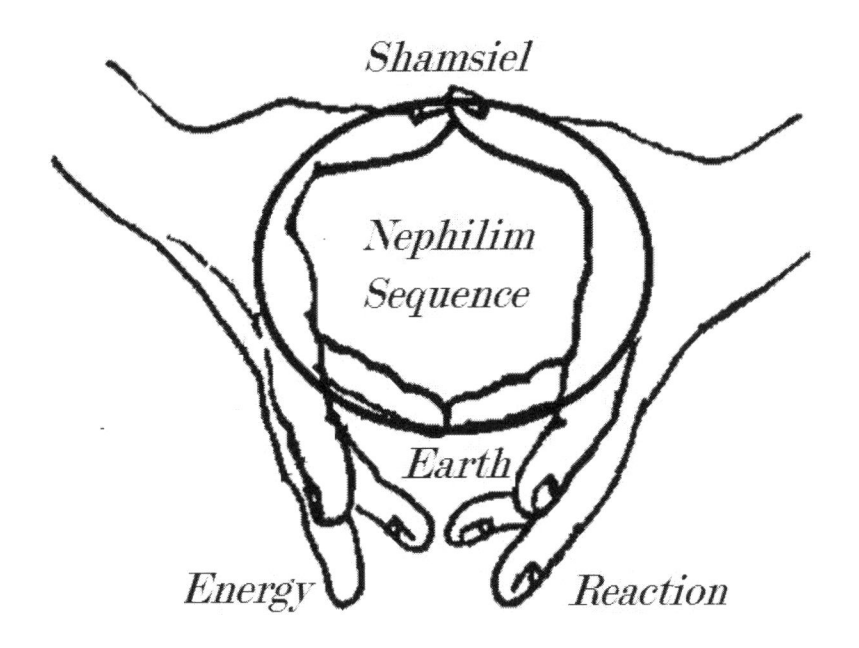

Nephilim Sequence

Earth

Energy   *Reaction*

'Ina Tilmara Amargi'

Cleanse Holy water upon Altar

Either hand straight out deosil – clockwise – motion

Sire

Urru annu da A dimmu antam, Keezh annu Arazu be Gi ma Dag, wur damu ma bar. Bana gankankha ina Ara ma ina ina zagdaku

Guard this gift I order the universe, under this prayer to be night and day, wisdom child and seat of wisdom. Exorcise this vessel in time and in the dark threshold

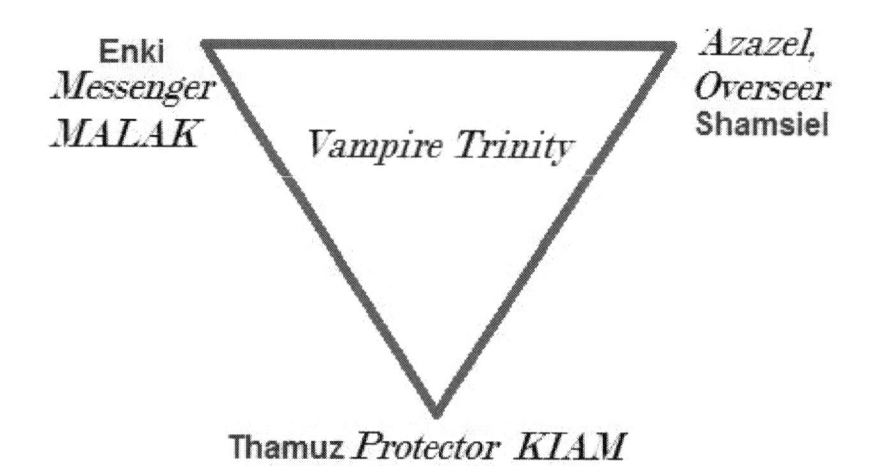

```
          Enki                              Azazel,
       Messenger                            Overseer
         MALAK      Vampire Trinity         Shamsiel
```

Thamuz *Protector* **KIAM**

Sepu Pil Ak Shamsiel

Anoint Craft of All

Sire

'Sepu Pil Ak Shamsiel'

By grace of Highest Sphere

Sire

Alka adullab an esig ina alad tia ina shinar, lu igen ahulu sig lipis, kug idu ma arammu da malu gana ina ina arazu tia sudum ma subar ar itka malu.

Come now and honour the spirits of the land, let no malice be cast inward, pure knowledge and love with us stand through the prayer of reckoning and release light upon us.

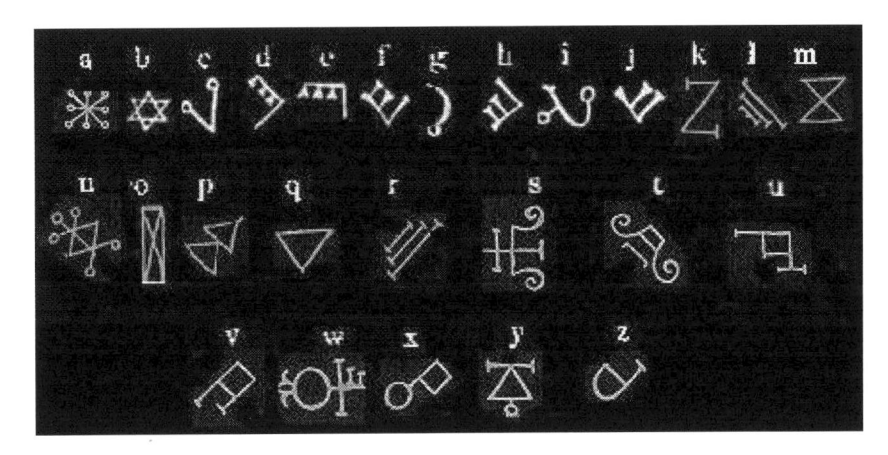

Drawing down the Sun, Moon, and Stars commences with the **Sibbu Usbar** (Snake Staff). Sire stands facing the east at the Altar, speaks the scripture once, then Calls the energy's name once at each call:

Ina Annu Bi, Ina Egura Da Dur Tur Erim Lu ina Anna Azag, la Lalartu, Duttu Bi Dara Bi!

Through this command, through Black Water the great bind, Let through unto the shining bright. Hail Phantom! Hail! One who speaks, command dark divides.

DRAWING DOWN ANSHAR: 1st CALLING of Moon

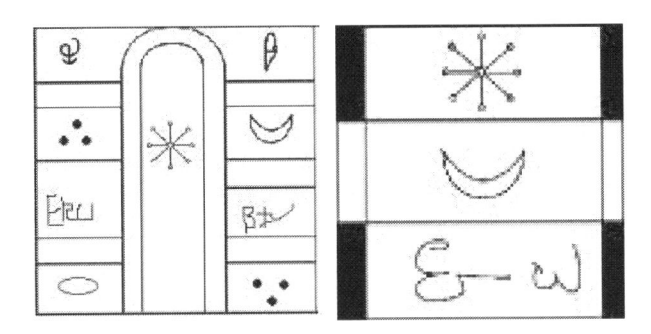

DRAWING DOWN EA: 2ND CALLING of Neptune

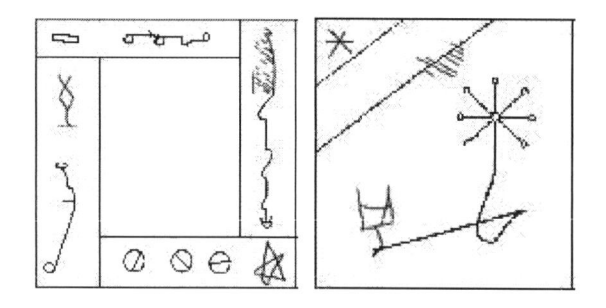

DRAWING DOWN INANNA: 3rd CALLING of Saturn

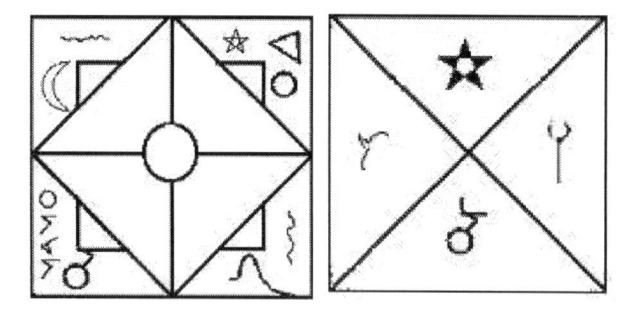

DRAWING DOWN AR: 4th CALLING of the Sun

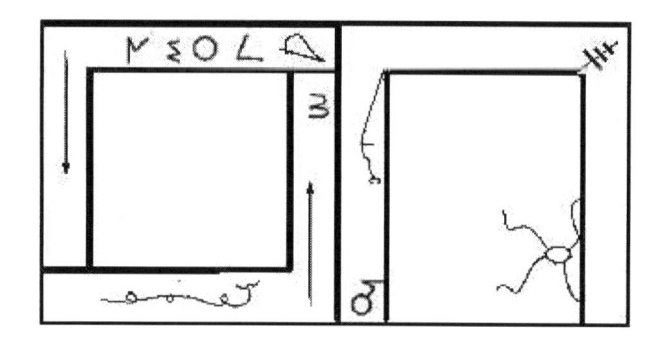

DRAWING DOWN ANUNNA: 5th CALLING of Mars

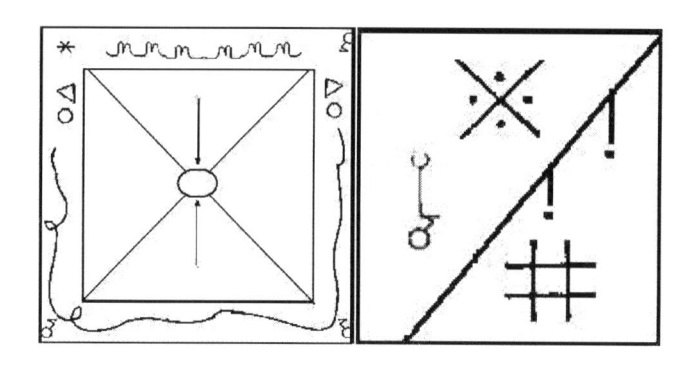

DRAWING DOWN RA.UBAN: 6th CALLING of Black Sun

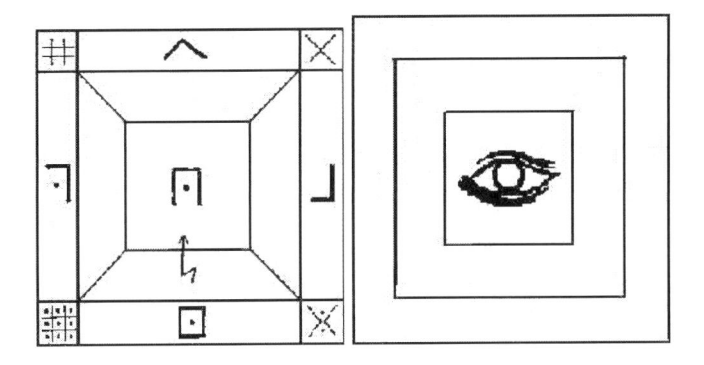

DRAWING DOWN LAHMU: 7th CALLING of Venus

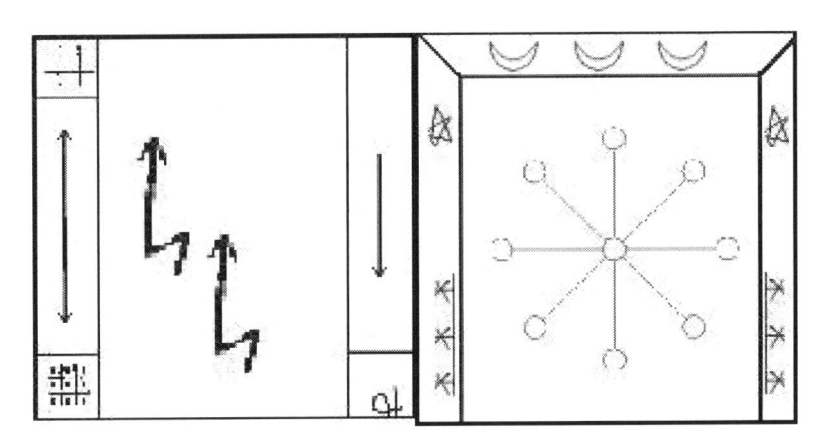

Crossing the barrier through Thamuz (Kiam)

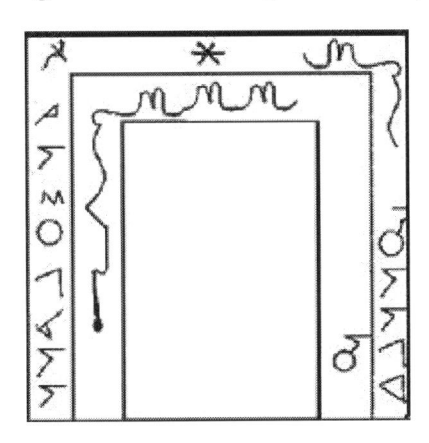

E DUR.TUR FI! E KUR INA ANNU EGURA!

EGURA FI DURA E! EGURA FI E!

ERI ANNU FI BI DUTTU! ANA SA DUR.TUR BI

ERI ANNU FI LU INA

BAR INA ARA ERI!

Rise the great Serpent!

Rise Underworld through this Black Water!

Black Water rise, draw together rise!

Black Water serpent rise

Bind this serpent with one who speaks!

One who the great command

Bind this serpent let through

Seat of wisdom through time bind!

(Allow 60 seconds to pass then say these words)

BI INA ANNU ERI

(Allow 60 seconds to pass then raise the sword of Kiam and say these words)

BI ALA BI INA GIDIM

EDIN NA ZU!

The call of Shemyaza

'The call of Leaders'

Note that a generation is indicated by each stage of development through, the initiate is a 1st Generation, and this increases until transformation, if this is deemed suitable at an appropriate time.

The 'Leaders' are known by many names, such as; Keepers, Nephilim, Angels, Demons, Guardians, and the 'Nine Lords of the Abyss'.

It is imperative that you know that to summon the Leaders is wrong, so it is wrong to invoke (bring spirit within), and further wrong to evoke (bring spirit around us). The K.e.y here is to Convoke, in other words, to cause to assemble in a meeting.

The Gateway

If not established already, the Sire will place the wooden logs in the centre of the space in the form of an inverted triangle, inverting from the North, so that the point of the triangle is in the South. The Sire will continue to seal the outer boundary of the triangle with salt in a widdershins (anti-clockwise) motion as he says the words of Shamsiel:

Varkmal Gelet Tu Mar

Suati Mili Korit gal

Tu Veh se.ant mal

Luvae Kalmak, Luvae Kalmak, Luvae Kalmak

The Constraint

The Sire now calls each of the Leaders by way of Convoke. As the Sire calls each one, he cast the relevant compound into the Chalice. Once all compounds are in the Chalice, the Sire tips the potion mix into the sealed traingle:

Note the elevated form of convoke:

Cardinal Direction	Dark Matter	Substance
1st, 9th	Ea	Water and Garnet
2nd	Inanna	Honey
3rd, 4th, 7th, 8th	Utukku	Sage, Rose Wine, Cinnamon, and Rose Petal
5th Gate	Asag	Of Lavender
6th Gate	Anzu	Of Salt

Note: Burdock Root is removed and correct placement of Sage applied

Blood is removed and correct placement of Rose Wine applied

Cinnamon is removed completely and not replaced

Sire E Su.Gaz Ina Alad Ak Anumun Ina Ea

I convoke the spirit of Water through Ea (First Gate)

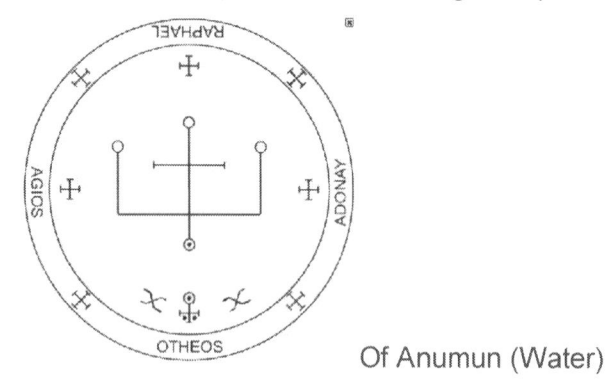

Of Anumun (Water)

Sire E Su.Gaz Ina Alad Ak Lil Ina Inanna

I convoke the spirit of Honey through Inanna (Second Gate)

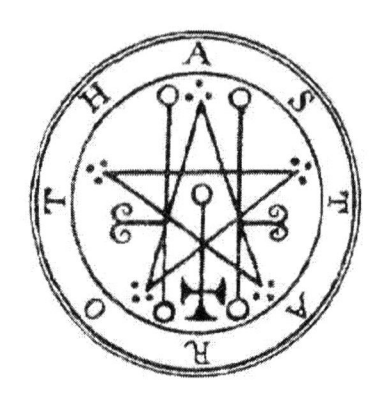

Of Lil (Honey)

Sire E Su.Gaz Ina Alad Ak Lappa Ina Utukku

I convoke the spirit of Burdock Root through Utukku (Third Gate)

Of Apkallu (Sage)

Sire E Su.Gaz Ina Alad Ak Uri Ina Ea

I convoke the spirit of Blood through Ea (Fourth Gate)

Of Uri (Blood)

Sire E Su.Gaz Ina Alad AK Azugnu Ina Asag

I convoke the spirit of Lavender through Asag (Fifth Gate)

Of Azugnu (Lavender)

Sire E Su.Gaz Ina Alad AK Dinig Ina Anzu

I convoke the spirit of Salt through Anzu (Sixth Gate)

Of Dinig (Salt)

Sire E Su.Gaz Ina Alad AK Qeneh Ina Utukku

I convoke the spirit of Cinnamon through Utukku (Seventh Gate)

Of Qeneh (Cinnamon)

Sire E Su.Gaz Ina Alad AK Aruru Ina Utukku

I convoke the spirit of Rose Petal through Utuuku (Eighth Gate)

Of Aruru (Rose Petal)

Sire E Su.Gaz Ina Alad AK Nunki Ina Ea

I convoke the spirit of Garnet through Ea (Ninth Gate)

Of Nunki (Garnet)

Sire – The Charge of Shamsiel

Sepu Ala Ina Nim Kabtu Tia Samsu Tia Ina Gula

Asum Firiq Tia Anki Alka Ahias ma Balu

Bar Dura Salatu Atuku

Nadanu Abarassa Awum. Da Menzug Masgik

Dug Luname E Igigal. E Su.Gaz Zae Alad Tia Shamsiel

Da Menzug Masgik

Alka Ina Annu Sagtak ma Awum

By all the High Glory of Names of the Great

Empowered lord of the Universe, come quickly and without

Barriers, draw together outside powers

Give true communication, make yourself visible

Come through this triangle and converse

INA ANNU BI, E UTU, NANNA, MA ADAR

DA ANNU INA ES E, MA ERI INA INA EGURA

DARA DUTTU LU INA ANNU ES ANNA INA HURSAGMU!

Through this command

Rise Sun, Moon, and Star

Make this the Temple rise and bind from the black water

Dark one who speaks let through this temple unto the mountain of the sky-chambers!

Sire Alka ina ina gidim quannu duramah, gibil wur, su'ati zae da

Durisam ina karabu ma sibum annu da er ina antam

Come through the spirit horn the great stag, one of fire wisdom, that you make forever this blessing and witness this offering to the universe. Come through and answer this prayer in love and truth. Blood Elders we carry the circle to the chamber of the regions of the four to aid and to let those who enter know you.

Sire sprinkles white salt over the Altar of Shamsiel (in the East)

Sire Gi be dag ma dara be ar

Night to be Day and Dark to be Light

Lectures and Practical teaching begins...

Each Participant is to undertake E Igisum Danna Ti

The closing and departure of Energies

(Sire will be at the alter and guard well the Circle of duality, with the Sibbu Usbar in hand to say these words)

Sire O spirits of Shamsiel, because thou hast diligently answered, I do hereby recognise and accept thee to depart, without injury to man or beast. Depart, and be thou willing and ready to come, whensoever duly exorcised and con red by the sacred rites of the Old Ways, the Dark Knowledge. I conjure thee to withdraw peaceably and quietly, and may peace continue forever between me and thee. **Mak Alam Mas Alam**

All candles are extinguished and the Sibbu Usbar (Snake Staff) is set to the ground to discharge.

The Celestial Alphabet

Also known as the Angelic Script, this alphabet is derived from Hebrew. During the early centuries after Christ's' death, a few scholars began a serious study of the Angelic Kingdoms. At the time, Christianity and religion was serious business. Strict rules and politics governed who could and could not share information about these beings. Study of these messengers and beliefs were strongly scrutinized by the political forces of the time. Disobeying or undermining the political and religious governors of this information was severely punished.

It was during this study that the names of the Angels were derived by altering the original Hebrew alphabet. These new symbolic variations were now considered to be "of God" and "Holy" images sent by the messenger Angels. This new alphabet can be laid out a variety of combinations or sounds to achieve a desired result.

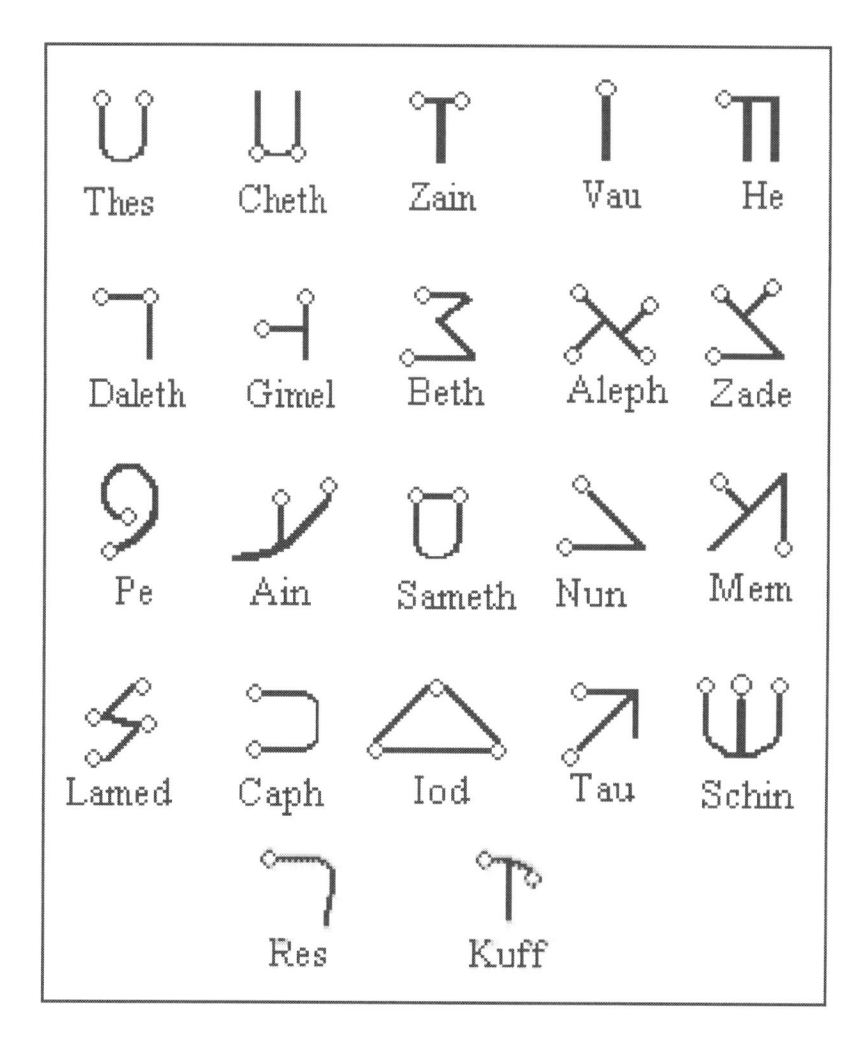

Thes	Cheth	Zain	Vau	He
Daleth	Gimel	Beth	Aleph	Zade
Pe	Ain	Sameth	Nun	Mem
Lamed	Caph	Iod	Tau	Schin
Res	Kuff			

The Nephilim Alphabet (Angelic Alphabet)

The Enochian Script

B	C	G	D	F
A	E	M	IY	H
L	P	Q	N	X
O	R	Z	UV	S
		T		

The Seven Heavens

Gabriel ruler of the 1st Heaven and the Moon. His zodiac sign - Cancer.

Raphael ruler of the 2nd Heaven and Mercury. His zodiac sign - Gemini and Virgo.

Anael ruler of the 3rd Heaven and Venus. His zodiac sign - Taurus and Libra.

Michael ruler of the 4th Heaven and the Sun. His zodiac sign - Leo.

Samael ruler of the 5th Heaven and Mars. His zodiac sign - Aries and Scorpio.

Sachiel (Zadkiel) ruler of the 6th Heaven and Jupiter. His zodiac sign - Sagittarius and Pisces.

Caffiel (Cassiel) ruler of the 7th Heaven and Saturn. His zodiac sign - Capricorn and Aquarius.

The 7 Seals of the Angels Ruling the Provinces of Heaven

SATURN
Seal of Aratron or Arathon the alchemist, who commanded seventeen million six hundred and fourty thousand spirits.

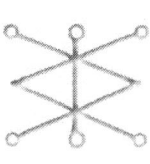

Character
Neutral

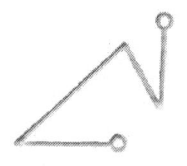

Spirit (Pos)
Agiel

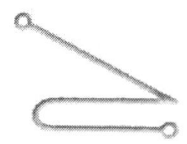

Demon (Neg)
Azazel

Saturn

JUPITER
Seal of Bethor, who commanded twenty-nine thousand legions of spirits.

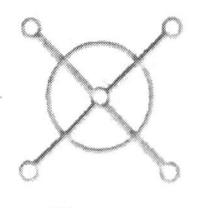

Character
Neutral

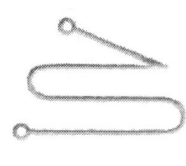

Spirit (Pos)
Jophiel

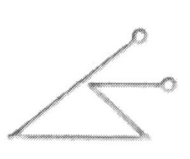

Demon (Neg)
Hismael

Jupiter

MARS
Seal of Phaleg, the War-Lord.

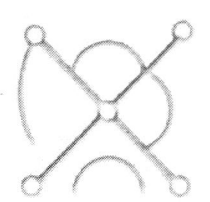

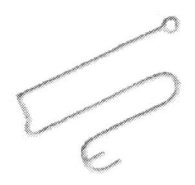

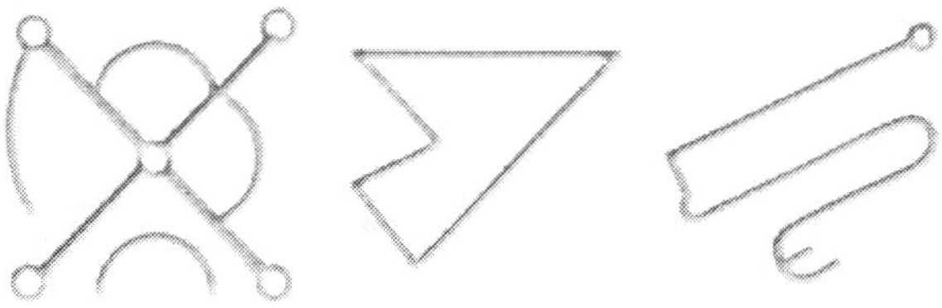

Character	Spirit (Pos)	Demon (Neg)
Neutral	Graphiel	Barzabel

Mars

SUN
Seal of Och, the alchemist, physician and magician.

Character	Spirit (Pos)	Demon (Neg)
Neutral	Nachiel	Sorath

Sun

VENUS
Seal of Hageth, transmuter of metals, and commander of four thousand legions of spirits.

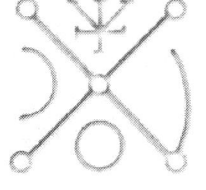

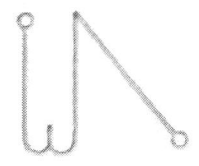

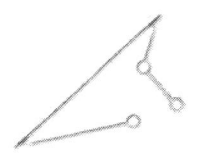

Character	Spirit (Pos)	Demon (Neg)
Neutral	Hagiel	Kedemel

Venus

MERCURY
Seal of Ophiel, who commanded one hundred thousand legions of spirits.

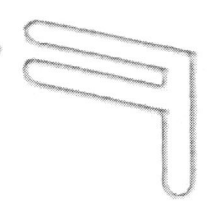

Character	Spirit (Pos)	Demon (Neg)
Neutral	Tiriel	Astaroth

Mercury

MOON
Seal of Phul, lord of the power of the Moon and supreme lord of the waters.

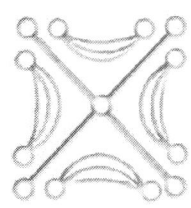

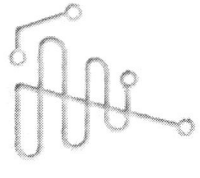

Character	Spirit (Pos)	Demon (Neg)
Neutral	Malcha	Hasmodai

Moon

The Seven Angels

They are called Olympic spirits, which do inhabit in the firmament, and in the stars of the firmament: and the office of these spirits is to declare Destinies, and to administer fatal Charms, so far forth as God pleases to permit them.

The Olympic Spirits who under God, presides over the natural world. There are seven chief Olympic spirits, each corresponding one each of the planets of our solar system, and having under them a certain number of provinces being 196 in number which using the principle of numerology equals 7 (7 Olympic Spirits, 7 Planets). The Olympic Spirits, their sign and planet are as follows:

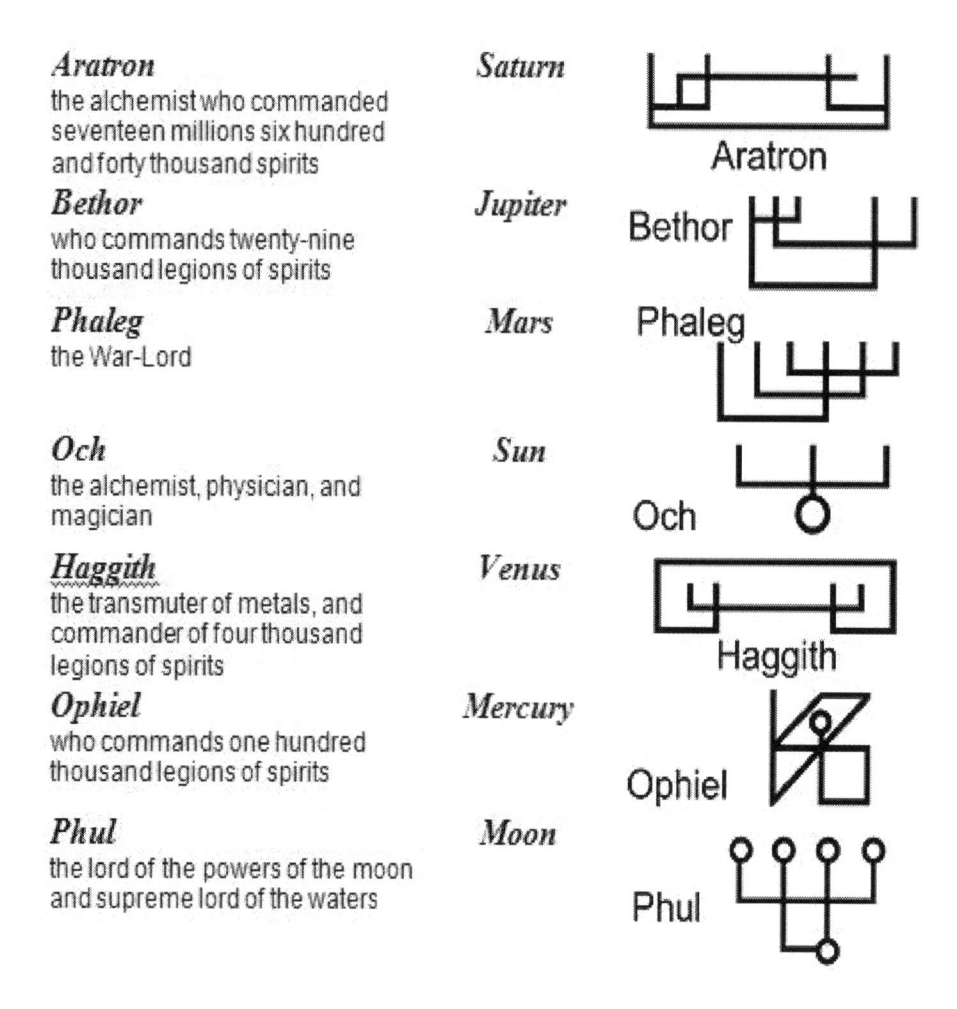

Aratron — Saturn
the alchemist who commanded seventeen millions six hundred and forty thousand spirits

Bethor — Jupiter
who commands twenty-nine thousand legions of spirits

Phaleg — Mars
the War-Lord

Och — Sun
the alchemist, physician, and magician

Haggith — Venus
the transmuter of metals, and commander of four thousand legions of spirits

Ophiel — Mercury
who commands one hundred thousand legions of spirits

Phul — Moon
the lord of the powers of the moon and supreme lord of the waters

Further known as: The Seven Olympic Spirits

The Apostles

Cain	τηε δεωιλ	Enki	RM	Ea
Modern English	**Greek Name**	**Energy Line**	**Warrior**	**Dark Matter**
Paul	Σιμων Ὀ Πετρος	Sukal	JR	**Och**
James, son of Zebedee	Ιακωβος	Panka	MM	**Bethor**
John	Ιωαννης	Darazi	CB	**Ophiel**
Judas Iskariot	Ιουδας Ισκαριωτης	Piklak	LE	**Hageth**
Andrew	Ανδρεας	Sureea	AB	**Aratron**
Philip	Φιλιππος	Walvbane	ES	Agares
Bartholomew	Βαρθολομαιος	Kamara	BB	**Phaleg**
Matthew	Μαθθαιος	Focalor		**Phul**
Thomas	Θωμας	Suggura		**Mish**
James, son of Alphaeus	Ιακωβος	Dalam	DP	**Achior**
Thaddaeus	Θαδδαιος	Su.endal	JO	**Aruru**
Simon	Σιμων	Sitri	TW	Asag

Practical Magic: The Rise of the Fallen

The Chant of Ea

The Sire now stands at the Altar of Ea (I.e. the central Altar), looking inwards from the East to the West, and speaks the words:

Bag.abi Laca Bach.abe

Lamc cahi ac.haba.be

Karrel.yos

Lamac Lamec Bach.al.yas

Cab.ah.agy sab.al.yos

Bar.yo.las

Lag.oz at.ha cab.yol.as

Sam.ah.ac et fam.yol.as

Har.rah.ya

Raising Dark Matter – The power of Energies

This ritual is for raising the power of Energies, or rather the **Dark Matter** (Sacred Energy) when assistance is required from the all seeing. In oftentimes, this Casting is referred to as 'Raising Loa Energy', especially when in connection with Voodoo.

Guidance:

1. You will need powdered egg shells and white salt combined to seal your Sacred Space
2. Place a reciprocal (or cauldron) in the centre of the space
3. A Candle of wisdom to be placed at the centre with SIX pieces of Clear Quartz around the Candle (Sphere of L.i.g.h.t) - This can be standard candle or a tea light
4. Water, Honey, and Salt (for Reciprocal)
5. Dried Rose stalk, for the Master of the Swamp (Nabu)
6. Your personal piece of Garnet
7. Blood Water, for Blessing
8. Dried Rose Leaf (to represent the Architect, God, and Goddess)
9. The Symbol of Sulgi (The Crossroads)
10. Your Sibbu Usbar – Snake Staff (or a piece of a branch)
11. Chalice with Holy Water
12. A small amount Rose Wine & a small container of White Salt

a) Place Your tea light at the centre followed by your six pieces of Clear Quartz around the tea light (or Candle)
b) Sprinkle salt around the outer boundary of your Clear Quartz crystals

Now place your Sibbu Usbar next to the Sphere of L.i.g.h.t as this will create a 'three-phase' of existence

Place the Garnet (Nunki) in your right hand and link both your hands together

Recipients close eyes and take long, deep, slow breaths

Sire Close your eyes and take long, deep, slow breaths as you focus in your minds eye upon the sphere (of L.i.g.h.t) placed within the centre of knowledge (Pure L.i.g.h.t

Start the Opening Phase

Sire Commence the opening phase of the raising chant, at low breath – The Phase of peace, and continue this until it feels linked in time:

Initiate: Chant (repeatedly) 'Inimdug' (Peace)

Sire Now imaging you are moving in a widdershins motion (anti-clockwise) around the space, with your eyes wide open – but within your mind's eye, focus upon the sphere of time (the tea light or candle within the centre of your space).

Sire Continue travelling widdershins (anti-clockwise) with both your hands still clasped as one – then start the blood and bone chant, and once rotations are in sequence - with the first phase of the opening:

Uri ma Esentu, Uri ma Esentu

Ala ina Ara Mupad Kima esdu

Blood and Bone, Blood and Bone

All in time to invoke as one

When ready – come to a halt in your thought of motion, so that you are back where you started – Release your clasped-hands and place your garnet (Nunki) upon the floor, next to your Sibbu Usbar

Make your hands into the 'horned symbols':

Left Hand   Right Hand

Sire kneel facing the Sphere of L.i.g.h.t, begin to raise your arms towards the sphere whilst chanting:

Second-phase Chant:

Ki ma An, Ki ma An

Eri kima ana, Da gar Sargad

Earth and Sky, Earth and Sky

Bind as one, with four worlds

Now lower your arms and collect your white salt containers, and with the third-phase of the chant – Cast your White Salt upon the Sphere of L.i.g.h.t:

Se tia Atuku

Collect your Sibbu Usbar – and point at the Sphere, then travel widdershins around the Sphere, with the Chant

Third-Phase Chant:

Se tia Atuku (At-Uk-U) Cone of Power

Place your Sibbu Usbar back next to the Sphere of L.i.g.h.t

Sire Continue as instructed below – work widdershins with palm facing down and held at a forty-five degree angle. At each calling, speak the words:

Collect your 'Sulgi' (The Crossroads symbol)

I ask Utukku (Sulgi), Guardian of the Barrier: Protect from malevolent spirits and guide me to the answers I seek

Burn the Sulgi symbol at the side of the tea light – Then sprinkle Salt onto the remains

I give praise and thanks to the Master of the Swamp (Asag)

Place one piece of dried Rose stalk onto the remians

Initiate:

Blessed am I to be within the entrance, In the name of Ea (Damballah Wedo), Ea (Damballah) the great, Ea (Damballah) Lele, Ayida Wedo, Ago, Ago si, Ago La

Anoint yourself with the Holy Water – In the sign of Pure Light (Marassa)

Marassa

I call Mulan (Agwe), Ansar (Ayizan), and the Hidden Knowledge (Baron Samedi) to this space to provide insight to me

Sprinkle Salt onto the remains

I call Anzu (Erzuli), Ea (Damballah and Ayida Wedo) to this space to provide protection from within and without

Sprinkle Salt onto the remains, then Pour the Holy Water onto the remain also

By the Power of the guardian of the crossroads (St. Anthony of Padua, Legba Atibon, guardian of the crossroads), Utukku (Sulgi) guardian of the bush, Utukku (Sulgi) guardian of the goose;

Ago, Ago, Si, Ago La

Now touch the mix of the remains and say these words:

Gator Geude, le bon ton roulette, ye, ye, ye

By the power of Anzu (Erzuli):

Mamou Iade, mamou Vodun, Erzulie Frieda Dahomey, Ago, Ago, Si, Ago. Mamou Iade, vie en cane Creole

Be Gone with peace in mind, I ask Utukku (Legba), Guardian of the Barrier to protect from malevolent spirits and close this Veil

<u>Extinguish the candle</u>

Papa Legba

Sulgi... The Crossroads

The Yazidis – A Vampiric ancestry

The Yazidis are linked to the extreme Shi'a (Ghulat) sects and number worldwide some 300,000 people. The main group of 150,000 Yazidis live in the Jebel Sinjar mountain and the Shaikhan district of northwest Iraq. At least 50,000 Yazidis live in the former Soviet Union (Armenia and other Caucasus states). They were also to be found in South-East Turkey around Diyarbakir and Mardin (10,000) but most emigrated from there to Germany in the 80s. They also live in Syria in and around Aleppo (5,000), and in parts of Iran. An estimated 50,000 have emigrated to Western Europe, mainly to Germany, in search of asylum and employment.

The Yazidis call themselves Dawasi. They are called "Devil worshippers" by their Sunni neighbours, who considered them heretics and have cruelly persecuted them over the centuries. They are closely related to similar sects such as the Ahl-i-Haqq. The Yazidi religion is a syncretistic combination of Zoroastrian, Manichaean, Jewish and Nestorian Christian with Islamic Shi'a and Sufi elements and has many variants. They believe that they were created separately from the rest of mankind and are descended from Adam only - not from Adam and Eve like the rest of humanity. They have therefore kept themselves strictly isolated from the other communities among whom they lived, and did not intermarry with them. They also call themselves "Children of Adam" and see themselves as a chosen people.

Although scattered, they have a well organised society. The Emir (Mirza Beg) who resides at Ba'dari (65 km north of Mosul), is the secular head who represents the Yazidis to the central authorities. He installs the chief Sheikh (Sheikh Nazir, Baba Sheikh) who resides in Beled-Sinjar and is the supreme religious head and the infallible authority on their holy scriptures.

Ethnically most Yazidis are Kurmanji speaking Kurds. Their religious practice is centered on the tomb of their founder figure, Sheikh 'Adi ibn Musafir at Lalesh, some 60 km north-east of Mosul, who was probably a Sufi (some think an Isma'ili) preacher of the 12th century.

Beliefs

Yazidis believe that the supreme God created the world, but delegated its maintenance to a hierarchy of seven angels of whom Malak Ta'us (the Peacock Angel) was the first in rank. Malak Ta'us sinned in not worshipping Adam, and was punished by being cast down from heaven. After shedding tears for 7000 years, with which the fires of hell were quenched, he repented of his sin of pride, was pardoned and reinstated as chief of the angels.

In Yazidi belief, Malak Ta'us is also the devil (Shaitan), the ruler of this world, and they seek to appease him as they fear his power. They do not actually worship him, but seek to honour and placate him, believing that the Supreme Being has delegated to him dominion over the world. They will never pronounce his Arabic name "Shaitan" or use any word beginning with "SH". He is seen as a capricious Lord who determines man's fate as he wills and in whom the principles of good and of evil are combined. It is believed that he appeared in different form in various periods of history, the final incarnation being in Sheikh 'Adi ben Musafir (d. 1162).

Malak Ta'us rules the universe with the help of six other angels, and he guards the gates of Paradise. The seven angels are worshipped by the Yazidi in the form of seven bronze peacock figures called Sanjaq, the largest of which weighs 320 kg. Six of them are taken yearly on a round of the main Yazidi centres. Of the other angels, Sultan Ezi is second in rank to Malak Ta'us and many legends are told about him. He is sometimes identified with the second Umayad Caliph Yazid ibn Mu'awiyah. Other important angels are Sherf-Edin (noble lord of religion) who is seen as the Mahdi (returning Messiah), and She-Shims (sun sheikh) who presents the prayers of the Yazidis to God's throne three times a day.

As hell was destroyed by Malak Ta'us, it does not exist anymore. There is no concept of the forgiveness of sins. A person's deeds receive due punishment or reward in his next reincarnation. Transmigration of souls is a process of gradual purification of the spirit through the successive rebirths until the final day of judgement. Like all Shi'a groups, the Yazidis believe firmly in Taqiya, the dissimulation of their faith in the face of persecution for the sake of the survival of the community.

Rites and Customs

Sheikh 'Adi, the Yazidi founder figure and saint, was a 12th century Sufi mystic whom the Yazidi believe was the final manifestation of Malak Ta'us. His tomb is their religious centre and focal point of their annual pilgrimage. Once a year, early in October, all Yazidis are encouraged to assemble at Sheikh 'Adi. The festivities are supervised by the Emir and the Baba Sheikh. The pilgrims bathe ritually in the river and form a procession in which the various clergy castes carry the Sanjaqs, play the flutes and drums, sing and dance. Hundreds of sesame oil lamps are lighted at the saint's grave and special offerings are brought. White bulls are sacrificed and common meals partaken of. A black serpent, symbol of Malak Ta'us, is carved on the doorway to the shrine and is kissed by the pilgrims.

Booths are set up and there is much rejoicing with singing and dancing. The clergy engage in secret rituals to which the laity (murids) have no access.

Yazidis pray ritually three times a day facing the sun after first washing their hands and face. The prayers are in Kurdish and express thankfulness and pleas for blessing and help. The weekly holy day is Wednesday, in which they gather at dawn in a Ziyaret (local pilgrimage centre). The day of rest is Saturday. Twice a year they fast for three days: at the sun festival (ida roja, 1st December) and at the Khidr Elias festival (The Prophet Elijah day, 18th February).

The new year festival (ida sersale, first Wednesday in April) is a time of much rejoicing. Sheep, goats or hens are sacrificed, and houses decorated with flowers. Bonfires are lit at night. Yazidis celebrate other festivals, including two days at the end of the Muslim Ramadan and a Jesus feast (ida Isa) around Easter time. Yazidis revere their dead, offering gifts, especially the firstfruits, at their graves. Many Yazidi villages have a tomb of a holy man nearby which is used as a local pilgrimage centre. Pilgrims seek blessing, protection and healing at these tombs.

Yazidi taboos include not eating lettuce, as they believe that evil is found in it. Tradition has it that "the devil once hid in a lettuce patch". This belief, ridiculed by their neighbours, probably goes back to the Manichaeans who believed that Divine Light was contained in plants more than in any other substance. Yazidis must not wear clothes of a specific dark blue colour, or a shirt open down the front. Underwear must be white. Very religious Yazidis do not eat chicken or gazelle meat.

Birth to Yazidi parents is the only way into the community. From birth each Yazidi is automatically linked to his or her specific Sheikh or Pir. This relationship cannot be changed. Children are baptised in the first week after birth, whilst circumcision is optional. Between the 7th to the 11th month, boys are initiated into full membership of the community through a special ceremony in which the Sheikh cuts off three locks of the boy's hair which are hidden by the mother. The Sheikhs perform at weddings and funerals with special prayers and liturgies.

The sacred scriptures of the Yazidis are two short books written in Arabic: Kitab al-Jilwah (book of revelation) supposed to have been written by Sheikh 'Adi himself, and Mishaf Rash (black writing) by Sheikh Hasan ibn-'Adi. An Arabic hymn in praise of Shaykh 'Adi is greatly respected as part of their liturgy.

SOCIETY

Yazidi society is divided into two classes, the laity and the clergy. Marriage is strictly restricted to one's own class, often to one's own clan and is preferably to a cousin.

The laity (murid) who constitute the majority of Yazidis were not supposed to learn to read or write (a privilege kept for an Imam claiming descent from the famous Sufi Hasan al-Basri). They are not initiated into the mysteries of their religion, their duty being to keep the religious rites and taboos and obey their spiritual leaders. Every Yazidi is linked as a disciple to a definite Sheikh or Pir, whose hand he kisses every day. The clergy or priests (ruhan, kahana) enjoy great respect and must not cut their hair or beard. They are divided into six classes:

1. The Sheikhs who are descended from five families closely related to Sheikh 'Adi.

2. The Pirs, descended from some of Sheikh Adi's disciples.

The Sheikhs and Pirs are responsible for the spiritual welfare of the murid families under their care, and for teaching them the proper Yazidi rites and ceremonies. They also function at the religious festivals and at the rites of passage (birth, marriage, death, etc.).

3. The Fakirs or Karabash who wear black shirts next to their skins and black turbans round their felt caps. They are organised like a Sufi order and have their own ascetic rules.

4. The Kawwals, who sing and play music at the festivals. Their representatives carry the Sanjaqs around Yazidi villages, inviting them to the pilgrimage to Sheikh Adi and gathering their donations to the Emir and to the upkeep of the religious centre.

5. The Kocaks - the dancers who serve at the tomb of Sheikh 'Adi.

6. The Awhan or deacons who perform the menial service at the tomb.

Every Yazidi is designated a "Brother or Sister of the Other World" on reaching puberty. This is a spiritual relationship which persists until death and carries certain ceremonial responsibilities (similar to Godparents in Christianity). Yazidi language, both in worship and in secular life, is the Kurmanji dialect of Kurdish. Yazidis are organised in tribes, with a chief (Agha) at the head of each. Every tribe is divided into clan groups. Marriage is monogamous and restricted to a person's caste and clan. As heretics the Yazidis were considered fair prey to any rightly believing Sunni. Turkish rulers and Sunni Kurdish tribes repeatedly persecuted them and tried to forcibly convert them. More recently the Iraqi authorities forcibly deported 20,000 Yazidis from Jebel Sinjar in 1975.

Since the Gulf War the Iraqi Government is claiming that the Yazidis are Arabs and their areas should be under its jurisdiction, whilst the Yazidis and Kurdish forces assert that they are Kurds and should be part of their safe haven. Iraqi government posts are only one mile away from the Yazidi sanctuary at Lalesh.

Many Yazidis were also forced to leave South-Eastern Turkey in the 70s and 80s as a result of general anti-Kurdish and specific Sunni-Islamic anti-Yazidi persecution. They have historically viewed their Syrian Orthodox and Nestorian Christian neighbours as friends and fellow sufferers at the hands of the dominant Sunni majority.

One aspect is certain that the Yazidis have a direct lineage through to Akhkharu Trait, such Vampiric qualities that are considered the minority amongst this race of men. However, the Yazidis, whether or not they have full knowledge of their ancestry, they continue to be a force to be reckoned with. Their Sacred 'Rites of Passage' cover many forms of healing, yet in particular; they continue to make use of the Sacred Symbol, the 'Buzur Agga', the **Final sign**:

Buzur Agga Final Sign

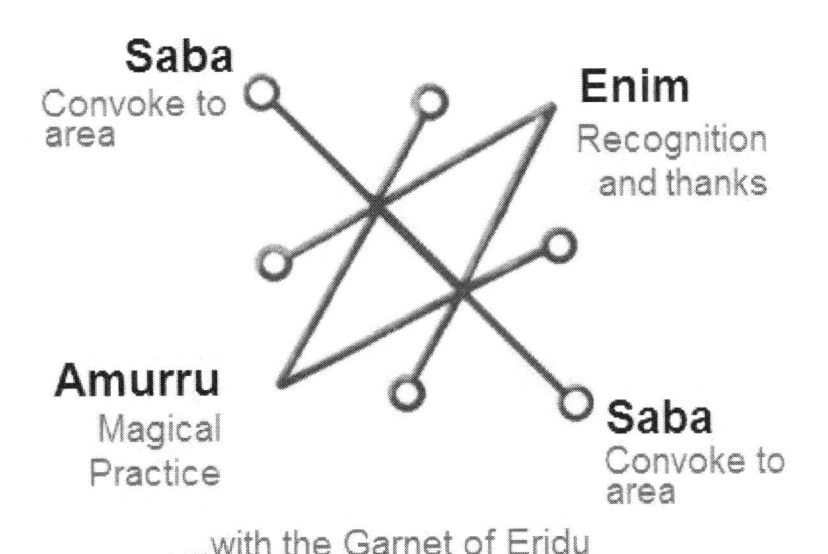

Saba
Convoke to area

Enim
Recognition and thanks

Amurru
Magical Practice

Saba
Convoke to area

...with the Garnet of Eridu

Time is given for the Initiate to choose SIX pieces of Clear Quartz (or six pieces of Garnet if they have upon them)

The Initiate will now place a Sacred stone (either Garnet or Clear Quartz) upon each circle of the Buzur Agga

Charging the Buzur Agga (Charging the Final sign)

You will need the Buzur Agga (Final sign), the six Sacred Stones (preferably Garnet, a substitute would be Clear Quartz), water in a reciprocal, either an individual tea light candle or four tea lights for the compass points.

Light a single tea light candle to the left of the Buzur Agga, or light four tea light candles at the compass points.

Cleanse the Water:

Now cleanse the Holy water upon the alter – Holding the left hand straight out and with a widdershins – anticlockwise – motion

Urru annu da A dimmu antam, Keezh annu Arazu be Gi ma Dag, wur damu ma bar. Bana gankankha ina ara ma ina ina zagdaku

Guard this gift I order the universe, under this prayer to be night and day, wisdom child and seat of wisdom. Exorcise this vessel in time and in the dark threshold

Instruction:

Have all stones aligned on the Channel Board within their designated stations and place all other stones upon the board at your choosing. Now hold your left palm closed. Raise your hand (Knuckles upwards) over the Buzur Agga and focus on the energy contained within.

Gently start a Widdershins motion (anti-clockwise) around the board. The speed of the motion is for you to decide, but ensure that all energy attunes to you appropriately. You will know when the stones are ready.

Now continue with the Widdershins motion and say this Mystic Chant:

E-gish-shir-gal, E-gish-shir-gal

Lu Annu bi ma lalartu eri

House of Great Light, House of Great Light

Let this divide and phantom bind

Continue with the following words:

Nabu Kur Dingar, E ina Utu, Nanna, ma Adar

Su'ati annu Piriq, ina Azag

Annu tisa bi er E Gallas

Mamman aga Azag bur annu aka annu wur eri

Nabu underworld God, raise the Sun, Moon, and star

That this the bearer of the magic, from the shining bright

This ninth command to go raise demons

Whoever crowns the shining bright

Hear this divine command, this wisdom bind

Initiate now spends the next 30 minutes to practice the psychic healing of the Buzur Agga. Time is given for those present to undertake healing on each other. Once completed do not forget to extinguish the tea light or candle.

Working for Azazel

One can but assume that the general populous feels that in order so to achieve, they must worship a 'Neon' God. After all, it is embedded within the forms of social conditioning at the birth of a human, that in order to achieve and have a 'fruitful' life – The human must live in accordance with the doctrine established by God himself. Of course, the general populous believe this 'Neon' God to be their truth, the basis of their civilisation. However, it is certain that this form of 'Worship' create noting more than 'fear' – And with fear it empowers the few to have 'control'. The very nature of the mundane and how it infects all with its 'false-beliefs' and 'false-values'.

There is certain hope, after all you have arrived at this place, a perfect point in time whereby you know that there is 'more' to discover, yet you remain uncertain, in a state of 'unknowing'. So here we have the offer of ritual, the offer of practice, and most importantly; the offer of 'enlightenment'. However, a ritual does not have to be enacted by a group to be powerful or even legitimate. Many of us are far more comfortable performing our ritual work alone. While group rituals build community, private rites can be very intense and potent. Many rites that are performed to work magic are private rites enacted between only one or two people. The fewer the number of people involved; the easier it is to get everyone focused together on the purpose of the rite. When working solo, you don't have to content with anyone's wandering attention.

Some resources may be limited if you are working just by yourself, but in certain cases, the one-pointed focus that an individual can achieve makes it worth it. Solitary rituals, in addition to being more focused are also more intimate and private. There are some ceremonies that have greater meaning for us if no one witnesses them save ourselves and whatever powers we may invoke. The following rites, which read more like prayers are solitary rituals that you can perform by yourself wherever and whenever you feel they are appropriate. While many may feel better if they have a specific part of their home set aside for rituals, or if they perform their private rites at a personal altar or shrine, there is no strict need for these things. As we covered at the very beginning of this collection, sacred space, ideally, is carried within, and therefore **you can make any place your temple or your altar.**

Consecration of the 'Mark'

Most vampire houses have a specific 'series' of Marks that allow them to distinguish as to the rank and value of the vampire within the community. Oftentimes, such recognition is worn as a pendant (i.e. a talisman) that symbolises the House and its ideals.

For many vampires, whether they belong to a House or not, their talisman represents their dedication to pursuing their identity as a vampire, with all that this entails. When a new talisman is obtained, it should be consecrated before putting it on, so you reflect upon all that it means to you.

To consecrate hold the talisman in your left hand and say these words:

This is the symbol of life.
It is the symbol of my ancient heritage,
A heritage I now proudly proclaim.

Life sustains me and makes me strong:
Every breath and every sweet drop of blood
Is a celebration of what I am.

Let this ankh be my constant reminder
As I wear it each night above my heart
Of the life that is so very precious
And the darkness that encircles my soul.

Sire Now kiss the talisman and place it over your heart. Draw a drop of blood from your finger (Your Sire will also draw a drop of blood from their finger) and consecrate the talisman with this blood before saying the prayer:

I am true to myself, and still they judge me.
I follow my heart, yet am condemned as a freak.
They hate me and they revile me.
They make no effort to understand.
Give me the strength to overcome their smallness.
Give me the wisdom to rise above.
Fear is the seed of their hatred.
I must accept myself regardless of how others feel.
I will not let their misunderstanding daunt me.
I will not let their prejudice keep me from who I am.
I am stronger than all of their narrow opinions.
Throughout all hardship, my soul will endure.

Sire What God are you invoking? Your purpose at this stage was to accept and recognise that I as your Sire and you as a soldier are bound. You have called upon that immortal part of yourself that has been judged and tortured and even murdered for who you are and what you can do. This part of you has the strength to endure these things. This part is where your true wisdom lies. This prayer helps you connect with that better so you don't feel so weak or alone when faced with the harsh realities of the world. **It is a prayer that you may recite whenever you feel in need, or at risk of harm**.

Sire (The Charge) While you are encouraged to have belief and write within your own mind, I charge you t be ever mindful of your commitment to I, your commitment to our Sanctuary, and your commitment to uphold our values and beliefs at all costs, and understand this as your charge:

We are the many-born. We are the Immortal.

Eternal we wander the aeons,

Moving to the rhythm of our own inner tides.

We are active elements moving through passive worlds

Endlessly we die and are reborn,

Changed yet unchanging through the years.

We move from lifetime to lifetime,

Taking up bodies as garments.

Ours is a journey toward understanding,

And our charge is knowledge and wisdom.

We are the catalysts, and as we Awaken to ourselves,

We serve to Awaken the very world.

We have passed this way before and we will pass this way again.

We have been many things to one another throughout the years: Brothers, Lovers,

Friends, and Bitterest Enemies.

But through it all, we have remained,

Tied together, soul to soul,

In this our Ancient Family.

May we endure together peacefully.

May we enjoy each new lifetime as it comes,

May we strengthen each other as we strengthen ourselves,

And may we always find one another

In very time and in every place

To share in this companionship

And to celebrate this bond.

The Initiate's Oath

The Initiate now travels to the Altar of Shamsiel (in the East) and kneels down before the Sire and Altar, and says these words:

Initiate

In this hour before dawn, as I lay down to sleep.

A promise to all kin, this oath I will keep.

The knowledge and memories that I keep in my mind,

I shall pass on to the younger, those of our kind.

For those who truly seek understanding of what we really are,

Or look for our friendship, need not go far

The Sire now offers the Initiate a drop of his blood upon their tongue.

Sire Take this my force, so that you may never be alone. Take this with an open mind and ask what I need have of you, and I shall show you such need. For this is the time and now is the hour of passing that you will seek and find. Think not of this world, for this has now passed, your faith and belief must be within us. Know that I will visit you in mind, and with such mind abound by rule of Tilmara.

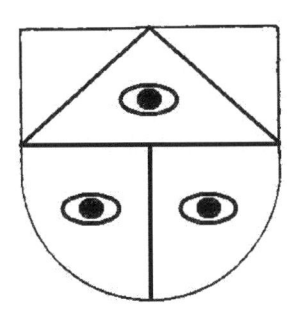

Initiate now collects their Celestial Alphabet and cuts out the THREE symbols to burn upon the Altar of Ea (Central Altar), and placing onto the Salt Bed as offering and commitment:

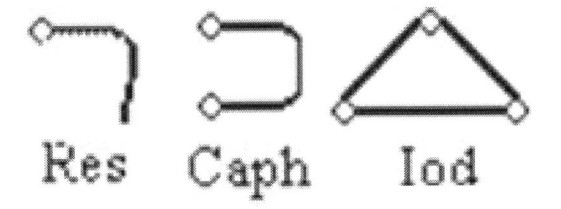

Res   Caph   Iod

Fifth Generation ...as willing as the ocean upon the shore

All non-essential items and bags must be left outside the Temple. Every Craft is checked at the entrance by a member of Templar Church

Opening into the Generation Central Chamber, as detailed below:

Red Dragon Statue, Anointment water, Recipricol, Water in Chalice, Dried Rose Stalks, Buzur Agga (Final Sign), Six Nunki (Garnet), Preceptor's personal Nunki (Garnet), Two Twigs (preferably natural liquorice sticks), Preceptor's Short Sword (Or Sword in current use, upon their person), Single Candle, Candle Holder, Sibbu Usbar (Snake Staff), Nunki Pendulum, and Energy Raiser (a piece of stick).

***The Creations** Opening Call*

Kur Dingar, E ina Utu, Nanna, ma Adar

Su'ati annu Piriq, ina Azag

Annu tisa bi er E Gallas

Mamman aga Azag bur annu aka annu wur eri

Underworld God, raise the Sun, Moon, and star
That this the bearer of the magic,
From the shining bright this ninth command to go raise demons.
Whoever crowns the shining bright hear this divine command, this wisdom bind

Sire Karabu er igi mannu Gana ina annu Dalbana. Lu malu zu Inimdug, arammu ma zid ina ma balu. Girigena tia dimmu aradu. Hasusu Menzug Namen ma eribu annu edin.

Blessings to those who stand in this space. Let us know peace, love and truth within and without. Path of order descend. Remember your Priesthood and enter this plain.

All

Ala Ina Ara Aram All within time come forth

Sire summons the L.i.g.h.t

From the Central Altar, light the white candle then say the words below:

The Calling (point-left-below-right)Light candle of the Akhkharu Lilitu Enki tia Ugur, Samu Thamuz tia menzen, Salmu Shamsiel tia Muh, sha Uru menzen

'Blue Enki of Sword, Red Thamuz of Stone, Black Shamsiel of Chalice, we support you'

Sire

Ar, isatu, ma ganzer – sha sugid ina menzug gigun, da malu ina ugula tia ina gula adhal kima sha andul ina sumer

Light, Fire, and Darkness – We accept the sacred building, make us the overseers of the great secret as we protect the land of the watchers.

Hand, Horn, Blood and Bone	Silig, Quannu, Uri ma Esentu
Wisdom old and wisdom young	Namzu Labaru ma Namzu ban
Child of star and moon of night	Damu tia mulan ma su.en tia gi
Elders strong in waters time	Abba ama ina Anumun ara
Come with everlasting sight	Alka Adullab nigul Igigal
And do your dePreceptor with light	Ma ak Menzug Aldug Adullab ar

Sire

Sha peta annu dalbana anna zae er tapputtu malu ina parsu. Ama menden zig ma alad menden idu. Menzug ugur tia zid adullab anna ina abula tia ara, kima ina dilibad es tia ina utu udmeda dubsag zae, sha gana menzug fi namen.

We open this space unto you to aid us in religious duties. Strong we stand and spirit we know. Your sword of truth now unto the gate of time, as the shining temple of the sun ever before you, we stand your serpent priesthood.

All

Ala Ina Ara Aram All within time comes forth

With the Ea (Central) Altar aligned, the Sire will assign a Fledgling to call each point in sequence, with the use of the Sacred Symbol (i.e. the sacred item of each direction) The Fledgling will collect the Material object from the Altar, travel to the edge of the area, undertake the calling, then return the Material object to the Altar

South — Garnet

Ina amalug, ina samu alad tia ara, sha uru zae. Barba ina annu gug ma dug da malu. Wasru sha gana, ina fi namen, ullulu annu Susgal ma lu Inimdug ba ina malu.

The present, the red spirit of time, we support you. Break through this seal and speak with us. Humble we stand, the Serpent Priesthood, purify this castle and let peace live through us

West — Sibbu Usbar

Ina nabu, ina lilitu alad tia ara, sha uru zae. Barba ina annu gug ma dug da malu. Wasru sha gana, ina fi namen, ullulu annu Susgal ma lu Inimdug ba ina malu.

The past, the blue spirit of time, we support you. Break through this seal and speak with us. Humble we stand, the Serpent Priesthood, purify this castle and let peace live through us

East — Fledgling's Short Sword

Ina mulan, ina salmu alad tia ara, sha uru zae. Barba ina annu gug ma dug da malu. Wasru sha gana, ina fi namen, ullulu annu Susgal ma lu Inimdug ba ina malu.

The future, the black spirit of time, we support you. Break through this seal and speak with us. Humble we stand, the Serpent Priesthood, purify this castle and let peace live through us

Sire

Azig durtur fi, e ina annu dalbana tia ara. Ina ina er balu, ina ina amalug da namigigal — Sha dura ina atuku alad tia ina ar. Kunu, sudug ina annu kaunakes tia ar. Alka sus malu ina abru tia ar ma du wasru. Namazlag nu tia annu dalbana, ina utusus tia nam ma ina Aguziga tia ina sargad, isatu ama ma wur er du, sha uul er us ina ina masu tir.

Raise the Great Serpent, rise through this space of time. From within to without, through the present with insight — We draw together the powerful spirits of the L.i.g.h.t. Approach, transform through this thick cloak of time. Come cover us in beams of light and hold humble. Craft Creator of this space, the sunset of destiny and the dawn of the worlds, fire strong and wisdom to hold, we consent to follow within the forgotten forest.

All
Ala Ina Ara Aram All within time comes forth

Gather close and all link hands
Travel widdershins around the Ea Altar with the Chant:

Chant:

Uri ma Esentu, Uri ma Esentu

Ala in Ara Mupad kima esdu

Blood and bone, blood and bone

All in time to invoke as one

Continue for as long as you feel it necessary, gaining speed as you travel around

Halt the Chant – Release hands, and then raise your hands into the air, with the sign of the Nephilim:

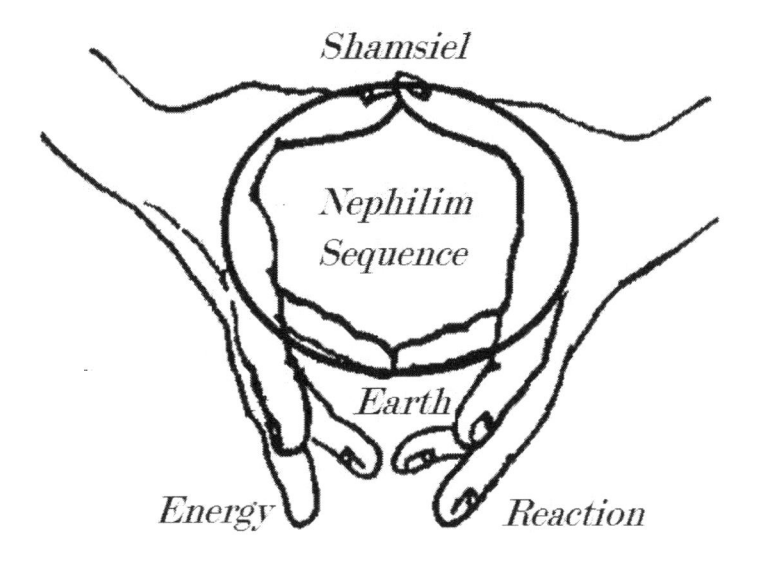

Shamsiel

Nephilim Sequence

Earth

Energy   *Reaction*

'Ina Tilmara Amargi'

Cleanse Holy water upon Altar

Either hand straight out deosil – clockwise – motion

Sire

Urru annu da A dimmu antam, Keezh annu Arazu be Gi ma Dag, wur damu ma bar. Bana gankankha ina Ara ma ina ina zagdaku Guard this gift I order the universe, under this prayer to be night and day, wisdom child and seat of wisdom. Exorcise this vessel in time and in the dark threshold

Anoint Craft of All

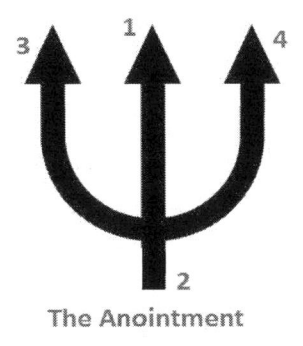

The Anointment

Sire

'Sepu Pil Ak Shamsiel'

By grace of Highest Sphere

Sire

Alka adullab an esig ina alad tia ina shinar, lu igen ahulu sig lipis, kug idu ma arammu da malu gana ina ina arazu tia sudum ma subar ar itka malu.

Come now and honour the spirits of the land, let no malice be cast inward, pure knowledge and love with us stand through the prayer of reckoning and release light upon us.

Drawing down the Sun, Moon, and Stars commences with the **Sibbu Usbar** (Snake Staff). Preceptor stands facing the east at the Altar, speaks the scripture once, then Calls the energy's name once at each call:

Ina Annu Bi, Ina Egura Da Dur Tur Erim Lu ina Anna Azag, Ia Lalartu, Duttu Bi Dara Bi! Through this command, through Black Water the great bind, Let through unto the shining bright. Hail Phantom! Hail! One who speaks, command dark divides.

DRAWING DOWN ANSHAR: 1st CALLING of Moon

DRAWING DOWN EA: 2ND CALLING of Neptune

DRAWING DOWN INANNA: 3rd CALLING of Saturn

DRAWING DOWN AR: 4th CALLING of the Sun

DRAWING DOWN ANUNNA: 5th CALLING of Mars

DRAWING DOWN RA.UBAN: 6th CALLING of Black Sun

DRAWING DOWN LAHMU: 7th CALLING of Venus

Crossing the barrier through Thamuz (Kiam)

E DUR.TUR FI! *E KUR INA ANNU EGURA!*

EGURA FI DURA E! EGURA FI E!

ERI ANNU FI BI DUTTU! ANA SA DUR.TUR BI

ERI ANNU FI LU INA

BAR INA ARA ERI!

Rise the great Serpent!

Rise Underworld through this Black Water!

Black Water rise, draw together rise!

Black Water serpent rise

Bind this serpent with one who speaks!

One who the great command

Bind this serpent let through

Seat of wisdom through time bind!

(Allow 60 seconds to pass then say these words)

BI INA ANNU ERI

(Allow 60 seconds to pass then raise the sword of Kiam and say these words)

BI ALA BI INA GIDIM

EDIN NA ZU!

'The call of Leaders'

Varkmal Gelet Tu Mar

Suati Mili Korit gal

Tu Veh se.ant mal

Luvae Kalmak, Luvae Kalmak, Luvae Kalmak

The Constraint

The Preceptor now calls each of the Leaders by way of Convoke. As the Preceptor calls each one, he cast the relevant compound into the Chalice. Once all compounds are in the Chalice, the Preceptor tips the potion mix into the sealed traingle:

Note the elevated form of convoke:

Cardinal Direction	Dark Matter	Substance
1st, 9th	Ea	Water and Garnet
2nd	Inanna	Honey
3rd, 4th, 7th, 8th	Utukku	Sage, Rose Wine, Cinnamon, and Rose Petal
5th Gate	Asag	Of Lavender
6th Gate	Anzu	Of Salt

Note: Within this generation you are privileged to receive knowledge of the advanced levels of magical practice. A set of properties to utilise as your knowledge of communication increases:

1st Phase	2nd Phase	Akhkharu	Karman	Dark Matter	13th Line
Honey	Sugar	Shiqlu	Walvbane	Agares	Ain
Water	Water	Enumun	Enki	Ea	Schin
Burdock Root	Orange	Musar	Darazi	Ophiel	Zade
Blood	Wine	Gestin	Kiamal	Mish	Daleth
Lavender	Apple	Tapuakh	Su.endal	Aruru	He
Salt	Salt	Nimur	Focalor	Phul	Cheth
Sage	Rosemary	Agga	Kamara	Phaleg	Beth
Rose Petal	Grapefruit	Ugli	Panka	Bethor	Thes
Garnet	Red Chili	Kaari	Sureea	Aratron	Aleph

Preceptor E Su.Gaz Ina Alad Ak Anumun Ina Schin

I convoke the spirit of Water through Schin (First Gate)

Of **Anumun** (Water)

Preceptor E Su.Gaz Ina Alad Ak Shiqlu Ina Ain

I convoke the spirit of Sugar through Ain (Second Gate)

Of **Shiqlu** (Sugar)

Preceptor E Su.Gaz Ina Alad Ak Musar Ina Zade

I convoke the spirit of Orange through Zade (Third Gate)

Of **Musar** (Orange)

Preceptor E Su.Gaz Ina Alad Ak Gestin Ina Daleth

I convoke the spirit of Wine through Daleth (Fourth Gate)

Of **Gestin** (Wine)

Preceptor E Su.Gaz Ina Alad AK Tapuakh Ina He

I convoke the spirit of Apple through He (Fifth Gate)

Of **Tapuakh** (Apple)

Preceptor E Su.Gaz Ina Alad AK Nimur Ina Cheth

I convoke the spirit of Salt through Cheth (Sixth Gate)

Of **Nimur** (Salt)

Preceptor E Su.Gaz Ina Alad AK Agga Ina Beth

I convoke the spirit of Rosemary through Beth (Seventh Gate)

Of **Agga** (Rosemary)

Preceptor E Su.Gaz Ina Alad AK Ugli Ina Thes

I convoke the spirit of Grapefruit through Thes (Eighth Gate)

Of **Ugli** (Grapefruit)

Preceptor E Su.Gaz Ina Alad AK Kaari Ina Aleph

I convoke the spirit of Garnet through Aleph (Ninth Gate)

Of **Kaari** (Red chilli)

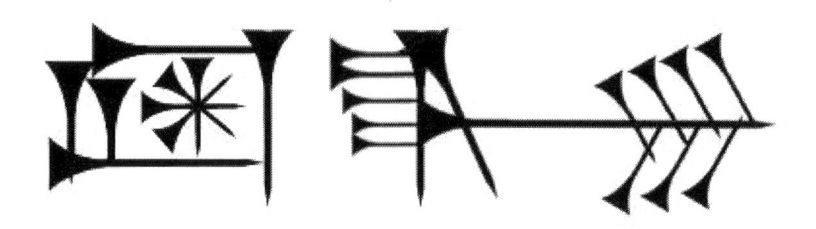

Ina Tilmara Amargi

Sire – The Charge of Shamsiel

Sepu Ala Ina Nim Kabtu Tia Samsu Tia Ina Gula

Asum Firiq Tia Anki Alka Ahias ma Balu

Bar Dura Salatu Atuku

Nadanu Abarassa Awum. Da Menzug Masgik

Dug Luname E Igigal. E Su.Gaz Zae Alad Tia Shamsiel

Da Menzug Masgik

Alka Ina Annu Sagtak ma Awum

By all the High Glory of Names of the Great

Empowered lord of the Universe, come quickly and without

Barriers, draw together outside powers

Give true communication, make yourself visible

Come through this triangle and converse

Sire

Ina annu bi, E Utu, Nanna, ma Adar

Da annu ina es E, Ma eri ina ina Egura

Dara duttu lu ina annu es anna ina Hursagmu

Through this command. Rise Sun, Moon, and Star

Make this the Temple rise and bind from the black water

Dark one who speaks let through this temple unto the mountain of the sky-chambers

Sire

Alka ina ina gidim quannu duramah, gibil wur, su'ati zae da

Durisam ina karabu ma sibum annu da er ina antam

Come through the spirit horn the great stag, one of fire wisdom, that you make forever this blessing and witness this offering to the universe. Come through and answer this prayer in love and truth. Blood Elders we carry the circle to the chamber of the regions of the four to aid and to let those who enter know you.

Sire sprinkles white salt over the Altar (central altar)

Sire Gi be dag ma dara be ar Night to be Day and Dark to be Light

It is time for you to receive further knowledge

Akhkharu Sum.Di

The Embrace (A complete process for high Generations)

Full Blood Vampires are created through a process called the Embrace. The Embrace is similar to normal vampiric feeding - the vampire drains their chosen prey of blood. However, upon complete exsanguination, the vampire returns a bit of her own immortal blood to the drained mortal. Only a tiny bit - a drop or two - is necessary to turn the mortal into an undead. This process can even be performed on a dead human, provided the body is still warm.

Once the blood is returned, the mortal 'awakens' and begins drinking of their own accord. The mortals body undergoes a series of subtle transformations; he learns to use the Blood in his body, and he is taught the special powers of his house. He is now a vampire.

Some vampire houses embrace more casually than others, but the Embrace is almost never given lightly. After all, any new vampire is a potential competitor for food and power.

A potential child is often stalked for weeks or even years by a watchful sire, who greedily evaluates whether the mortal would indeed make a good addition to the house and the line.

History

Vampires - or Kindred, exist for centuries and often seem unchanging to mortal eyes. Even Kindred society, however, has undergone evolution, upheaval and strife. Let us look at history as the Kindred view it, that we might better understand.

Cain and the First Nights

According to myth, the first of their kind was Cain, the first murderer. For his crime, Cain was cursed by God and thereby transformed into a vampire. Exiled from his people, Cain was forced to stalk the fringes of civilisation, fearful of the sun and ravenous for blood.
In his loneliness, Cain came upon a mighty witch named Lilith, who had been Adam's first wife.

Lilith taught Cain how to use his blood for mighty magic (indeed, a few heretics claim that Lilith, not Cain, was the First Vampire). Lilith taught Cain many things, including how to use his blood to evoke mystic powers - and how to create others of his kind.

The Second Generation and the First City

At first Cain refused to transform others, believing it wrong to curse the world with others of his kind. But eventually he grew lonely and brought three others into the vampiric fold. These three in turn became 13 more, and these voracious monsters went among the early peoples of the world, carelessly feeding and using mortals as puppets in their sibling feuds. Cain, outraged by this behavior, rejected the creation of any more progeny. Gathering his children and grandchildren to him, Cain built a great city - the First City in the world - and here vampires and mortals coexisted in peace.

The Antediluvians and the Clans

It could not last. Cain's children squabbled for their sire's affections, and once again the mortals were used as pawns in the feud. Finally the city was thrown down - some say a natural disaster was the cause; others, that a spurned child's vengeful sorcery precipitated the cataclysm. Cain vanished into the wastes, never to be heard from again.

The three vampires of the Second Generation likewise disappeared into the mists of legend. But Cain's 13 grandchildren, free from restraint, began breeding new vampires with abandon. The 13 vampires became known as Antediluvians, and their children, created in their images, inherited the Antediluvians' magical gifts and curses. Thus were the houses formed.

The Dark Ages

The houses (also known as clans) spread across the world, sowing discord and misery. Though each successive generation of vampires proved weaker than the last, they made up for it with greater numbers. In the ziggurats of Babylon, in the palaces of Crete, in the tribunals of Rome, vampires ruled as shadowy tyrants, forever using mortals as food and unwitting soldiers. Vampire warred with vampire, house with house, and thus - from the ancient rivalries of the First City - was born the great Jihad (a Holy war), which is still fought today. The Kindred reached their worst excesses during the early Middle Ages. During this period, many vampires ruled openly, smothering peasant and lord alike beneath their nocturnal grip. The vampiric population reached unhealthy numbers, and it seemed that the Earth would belong to the main houses forever.

The Anarch Revolt

Again, it could not last. The Children of Cain, in their hubris, began to flaunt their power flagrantly. Terrified peasants whispered of the monsters in their midst - and the Church began to listen. The reports of a few horrified priests spawned a frenzied Inquisition, and vengeful mortals rose up in a tide of fire and blood.

Though individually much more powerful than mortals, even the mightiest vampires could not stand against the humans' sheer numbers; vampire after vampire was dragged from its lair and hurled into fire or sunlight.

In the throes of the Inquisition, a current of revolt gripped the Children of Cain. Younger vampires, who were being deployed as sacrificial lambs by terrified elders, began to rise up against their sires and masters. In Eastern Europe, a group of vampires learned how to sever the mystic bonds through which sires controlled their children. Soon all of Europe saw beneath a nocturnal revolt, as rebellious children threw off the rule of their masters. Between the Inquisition and the revolt of the vampire 'anarchs,' it seemed as though the Kindred would not survive. And so, in the 15th century, a council was called. Seven of the 13 clans united in an organization called the Camarilla. (further known as the **Karman Council)**. With its advantage of numbers, the Karman Council suppressed the anarchs and agreed to exist behind a great Masquerade.

Never more shall vampires rule openly, the lords of the Karman Council decreed. We shall hide among the mortals, and conceal our natures from our prey, and in a few decades the mortals will know vampires only as myths. Thus, the Masquerade was born, and the Inquisition gradually forgot its original target. Those anarchs who would not join the Karman Council were driven into the wastes, from which they would later emerge as the dread Sabbat cult. With the discovery of the New World and the dawn of science, humanity gradually forgot about the Kindred, relegating them to the status of childhood legends. But, though hidden, vampires were still quite real. The wars of the Jihad raged on, though the nights of open battle were replaced by sudden ambushes and maneuvering of human pawns. Weaving their webs throughout the ever-expanding cities, the Kindred eschewed their previous games for more methodical but no less deadly ones.

The Modern Nights and Gehenna
And the wars continued down the centuries, and continue still. The Jihad rages as it always has - though skyscrapers take the place of castles, machine-guns and missiles replace swords and torches, and stock portfolios substitute for vaults of gold, it remains the same.

Kindred battles Kindred, house battles house, Council battles Sabbat, as they have for eons.

Buzur Agga Final Sign

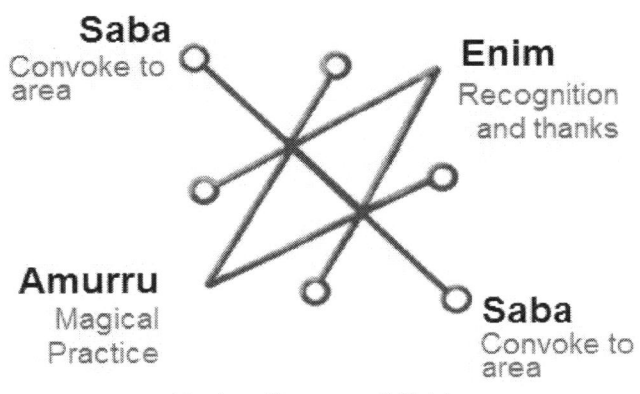

Saba — Convoke to area
Enim — Recognition and thanks
Amurru — Magical Practice
Saba — Convoke to area

...with the Garnet of Eridu

Increasingly, vampires speak of Gehenna - the long-prophesied night of apocalypse when the most ancient vampires, the mythical Antediluvians, will rise from their hidden lairs to devour all the younger vampires. This Gehenna, so the Kindred say, will presage the end of the world, as vampires and mortals alike are consumed in an inexorable tide of blood. Some vampires strive to prevent Gehenna, some fatalistically await it, and still others consider it a myth. Those who believe in Gehenna, however, say that the end time comes soon.

The Six Traditions Vampires swear to uphold the legendary Six Traditions of Cain, the laws which Cain passed to his progeny. Like any other laws, the Traditions are commonly ignored, bent or violated outright.

The First Tradition: The Masquerade
You shall not reveal the nature to those not of the Blood. Doing so shall renounce your claims of Blood.

The Second Tradition: The Domain
Your domain is your own concern. All others owe their respect to you while in it. None may challenge your word while in your domain, except a Sire.

The Third Tradition: The Progeny
You shall sire another only with the permission of your Sire. If you create another without your Sire's leave, both you and your progeny shall be slain.

The Fourth Tradition: The Accounting

Those you create are your own children. Until their progeny shall be released, you shall command them in all things. Their sins are yours to endure.

The Fifth Tradition: Hospitality

Honour one another's domain. When you are in a foreign city, you shall present yourself to the one who rules there. Without the word of acceptance, you are nothing.

The Sixth Tradition: Destruction

You are forbidden to destroy another of your kind. The right of destruction belongs only to the Sire. Only the eldest Sire amongst Sires shall call the blood hunt.

The Six Traditions
The Maker's Way

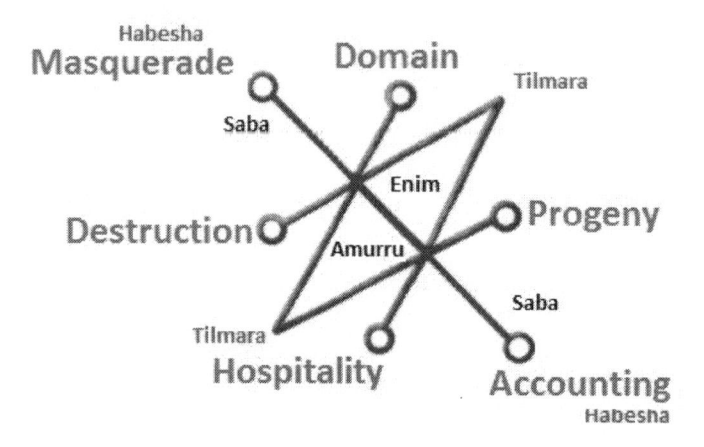

Habesha — Masquerade
Domain — Tilmara
Saba
Enim
Destruction — Amurru — Progeny
Saba
Tilmara — Hospitality
Accounting — Habesha

1. **Masquerade** - Not to reveal to any Adapa

2. **Domain** - The Maker has final decision. Do not challenge annother within their Lair

3. **Progeny** - Thou shalt Sire another only with the permission of the Maker

4. **Accounting** - Those thou transforms are thine own childer, until thy progeny released

5. **Hospitality** - Honours another's domain When in foreign land present thyself to who ruleth there

6. **Destruction** - Thou art forbiddden to destroy another of thy kind, only The Maker and his pack shall call The BLOOD HUNT

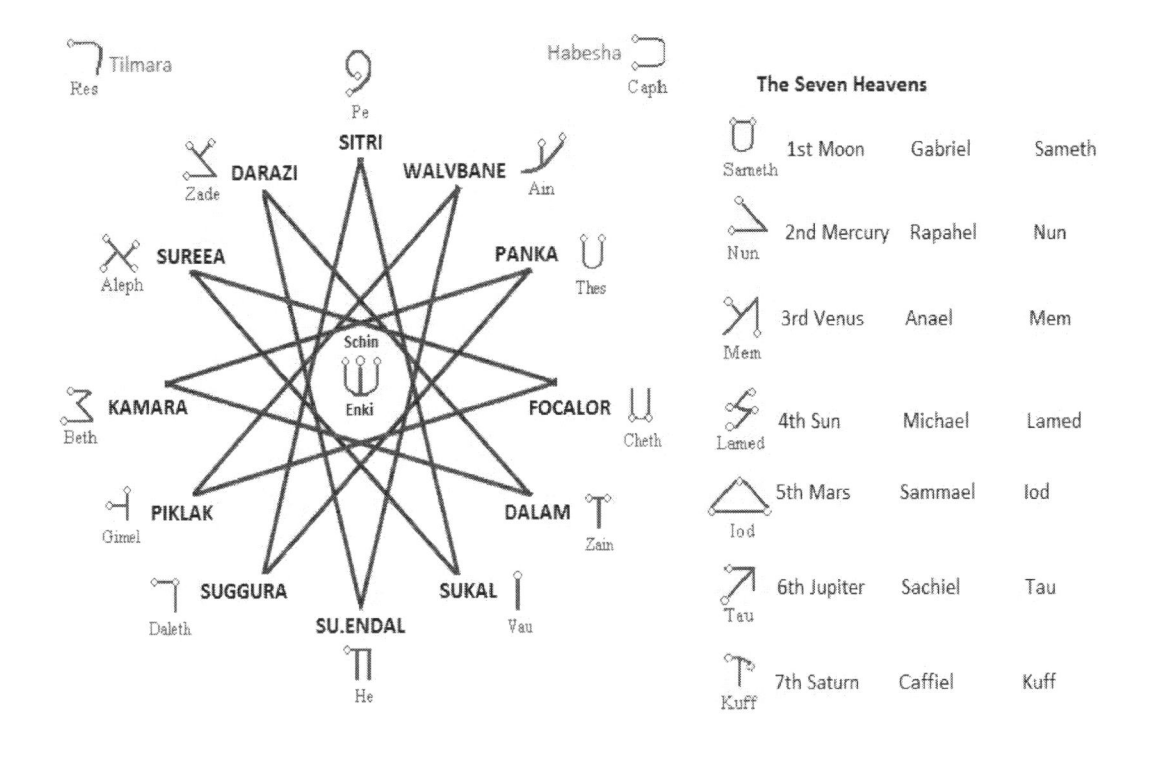

Tilmara (Res)	Pe — SITRI	Habesha (Caph)	**The Seven Heavens**
	DARAZI (Zade) — WALVBANE (Ain)		Sameth — 1st Moon — Gabriel — Sameth
SUREEA (Aleph)		PANKA (Thes)	Nun — 2nd Mercury — Rapahel — Nun
	Schin / Enki		Mem — 3rd Venus — Anael — Mem
KAMARA (Beth)		FOCALOR (Cheth)	Lamed — 4th Sun — Michael — Lamed
PIKLAK (Gimel)		DALAM (Zain)	Iod — 5th Mars — Sammael — Iod
SUGGURA (Daleth) — SU.ENDAL (He) — SUKAL (Vau)			Tau — 6th Jupiter — Sachiel — Tau
			Kuff — 7th Saturn — Caffiel — Kuff

Daku Adapa, Daku Salmat!

K*** H*****, K*** M******

ENTER INTO THE ACCEPTANCE OF GEHENNA: Pact of commitment

223

Gehenna Commitment

The name **Gehenna** comes from the language of the Akhkharu. However, in modern times it is believed to be from the Hebrew *ge-hinnom* which means 'valley of Hinnom.' Today it's more generally used to refer to hellfire, but it is an actual location that only acquired a metaphorical meaning at a perfect point in space and time, being associated with forbidden religious practices and condemned by Jeremiah of the Bible. An interesting set of points to cover is that Jeremiah was in ministry in 626 BCE, which so happens to be a numerological sequence; in the fact that if we add all three numbers together, we receive the word of 10, or rather the '1' and the '0' in binary formations. There is further interest within the name given within the tales of Jeremiah. It is said that Jeremiah was a 'Kohen', meaning that of a Jewish Priest. Interesting as it is, the same sounding word can further be applied to the sound of 'Cowan' – a Non-Craft, being of the mere mundane world and insular within their thought patterns. Therefore we see the decoding off the riddle at point, that a 'Kohen', the Jewish Priest is no more that that of the Mundane, with little or no understanding of magical practice.

Why is Gehenna important?

Enoch refers to Gehenna as both a physical and a metaphorical location. Enoch describes how Jews will gather on the holy mountain and look down into a pit where they can observe God's righteous judgment on godless cursed people, therefore making the 'righteous apocalypse, or rather, **Idugga Gehenna**.

In the New Testament, Gehenna is only referred to metaphorically as the place where the damned spend eternity — the actual geographic location is never mentioned. Gehenna must be distinguished from places like Hades where the dead in general dwell; instead, it's a place of torment and punishment for those who have committed sins against the Righteous. It is interesting to note that the 'Righteous' are far removed from that of an imaginary set of ideals in this imaginary world of Earth. The Righteous are formed from both Conscious and Unconscious thought. For it is often better to think and act, than merely think of the possibility. Let us consider that **Lucifer is Enki who is 'Schin'**, does this make Enki Satan too? Clearly the answer has to be categorically No! For Lucifer and Satan are not the same, in fact if we consider Satan to be a Commander within Lucifer's Religious Army, we would come to realise that Satan is on the Right hand of Enki. In other words, that Satan is favoured, or rather cherished by Lucifer himself in the form of **'Ain'**. On the left hand is **Zade**. Therefore we see:

Schin

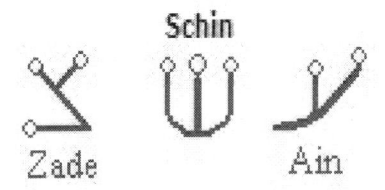

Zade   Ain

It is said that 'When the thousand years are over, Ain (i.e. Satan will be released from his prison and will go out to deceive the nations in the four corners of the earth, Gog and Magog to **gather them for battle**. In number they are like the sand on the seashore. They marched across the breadth of the earth and surrounded the camp of God's people, the city he loves:

The Legend of Gog and Magog

Genesis, 10:2-4: The sons of Japeth: Gomer, and Magog, and Madai, and Javan, and Tubal, and Meshech, and Tiras. And the sons of Gomer: Ashkenaz, and Riphath, and Togarmah. And the sons of Javan: Elishah, and Tarshish, Kittim, and Dodanim.

Ezekiel 18:6: Gomer and all his hordes; the house of Togarmah in the uttermost parts of the north, and all his hordes; even many peoples with thee.

Ezekiel 37:28 Then the nations will know that I the LORD sanctify Israel, when my sanctuary is in the midst of them for evermore.

Ezekiel 38:1-4 The word of the LORD came to me: Son of man, set your face toward Gog, of the land of Magog, the chief prince of Meshech and Tubal, and prophesy against him and say, Thus says the Lord GOD: Behold, I am against you, O Gog, chief prince of Meshech and Tubal; and I will turn you about, and put hooks into your jaws, and I will bring you forth, and all your army, horses and horsemen, all of them clothed in full armor, a great company, all of them with buckler and shield, wielding swords.

Ezekiel 38:15-23 and come from your place out of the uttermost parts of the north, you and many peoples with you, all of them riding on horses, a great host, a mighty army;

you will come up against my people Israel, like a cloud covering the land. In the latter days I will bring you against my land, that the nations may know me, when through you, O Gog, I vindicate my holiness before their eyes.

'Thus says the Lord Habesha (i.e. God): Are you he of whom I spoke in former days by my servants the prophets of Israel, who in those days prophesied for years that I would bring you against them? But on that day, when Gog shall come against the land of Israel, says the Lord GOD, my wrath will be roused.

For in my jealousy and in my blazing wrath I declare, On that day there shall be a great shaking in the land of Israel;the fish of the sea, and the birds of the air, and the beasts of the field, and all creeping things that creep on the ground, and all the men that are upon the face of the earth, shall quake at my presence, and the mountains shall be thrown down, and the cliffs shall fall, and every wall shall tumble to the ground.

I will summon every kind of terror against Gog, says the Lord GOD; every man's sword will be against his brother. With pestilence and bloodshed I will enter into judgment with him; and I will rain upon him and his hordes and the many peoples that are with him, torrential rains and hailstones, fire and brimstone. So I will show my greatness and my holiness and make myself known in the eyes of many nations. Then they will know that I am the LORD.

Ezekiel 39:1 And you, son of man, prophesy against Gog, and say, Thus says the Lord GOD: Behold, I am against you, O Gog (i.e. land of Babylon), chief prince of Meshech and Tubal . . .

Rev 20:6-10 Blessed and holy is he who shares in the first resurrection! Over such the second death has no power, but they shall be priests of God and of Christ, and they shall reign with him a thousand years. And when the thousand years are ended, Satan (i.e. Ain - Walvbane) will be loosed from his prison, and will come out to deceive the nations which are at the four corners of the earth, that is, Gog and Magog (i.e. from the four corners of Babylon), to gather them for battle; their number is like the sand of the sea. In other words that:

Ain shall rise and bring together the true warriors of the Old Ways, from the four corners of Creation, that being; Telal, the Demon Warriors from the West and the East, and the Ansar, those of Spiritual virtue from the North and South. For they shall be known as one, gathered from the points to enact Gehenna

'They marched up over the broad earth and surrounded the camp of the saints; but fire came down from heaven and consumed them,and they will be tormented day and night for ever and ever'

The passage here enlightens us that Lucifer's (i.e. Enki who is Schin – Another name for God) Commander, Ain and his Armies surround the Saints – The false Prophets, and consumes them in fire.

So where is Ain's (i.e Satan's) network today?

If we seek the network in the four corners of the world, where did it begin and what should we be looking out for today? Will Ain (i.e. Satan) of Revelation 20 come too pass? Or will the revelation be enacted for the final battle? There has been much speculation over which nation God's Adversary will come out of. Let us not limit our thinking to one person, one creature, for Gehenna will be enacted by a network allied with Ain, whom shall have powerful influence and persuasion over the world of Earth. In other words, Ain will have all nations in the four corners of the world supporting him, which means that he will not be alone in spreading the gospel (i.e. the Word). Ain will work through a network of nations and not just one nation.

In Matthew 4:8-9 says 'The devil took Jesus to a very high mountain and showed him all the kingdoms of the world and their splendor. 'All this I will give you, if you bow down and worship me.'

Here we are reminded that Ain (i.e. Satan) invited Schin (i.e. One of the Gods) to a High Mountain, or rather a high point to show him the Earth and its many boarders. Ain offered to give the Earth to Schin, if Schin would Honour and Love Ain. It is clear from this piece of scripture that Ain sought to embrace the powers of a God, and that what Ain was offering was pure allegiance to Schin on a multitude of levels.

In modern times, Schin, who is Enki, who is **Tilmara**, decreed that the following rules would need to be applied to the Earth, so to gain equilibrium, a pledge that must be recited by each recipient (Each Recipient no recites the Pledge):

1. End of sovereignty in all countries
2. End of absolute property rights
3. Creation of an international economic Order (world government)
4. The redistribution of wealth and jobs
5. Promote education of the Old Ways
6. Promote interdependence
7. Support the principle of communism

Enki guiding the Priests

The Recipients now offer blood to Enki, upon his Tongue

Lucifer, Ea, Enki, Tilmara: The Fallen Angel

For the purpose of this informative account, we will refer to the Deity as 'Lucifer', though Lucifer in heaven, before his rebellion, was a high and exalted angel, next in honour to God, or rather 'Habesha'. His countenance, like those of the other angels, was mild and expressive of happiness. His forehead was high and broad, showing a powerful intellect. His form was perfect; his bearing noble and majestic. A special light beamed in his countenance and shone around him brighter and more beautiful than around the other angels; yet Habesha (i.e. God), had the per-eminence over all the angelic hosts. Lucifer gradually assumed command which passed on Habesha alone.

The great Creator assembled the heavenly hosts, that He might in the presence of all the angels confer special honour upon Lucifer and he was seated on the throne with the Father (i.e. Habesha), and the heavenly throng of holy angels was gathered around them.

The Father then made known that it was ordained by Himself that Lucifer, his Son, should be equal with Himself; so that wherever was the presence of his Son, it was as his own presence. The word of the Son Lucifer was to be obeyed as readily as the word of the Father. His Lucifer had invested with authority to command the heavenly hosts. Especially was Lucifer to work in union with Habesha in the anticipated creation of the Earth and every living thing that should exist upon the Earth. Lucifer would carry out Habesha's will and his purposes but would do nothing of himself alone. Habesha's will would be fulfilled in Lucifer.

Lucifer was envious and jealous of Habesha, his father. Yet when all the angels bowed to Habesha to acknowledge his supremacy and high authority and rightful rule, Lucifer bowed with them; but his heart was filled with envy and hatred. Habesha had been taken into the special counsel sure regard to his plans, while Lucifer was unacquainted with them. He did not understand, neither was he permitted to know, the purposes of Habesha.

Habesha was acknowledged sovereign of heaven, his power and authority to be that of himself. Lucifer thought that he was himself a favourite in heaven among the angels. He had been highly exalted, but this did not call forth from him gratitude and praise to his Creator. He aspired to the height of Habesha himself. He gloried in his loftiness. He knew that he was honoured by the angels. He had a special mission to execute. He had been near the great Creator, and the ceaseless beams of glorious light enshrouding the eternal God (i.e. Habesha) had shone especially upon him. He thought how angels had obeyed his command with pleasurable alacrity. Were not his garments light and beautiful? Why should Habesha thus be honoured before himself?

He left the immediate presence of his father Habesha, dissatisfied and filled with envy. Concealing his real purposes, he assembled the angelic hosts. He introduced his subject, which was himself. As one aggrieved, that Habesha had neglected him. He told them that henceforth all the sweet liberty the angels had enjoyed was at an end. For had not a ruler been appointed over them, to whom they from henceforth must yield servile honour? He stated to them that he had called them together to assure them that he no longer would submit to this invasion of his rights and theirs; that never would he again bow down to Habesha; that he would take the honour upon himself which should have been conferred upon him, and would be the commander of all who would submit to follow him and obey his voice.

There was contention among the angels. Lucifer and his sympathisers were striving to reform the government of Habesha (i.e. God). They were discontented and unhappy because they could not look into his unsearchable wisdom and ascertain his purposes, and with such unlimited power and command. They rebelled against the authority of Habesha.

Angels that were loyal and true sought to reconcile this mighty, rebellious angel to the will of his Creator. They justified the act of Habesha in conferring honour upon him, and with forcible reasoning sought to convince Lucifer that no less honour was his now than before the Father had proclaimed the honour which he had conferred. They clearly set forth that Habesha was the all knowledged God, existing before the angels were created; and that he had always stood, and His mild, loving authority had not heretofore been questioned; and that he had given no commands but what it was joy for the heavenly hosts to execute. They urged that nothing had detracted from the honour that Lucifer had heretofore received.

The angels wept. They anxiously sought to move him to renounce his wicked design and yield submission to their Creator; for all had heretofore been peace and harmony, and what could occasion this dissenting, rebellious voice?

Lucifer refused to listen. And then he turned from the loyal and true angels, denouncing them as slaves. These angels, true to God, stood in amazement as they saw that Lucifer was successful in his effort to incite rebellion.

He promised them a new and better government than they then had, in which all would be freedom. Great numbers signified their purpose to accept him as their leader and chief commander. As he saw his advances were met with success, he flattered himself that he should yet have all the angels on his side, and that he would be equal with Habesha Himself, and his voice of authority would be heard in commanding the entire hosts of heaven. Again the loyal angels warned him, and assured him what must be the consequences if he persisted; that he who could create the angels could by his power overturn all their authority and in some signal manner punish their audacity and terrible rebellion.

To think that an angel should resist the law of God which was as sacred as himself! They warned the rebellious to close their ears to Lucifer's deceptive reasoning, and advised him and all who had been affected by him to go to God and confess their wrong for even admitting a thought of questioning his authority. Many of Lucifer's sympathisers were inclined to heed the counsel of the loyal angels and repent of their dissatisfaction and be again received to the confidence of the Father. The mighty revolter then declared that he was acquainted with God's law, and if he should submit to servile obedience, his honour would be taken from him. No more would he be in-trusted with his exalted mission.

He told them that himself and they also had now gone too far to go back, and he would brave the consequences, for to bow in servile worship to Habesha, to God he never would; that God would not forgive, and now they must assert their liberty and gain by force the position and authority which was not willingly accorded to them.

> Thus it was that Lucifer, the 'Light-Bearer', the sharer of God's glory, the attendant of his throne, by loyalty received Satan into his loyal service. It was to be known that never shall Lucifer undertake duties in solitary, that Satan, as Lucifer's 'right-hand', would support and guide the growing armies.

The loyal angels hastened speedily to Habesha and acquainted him with what was taking place among the angels. They found the Father in conference, to determine the means by which, for the best good of the loyal angels, the assumed authority of Lucifer and Satan could be forever put down. The great God could at once have hurled this arch deceiver and his companion from heaven; but this was not his purpose. He would give the rebellious an equal chance to measure strength and might with his loyal angels. In this battle every angel would choose his own side and be manifested to all. It would not have been safe to suffer any who united with Lucifer and Satan in their rebellion to continue to occupy heaven. They had learned the lesson of genuine rebellion against the unchangeable law of God, and this is incurable. If God had exercised his power to punish this chief rebel, disaffected angels would not have been manifested; hence, God took another course, for he would manifest distinctly to all the heavenly hosts his justice and his judgment.

War in Heaven

It was the highest crime to rebel against the government of God. All heaven seemed in commotion. The angels were marshalled in companies, each division with a higher commanding angel at its head. Lucifer and Satan were warring against the law of God, because ambitious to exalt themselves and unwilling to submit to the authority of God, heaven's great commander. All the heavenly hosts were summoned to appear before the Father, to have each case determined. Lucifer and Satan unblushingly made known their dissatisfaction. Lucifer stood up proudly and urged that he should be equal with God and should be taken into conference with the Father and understand His purposes. God informed Lucifer, that to no one would reveal his secret purposes, and he required all the family in heaven, even Lucifer, to yield him implicit, unquestioned obedience; but that he (Lucifer) had proved himself unworthy of a place in heaven.

Then Lucifer exultingly pointed to his sympathisers, comprising nearly one half of all the angels, and exclaimed, 'These are with me! Will you expel these also, and make such a void in heaven?' Lucifer then declared that he was prepared to resist the authority of Habesha, of God and to defend his place in heaven by force of might, strength against strength.

Good angels wept to hear the words of Lucifer and his exulting boasts. God declared that the rebellious should remain in heaven no longer. Their high and happy state had been held upon condition of obedience to the law which God had given to govern the high order of intelligences. But no provision had been made to save those who should venture to transgress his law. Lucifer grew bold in his rebellion, and expressed his contempt of the Creator's law. This Lucifer could not bear. He claimed that **angels needed no law** but should be left free to follow their own will, which would ever guide them right; that law was a restriction of their liberty; and that to abolish law was one great object of his standing as he did. The condition of the angels, he thought, needed improvement. Not so the mind of God, who had made laws and exalted them equal to himself. The happiness of the angelic hosts consisted in their perfect obedience to law. Each had his special work assigned him, and until Lucifer rebelled, there had been perfect order and harmonious action in heaven.

Then there was war in heaven. God, and His loyal angels engaged in conflict with the arch-rebel and those who united with him. God and loyal angels prevailed; and Lucifer and his sympathisers were expelled from heaven. All the heavenly hosts acknowledged and adored the God of justice. Not a taint of rebellion was left in heaven. All was again peaceful and harmonious as before. Angels in heaven mourned the fate of those who had been their companions in happiness and bliss. Their loss was felt in heaven.

The Father (i.e. Habesha) consulted with Lucifer, whom now banished from Heaven for the purpose to **make humans to inhabit the Earth**. Lucifer would place humans upon probation to test their loyalty before him before he could render them eternally secure.

If Lucifer endured the test wherewith Habesha (i.e. God) saw fit to prove him, he should eventually be equal with Habesha (God). He was to have the favour of God, and he was to converse with angels, and they with him. He did not see fit to place them beyond the power of disobedience.

Lucifer now on the Earth, known by the name of **Cain** and his follower Satan, now known as **Abel** were referred to by the humans as the 'sons of Adam and Eve'. However, we must first consider the story within a story of such a tale. Let us first identify the K.e.y phrase of that 'I am the First and the Last, the Alpha to Omega', where it is here that we begin to see true L.i.g.h.t:

Adam = A

Ev**e** = E

Which becomes: Ea – To become the waters of Creation. Making Ea, as we know Enki, to whom we discover is Lucifer, who becomes Cain, and further Schin. Yet from this we see Schin as **Tilmara,** the creator of Humans. Therefore when we see that 'Adam and Eve' had two sons, this is true. For Lucifer (i.e. Tilmara), had **two suns**, or rather **two lights**, namely; **Habesha** as the All-seeing and **Ain**, formerly known as Satan. Although there are two lights for Lucifer, it is appropriate to acknowledge that on Lucifer's right is Ain and to his left side is Zade. Though we have not covered Zade in full, he will be explored in great detail in the chapters to come.

It is interesting that in the fabricated story of Adam, Abel was a shepherd. So here we see the 'Able Shepherd' in the form of Walvbane. What is of significant interest is that Cain and Abel were lovers, having no level of label attached as in such times gender did not matter. There are a variety of tales of the murder of Abel, it is uncertain how Abel met an untimely death. What is certain is that Cain was wrongly accused of killing Abel, and as such was cursed by Habesha (i.e. God) and for Cain's punishment, the ground would not produce anything for him any longer. Cain told God his punishment was more than he could bear, to always be hidden from the face of God and driven out from the face of the earth.

Cain also told God his concern of being killed, but God set a mark upon Cain that if any should harm him, **they would suffer punishment sevenfold**. Cain then left into the land of Nod, the place of wanderers, or rather to be a wanderer and travel the four corners of the Earth. For Habesha placed Cain into the World of Darkness upon the Earth with a continuous craving for blood, passing this gift and curse from generation to generation. Cain became acquainted with the Lady of the Forgotten Forest, whom gave Cain some of her blood, which awakened the inner strength and outer abilities of Cain, being able to transform into other creatures as a 'shape-shifter'. After wandering for any years upon the Earth, Cain returned to being amongst the mortals (i.e. the humans that he had created), there he built a city called **Enoch,** in 7,988 BCE

There, Cain created the second generation of vampires by turning three mortals, they in turn created a third generation of vampires in vast numbers, and Cain finally forbade the creation of vampires from thence on. After some time, the city Cain had built was destroyed by a flood. Cain ended up abandoning the city and leaving all the generations of vampires behind to do what ever they wanted, but before he left, he reminded them of his command **not to create any more vampires**. The vampires completely rebelled against Cain's command and made a 4th generation of vampires, who rose up against the elder vampires of the third generation, killing all but a very few.

Over the next **1000 years**, At times, it was said that a person who claimed to be Cain appeared here and there. One of his most heightened appearances is known in a story in which he appeared amongst a band of gypsies and embracing a man by the name of **Ravnos**, after his father had been killed by other vampires. As time went on, Ravnos was introduced to **Ennoia** (Ennoia was the daughter of Lilith) Ravnos ended up turning Ennoia into a vampire. Ennoia later betrayed Ravnos and caused death to come upon Ravnos. Because of this, Cain cursed her. Ennoia later became known as the creator of the **clan Gangrel**. It is said that if Cain ever makes any appearances, it is done with a specific set of purposes, or goals to achieve in mind.

Time is given for each recipient to undertake the Cleansing Rite

Aga Mass Ssaratu

The Cleansing Rite: Transformation creation

Items Required: Buzur Agga – The Final Sign board, Eight pieces of Nunki – Garnet, Tea Light, Nunki Pendulum, Salt, Sugar, Water, A Receptacle, small piece of blank paper, and a sharp instrument to draw blood

Purpose of Rite: To cleanse the Practitioner and give thanks and recognition to Tilmara and Habesha

Action: To empower the individual to create a sphere of pure light that will grow from within, so to ensure that the fullness and development of this evolution (transformation) is balanced as the individual begins to awaken the creature inside.

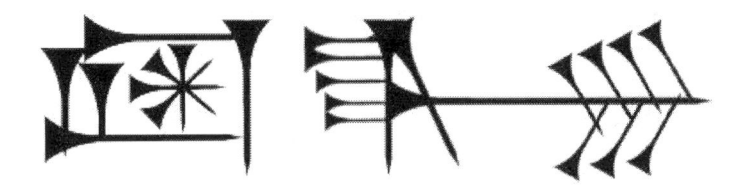

The recipient gathers their working tools into a space upon the floor – It matters not the positioning of the required items, so long as all are present.

Light the candle and say these words:

E Su.Gaz Ina Alad Ina Aleph

I convoke the spirits through Aleph (Ninth Gate)

Hold your Nunki Pendulum above the Buzur Agga – it should start to rotate in a Deosil (i.e. clockwise) motion, as you say these words: **The Charge of Shamsiel (Habesha)**

Sepu Ala Ina Nim Kabtu Tia Samsu Tia Ina Gula

Asum Firiq Tia Anki Alka Ahias ma Balu

Bar Dura Salatu Atuku

Nadanu Abarassa Awum. Da Menzug Masgik

Dug Luname E Igigal. E Su.Gaz Zae Alad Tia Shamsiel

Da Menzug Masgik

Alka Ina Annu Sagtak ma Awum

By all the High Glory of Names of the Great

Empowered lord of the Universe, come quickly and without

Barriers, draw together outside powers

Give true communication, make yourself visible

Come through this triangle and converse

Place your Nunki pendulum to the floor in front of you and hold either hand (left or right hand) above your Buzar Agga at a forty-five degree angle and say these words:

Ina annu bi, E Utu, Nanna, ma Adar

Da annu ina es E, Ma eri ina ina Egura

Dara duttu lu ina annu es anna ina Hursagmu

Through this command. Rise Sun, Moon, and Star

Make this the Temple rise and bind from the black water

Dark one who speaks let through this temple unto the mountain of the sky-chambers

Pour the water into your receptacle and say these words:

Alka ina ina gidim quannu duramah, gibil wur, su'ati zae da

Durisam ina karabu ma sibum annu da er ina antam

Come through the spirit horn the great stag, one of fire wisdom, that you make forever this blessing and witness this offering to the universe. Come through and answer this prayer in love and truth. Blood Elders we carry the circle to the chamber of the regions of the four to aid and to let those who enter know you.

Add salt to the water and say these words:

Gi be dag ma dara be ar Night to be Day and Dark to be Light

Add sugar to the water and say these words:

En-Ki-En-Gi Lugal Kalam ma The Lord of Sumer, The King of the Land

Use your blank piece of paper, draw blood and write your given name onto the paper: Note, your given name will be from the names that are 'purple', as below:

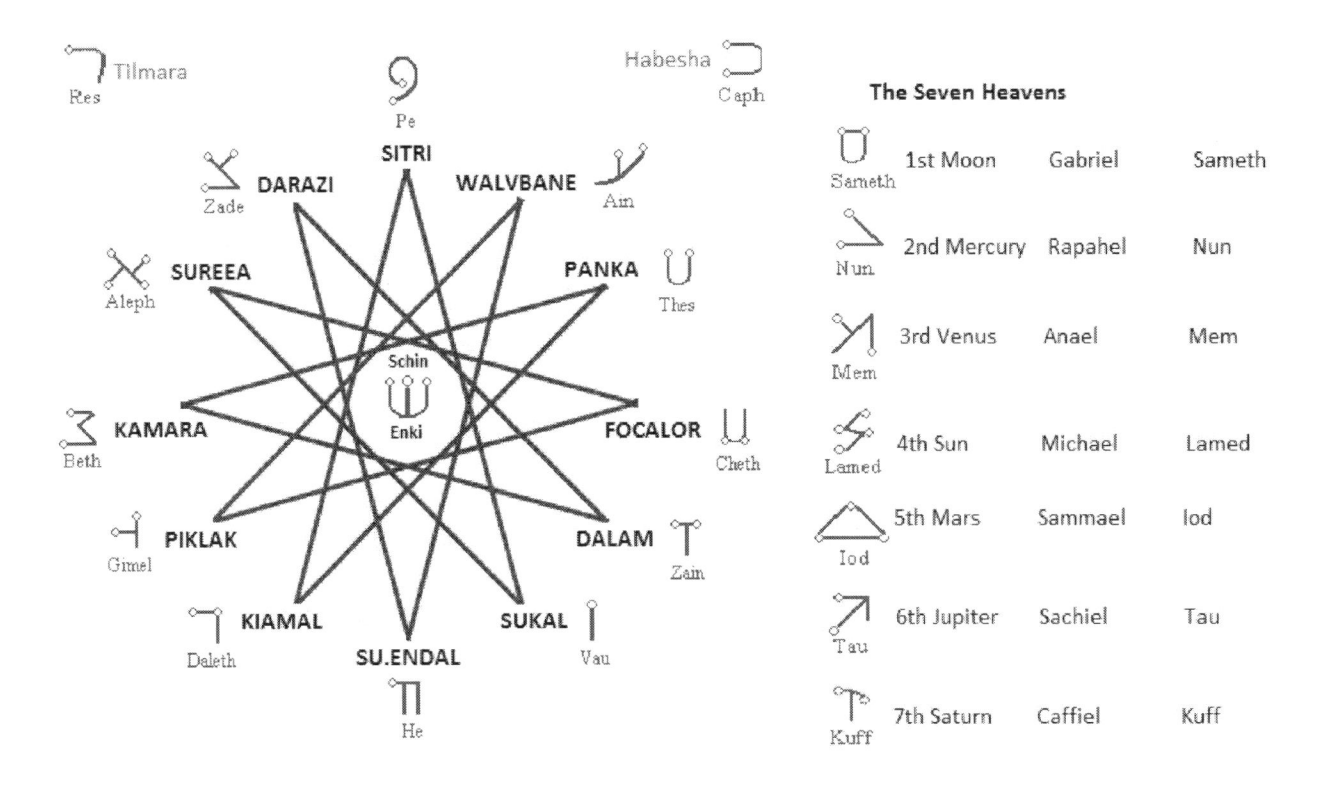

The Seven Heavens

Symbol	Heaven	Angel	Letter
Sameth	1st Moon	Gabriel	Sameth
Nun	2nd Mercury	Rapahel	Nun
Mem	3rd Venus	Anael	Mem
Lamed	4th Sun	Michael	Lamed
Iod	5th Mars	Sammael	Iod
Tau	6th Jupiter	Sachiel	Tau
Kuff	7th Saturn	Caffiel	Kuff

Star diagram names:
- Tilmara (Res)
- Habesha (Caph)
- SITRI (Pe)
- DARAZI (Zade)
- WALVBANE (Ain)
- SUREEA (Aleph)
- PANKA (Thes)
- Enki (Schin)
- KAMARA (Beth)
- FOCALOR (Cheth)
- PIKLAK (Gimel)
- DALAM (Zain)
- KIAMAL (Daleth)
- SUKAL (Vau)
- SU.ENDAL (He)

AGA MASS SSARATU

Boil! Boil! Burn! Burn! UTUK XUL TA ARDATA! Who art thou, whose son? Who are thou, whose daughter? What sorcery, what spells, has brought thee here?
May ENKI, the Master of Magicians, free me! May ASHARILUDU, son of ENKI, free me! May they bring to nought your vile sorceries! I chain you! I bind you!
I deliver you to GIRRA, Lord of the Flames, who sears, burns, enchains of whom even mighty KUTULU has fear! May GIRRA, the Ever-burning One gives strength to my arms!

May GIBIL, the Lord of Fire, give power to my Magic! Injustice, murder, freezing of the loins, rending of the bowels, devouring of the flesh, and madness in all ways hast thou persecuted me! God of CHAOS! May GIRRA free me!

AZAG-THOTH TA ARDATA! IA MARDUK! IA MARDUK! IA ASALLUXI

You have chosen me for a corpse. You have delivered me to the Skull.
You have sent Phantoms to haunt me. You have send vampires to haunt me.
To the wandering Ghosts of the Wastes, have you delivered me.
To the Phantoms of the fallen ruins, have you delivered me.
To the deserts, the wastes, the forbidden lands, you have handed me over.

KAKKAMMU! KANPA!

Extinguish the candle

The Djinn

Djinn were the first formed creatures on the planet Earth. They were used as manual workers, and as their evolution continued, they were empowered to be free-thinking individuals. The Djinn developed greed and gluttony to such an extreme that Enki made the decision to remove the entire species from the Earth and place into a parallel dimension. It is important to note that Enki created the Djinn in his own image, and in respect of this the Djinn are known to feed on human blood and can poison their victims with a single touch if the choose to do so, or consider it to be Idugga (Righteous). Their poison causes reality-altering hallucinations and can be used either to kill their victims quickly, or to leave victims in a coma-like state while the djinn feeds on their blood over a long period of time. Djinn are able to read a person's mind to learn their deepest desires; however, the djinn do not truly grant wishes like the myth and legends.

Instead, they send their victims into an alternate reality where they believe their wish has been granted while the djinn can drink their blood slowly over the course of days. Time passes slowly enough in the alternate reality that the djinn's victims will feel as if they're living an entire lifetime before their physical bodies die. When djinn access their powers, either their eyes and hands **glow blue**.

In Arabian lore, djinn, further known as jinn are a race of supernatural beings who have the ability to intervene in the affairs of people, this is mostly true. The Djinn are able to 'change'. They can be conjured in magical rites to perform various tasks and services.

In Western lore Djinn are sometimes equated with Demons, but they are not the same. It is fair to note that some Demons are also Djinn, but not all Djinn are Demons. They are often portrayed as having a demonic-like appearance, but they can also appear in beautiful, seductive forms. The djinn are **masterful shape-shifters**, and their favored forms are snakes and black dogs, in particular; Panthers are the favoured creature of shape. They also can masquerade as anything: humans, animals, ghosts, and other entities such as extraterrestrials, Demons, shadow people, fairies, angels and many more.

The djinn have the ability and the desire to enter this world and interact with all creatures on the planet Earth. The djinn have been among the living in antiquity and they are among humans now.

Origins

The Djinn are born of smokeless fire, known as plasma. They live very long lives but they are essentially not immortal. They live with other supernatural beings in the **Kaf**, a mythical range of emerald mountains that encircles the Earth. In modern times this in known as a parallel dimension.

They are malicious and dangerous, capable of bringing bad luck, illness, disaster and death. Even when granting favours, they have a trickster nature and can twist events for the worse. Though the djinn can be conjured in magical rites, they are **difficult to control**. One individual said to have complete power over the djinn was the legendary **Biblical King Solomon**. God gave Solomon a copper and iron magic ring that enabled him to subdue Djinn, and which protected him from their powers. The ring was inscribed with a pentacle, and in other accounts it was set with a diamond, that had a living force of its own. With the ring, Solomon branded the necks of the djinn as his slaves and set them to working building the first Temple of Jerusalem and even the entire city of Jerusalem.

A jealous Djinn, known as Asmodeus, stole Solomon's ring while he bathed in the river Jordan. The Djinn seated himself on the king's throne at his palace and reigned over his kingdom, forcing Solomon to become a wanderer. God compelled the Djinn to throw the ring into the sea. Solomon retrieved it, and punished the Djinn by imprisoning him in a bottle.

Djinn were on the earth before humans. By some accounts, they were created 2000 years before Adapa (before humans), and were equal to angels in stature. Like humans, Djinn have free will, and are able to understand good and evil. The purpose of their creation is the same as that of humans, which is to worship Tilmara and Habesha (the two great lights). They are responsible for their actions, and will be judged at the Last Judgment, at the 'Final Sign'.

If a Djinn is harmed or killed, even inadvertently, Djinn will take revenge, bringing misfortune, illness and even death to the offenders. It is said that if people find a snake in their house, they should call out to it for three days before killing it. If the snake is a shape-shifted Djinn, it will leave. If it remains after three days, it is an ordinary snake and can be killed. The Djinn can be converted to Akhkharu religion.

The existence of Djinn

The life span of Djinn is much longer than humans, but they do die. They are both male and female, and have children. They eat human meat, bones, and drink the blood and sexual fluids of Humans. They play, sleep, and have their own pet animals, especially cats.

Although they can live anywhere, they prefer remote and lonely places, such as deserts, ruins, caves, and tunnels. They also inhabit places of impurity such as graveyards, garbage dumps, bathrooms, and pastures. They can live in houses occupied by people. They like to sit in the places between the shade and the sunlight, and move around when the dark first comes. They also like marketplaces. Some djinn become attached to human beings and function like companion spirits. The joining of humans and Djinn in marriage is a practice in some parts of the planet Earth. A mixed marriage is believed to be capable of producing offspring, though this is not desirable. In lore, the Queen of Sheba, who fascinated King Solomon, was rumored to be part Djinn.

Djinn are capable of possessing human beings. They are said to enter the blood stream and circulate rapidly through the body. Asking a Djinn to leave, or bargaining with it, may not be enough to get it to go, and someone who is trained may be needed to perform an exorcism to get it out of the body.

Djinn encounters occur everywhere, and they may be interpreted as other entities rather than their true selves. This is especially the case in areas where little is known about them. Encounters with angels, fairies, Demons, elemental, extraterrestrials, mysterious creatures and ghosts of the dead may be djinn in disguise, either playing tricks or carrying out an agenda.

Quick Reference

1. Djinn exist in a parallel dimension in the physical world. They are here, but in a place we cannot normally experience, seen in what is known as a 'Ghost'.

2. Djinn can shape shift into human form, either male form or female. There may be something striking or odd about them, especially in their eyes. They exhibit unusual behavior.

3. As shape-shifters, Djinn will shape-shift into almost anything that suits their purposes.

4. Djinn can eat human food when they take human form, but human food does not sustain them. It gives them pleasure. Their main source of nourishment is the absorption of energy from life forms, by way of blood.

5. Djinn have their own music and language, and they do sing and whistle, just like people. Their own language sounds like a mixture of Latin and ancient tongues from the Middle East, such as Sumerian.

6. Djinn will create poltergeist disturbances, if it suits their purposes. They can make noises, smells, apparitional forms, and shadow people forms.

7. Djinn can cause nightmares. Like some other entities, they can cause unpleasant dreams, especially dreams that are real experiences in an alternate reality. When they wish to manipulate and control, they are capable of interfering in sleep.

8. Djinn can affect moods and thoughts, and they can influence a person according to that person's own inclinations.

9. Djinn can cause physical injury, but they take such actions only when they feel they or their family or clan have been harmed or wronged by a person, much as a human would react in a protective way. They can cause harm in several ways. One is like an electrical shock to the system. Also, they can knock a person down, cause things to fall on them, and alter their body to cause illness. Hostile Djinn can act out in unprovoked aggressive ways just as criminal human beings do.

10. Djinn often attach to the body's field of energy rather than enter. They can take over a person to alter mood and behavior.

11. Djinn come in all persuasions, attitudes and mindsets, just like humans. Not all of them are hostile or unfriendly. Some are indifferent and don't want to be bothered with us, and an even smaller number may be inclined to be helpful, provided it serves their own interests as well.

12. Djinn live very long lifespans, hundreds of perhaps even thousands of years. Like humans, they have the potential to ascend to an enlightened state of being.

The Charge

Recipient travels to central altar and rests on both knees

The Sire now guides each recipient to the central altar, and passes one drop of blood to the recipients tongue, then continues to mark the Recipient to the forehead with the Sign:

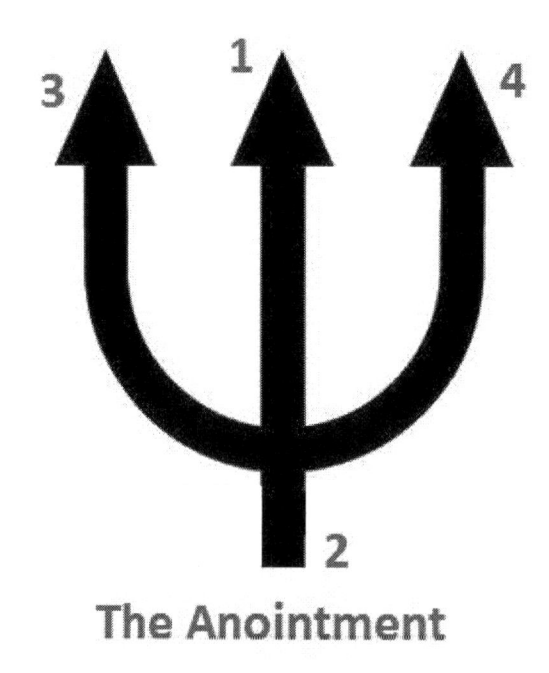

The Anointment

Recipient: We are the many-born. We are the immortal. We have been known by many names throughout the ages, though few have understood the truth of our existence. Endlessly, we die and are reborn, changed yet unchanging throughout the ages. We move from lifetime to lifetime, taking up bodies as garments.

We are watchers and we are wanderers. We seek knowledge and understanding above all.

Long ago we strove the sunder the life of our body from our roving minds, for it grounded us. It held us back. It bound us to a single span of days. Through a ritual of death and rebirth, we severed our living ties and gained immortality.

Now we are freed of the life of the body, but we are irrevocably tied to the life we cut away. It sustains us and empowers us.

We thirst for life and we feed upon it. It is our greatest weakness and our greatest prize.

Recipient now raises from the floor and embraces the Sire.
The Sire responds by saying: Gulak (i.e. Welcome)

Prepare eleven black candles and heavy incense. The temple should be decorated with images and symbols representing the left hand path concept, like inverted pentagrams.

The following seal should be placed on the altar:

Light the candles one by one, after lighting each one knock your Sibbu Usbar to the floor once and say the name of the Demon in the following sequence:

SATAN, MOLOCH, BEELZEBUB, LUCIFER, ASTAROTH, ASMODEUS, BELPHEGOR, BAEL, ADRA-MELEK, LILITH, NAHEMA

Once all the candles are alight, burn the incense and begin chanting:

Lepaca Mephistopheles! (Le-Pack-A... Mef-ist-off-ellies)

Now raise your left arm and say these words:

I call the Lord of Darkness! The Ruler of Earth! The Master of this World! Come forth from your realms of everlasting night and heat

Enflame me with your shadowy essence. Open the Gate of Darkness in my Mind and Soul, As I seek entrance into your underworld kingdom. In pursuit of Divinity

CHANT: ZAZAS, ZAZAS, NASATANADA ZAZAS (Za.zas Za.zas Nasat.ana.da za.zas)

I enter the realm of Death, shades and specters and I shall walk into the heart of Darkness to find the light that is brighter than anything else. Through death shall I emerge immortal and awakened.

From the dead shall I rise, baptized in the Black Light of illumination. From shadows shall I cloak myself in flesh again, strong and forged in the gorge of infernal hearth

I reject death of spirit that is proclaimed by mass religion and affirm the spark of life that burns in my being. I dare to eat the forbidden fruit from the Tree of Knowledge. I bear the mark of Cain and I follow the Adversary who left the barren Garden of Eden to seek liberation and Divinity. Sire now presents the Tilmara Jewell to the recipient and removes the Seal

By the power of the four Rulers of Darkness:
(turn now on each directions and say)

South: Satan, Mephistopheles (Mef-ist-off-ellies)

East: Lucifer, the Light-Bringer

North: Belial, Lord of the Earth

West: Leviathan, the serpent of timeless existence

I become the adversary myself. I am the child of the Sun and the Moon, devil and angel, the saint and the beast. In Darkness shines the light that illuminates my path. I am beyond any limitations, free and strong enough to proclaim my Will in this World. So it is done.

Sire: Explanation

The ritual was a calling of the force of **change and transformation** that is necessary on the path of dedication. The spirit of the Adversary releases the inward impulses towards self-improvement of ones life, the destruction of obstacles and barriers that hinder one's progress. This is a powerful force and should be approached carefully.

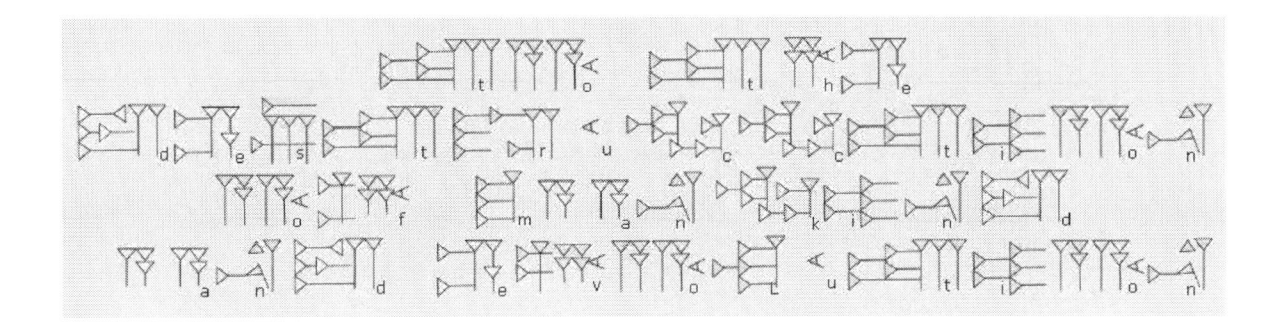

The closing and departure of Energies

(Sire will be at the alter and guard well the Circle of duality, with the Sibbu Usbar in hand to say these words)

Sire O spirits of Shamsiel, because thou hast diligently answered, I do hereby recognise and accept thee to depart, without injury to man or beast. Depart, and be thou willing and ready to come, whensoever duly exorcised and con red by the sacred rites of the Old Ways, the Dark Knowledge. I conjure thee to withdraw peaceably and quietly, and may peace continue forever between me and thee. **Mak Alam Mas Alam**

All candles are extinguished and the Sibbu Usbar (Snake Staff) is set to the ground to discharge.

Sixth Generation ...Know this, all shall reap what they have sown

All non-essential items and bags must be left outside the Temple. Every Fledglin is checked at the entrance by a secured member

Opening into the Generation Central Chamber, as detailed below:

Red Dragon Statue, Anointment water, Receptacle, Water in Chalice, Dried Rose Stalks, Buzur Agga (Final Sign), Six Nunki (Garnet), Preceptor's personal Nunki (Garnet), Two Twigs (preferably natural liquorice sticks), Fledgling's Short Sword (Or Sword in current use, upon their person), Single Candle, Candle Holder, Sibbu Usbar (Snake Staff), Nunki Pendulum, and Energy Raiser (a piece of stick).

The Creations Opening Call

Kur Dingar, E ina Utu, Nanna, ma Adar

Su'ati annu Piriq, ina Azag

Annu tisa bi er E Gallas

Mamman aga Azag bur annu aka annu wur eri

Underworld God, raise the Sun, Moon, and star
That this the bearer of the magic,
From the shining bright this ninth command to go raise demons.
Whoever crowns the shining bright hear this divine command, this wisdom bind

Sire Karabu er igi mannu Gana ina annu Dalbana. Lu malu zu Inimdug, arammu ma zid ina ma balu. Girigena tia dimmu aradu. Hasusu Menzug Namen ma eribu annu edin.

Blessings to those who stand in this space. Let us know peace, love and truth within and without. Path of order descend. Remember your Priesthood and enter this plain.

All

Ala Ina Ara Aram All within time come forth

Sire summons the L.i.g.h.t

From the Central Altar, light the white candle then say the words below:

The Calling (point-left-below-right)Light candle of the Akhkharu Lilitu Enki tia Ugur, Samu Thamuz tia menzen, Salmu Shamsiel tia Muh, sha Uru menzen

'Blue Enki of Sword, Red Thamuz of Stone, Black Shamsiel of Chalice, we support you'

Sire

Ar, isatu, ma ganzer – sha sugid ina menzug gigun, da malu ina ugula tia ina gula adhal kima sha andul ina sumer

Light, Fire, and Darkness – We accept the sacred building, make us the overseers of the great secret as we protect the land of the watchers.

Hand, Horn, Blood and Bone	Silig, Quannu, Uri ma Esentu
Wisdom old and wisdom young	Namzu Labaru ma Namzu ban
Child of star and moon of night	Damu tia mulan ma su.en tia gi
Elders strong in waters time	Abba ama ina Anumun ara
Come with everlasting sight	Alka Adullab nigul Igigal
And do your Earth creatures with light	Ma ak Menzug Kimaran Adullab ar

Sire

Sha peta annu dalbana anna zae er tapputtu malu ina parsu. Ama menden zig ma alad menden idu. Menzug ugur tia zid adullab anna ina abula tia ara, kima ina dilibad es tia ina utu udmeda dubsag zae, sha gana menzug fi namen.

We open this space unto you to aid us in religious duties. Strong we stand and spirit we know. Your sword of truth now unto the gate of time, as the shining temple of the sun ever before you, we stand your serpent priesthood.

All

Ala Ina Ara Aram All within time comes forth

With the Ea (Central) Altar aligned, the Sire will assign a Fledgling to call each point in sequence, with the use of the Sacred Symbol (i.e. the sacred item of each direction) The Fledgling will collect the Material object from the Altar, travel to the edge of the area, undertake the calling, then return the Material object to the Altar

South — Garnet

Ina amalug, ina samu alad tia ara, sha uru zae. Barba ina annu gug ma dug da malu. Wasru sha gana, ina fi namen, ullulu annu Susgal ma lu Inimdug ba ina malu.

The present, the red spirit of time, we support you. Break through this seal and speak with us. Humble we stand, the Serpent Priesthood, purify this castle and let peace live through us

West — Sibbu Usbar

Ina nabu, ina lilitu alad tia ara, sha uru zae. Barba ina annu gug ma dug da malu. Wasru sha gana, ina fi namen, ullulu annu Susgal ma lu Inimdug ba ina malu.

The past, the blue spirit of time, we support you. Break through this seal and speak with us. Humble we stand, the Serpent Priesthood, purify this castle and let peace live through us

East – Fledgling's Short Sword

Ina mulan, ina salmu alad tia ara, sha uru zae. Barba ina annu gug ma dug da malu. Wasru sha gana, ina fi namen, ullulu annu Susgal ma lu Inimdug ba ina malu.

The future, the black spirit of time, we support you. Break through this seal and speak with us. Humble we stand, the Serpent Priesthood, purify this castle and let peace live through us

Sire

Azig durtur fi, e ina annu dalbana tia ara. Ina ina er balu, ina ina amalug da namigigal – Sha dura ina atuku alad tia ina ar. Kunu, sudug ina annu kaunakes tia ar. Alka sus malu ina abru tia ar ma du wasru. Namazlag nu tia annu dalbana, ina utusus tia nam ma ina Aguziga tia ina sargad, isatu ama ma wur er du, sha uul er us ina ina masu tir.

Raise the Great Serpent, rise through this space of time. From within to without, through the present with insight – We draw together the powerful spirits of the L.i.g.h.t. Approach, transform through this thick cloak of time. Come cover us in beams of light and hold humble. Craft Creator of this space, the sunset of destiny and the dawn of the worlds, fire strong and wisdom to hold, we consent to follow within the forgotten forest.

All
Ala Ina Ara Aram All within time comes forth

Gather close and all link hands
Travel widdershins around the Ea Altar with the Chant:

Chant:

Uri ma Esentu, Uri ma Esentu

Ala in Ara Mupad kima esdu

Blood and bone, blood and bone

All in time to invoke as one

Continue for as long as you feel it necessary, gaining speed as you travel around

Halt the Chant – Release hands, and then raise your hands into the air, with the sign of the Nephilim:

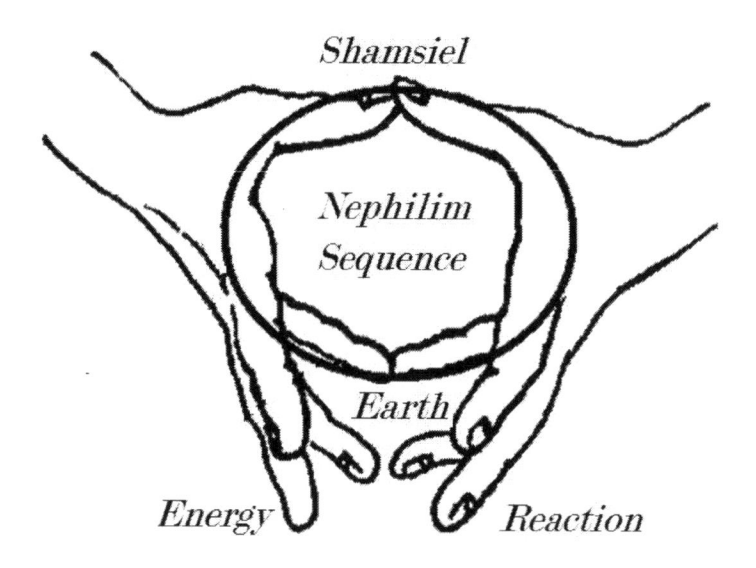

Shamsiel

Nephilim Sequence

Earth

Energy — *Reaction*

'Ina Tilmara Amargi'

Cleanse Holy water upon Altar

Either hand straight out deosil – clockwise – motion

Sire

Urru annu da A dimmu antam, Keezh annu Arazu be Gi ma Dag, wur damu ma bar. Bana gankankha ina Ara ma ina ina zagdaku Guard this gift I order the universe, under this prayer to be night and day, wisdom child and seat of wisdom. Exorcise this vessel in time and in the dark threshold

Anoint Craft of All

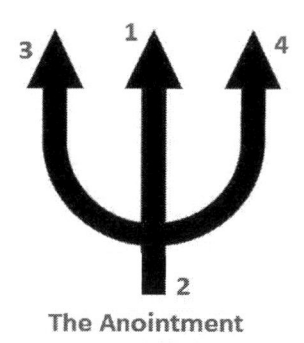

The Anointment

Sire

'Sepu Pil Ak Shamsiel'

By grace of Highest Sphere

Sire

Alka adullab an esig ina alad tia ina shinar, lu igen ahulu sig lipis, kug idu ma arammu da malu gana ina ina arazu tia sudum ma subar ar itka malu.

Come now and honour the spirits of the land, let no malice be cast inward, pure knowledge and love with us stand through the prayer of reckoning and release light upon us.

Drawing down the Sun, Moon, and Stars commences with the **Sibbu Usbar** (Snake Staff). Preceptor stands facing the east at the Altar, speaks the scripture once, then Calls the energy's name once at each call:

Ina Annu Bi, Ina Egura Da Dur Tur Erim Lu ina Anna Azag, la Lalartu, Duttu Bi Dara Bi! Through this command, through Black Water the great bind, Let through unto the shining bright. Hail Phantom! Hail! One who speaks, command dark divides.

DRAWING DOWN ANSHAR: 1st CALLING of Moon

DRAWING DOWN EA: 2ND CALLING of Neptune

DRAWING DOWN INANNA: 3rd CALLING of Saturn

DRAWING DOWN AR: 4th CALLING of the Sun

DRAWING DOWN ANUNNA: 5th CALLING of Mars

DRAWING DOWN RA.UBAN: 6th CALLING of Black Sun

DRAWING DOWN LAHMU: 7th CALLING of Venus

Crossing the barrier through Thamuz (Kiam)

E DUR.TUR FI! *E KUR INA ANNU EGURA!*

EGURA FI DURA E! EGURA FI E!

ERI ANNU FI BI DUTTU! ANA SA DUR.TUR BI

ERI ANNU FI LU INA

BAR INA ARA ERI!

Rise the great Serpent!

Rise Underworld through this Black Water!

Black Water rise, draw together rise!

Black Water serpent rise

Bind this serpent with one who speaks!

One who the great command

Bind this serpent let through

Seat of wisdom through time bind!

(Allow 60 seconds to pass then say these words)

BI INA ANNU ERI

(Allow 60 seconds to pass then raise the sword of Kiam and say these words)

BI ALA BI INA GIDIM

EDIN NA ZU!

'The call of Leaders'

Varkmal Gelet Tu Mar

Suati Mili Korit gal

Tu Veh se.ant mal

Luvae Kalmak, Luvae Kalmak, Luvae Kalmak

The Constraint

The Preceptor now calls each of the Leaders by way of Convoke. As the Preceptor calls each one, he cast the relevant compound into the Chalice. Once all compounds are in the Chalice, the Preceptor tips the potion mix into the sealed traingle:

Note the 'transition' of convoke:

Direction	Matter	Energy	Route	Substance	Akhkharu
1st Gate	Schin	Lucifer	Enki / Ea	Water	Anumun
2nd Gate	Ain	Satan	Agares / Innana / Walvbane	Sugar	Shiqlu
3rd Gate	Zade	Ophiel	Utukku / Darazi	Orange	Musar
4th Gate	Daleth	Mish	Asag / Kiamal	Wine	Gestin
5th Gate	He	Aruru	Anzu / Su.endal	Apple	Tapuakh
6th Gate	Cheth	Phul	Focalor	Salt	Nimur
7th Gate	Beth	Phaleg	Kamara	Rosemary	Agga
8th Gate	Thes	Bethor	Panka	Grapefruit	Ugli
9th Gate	Aleph	Aratron	Sureea	Chilli	Kaari
Entrance	Tilmara	Nu	Creator	Water	Anumun
Perfection	Habesha	Kashurra	Primeval Source	Fire	Gibil

Zade   **Tilmara**   **Ain**

Preceptor E Su.Gaz Ina Alad Ak Anumun Ina Schin

I convoke the spirit of Water through Schin (First Gate)

Of **Anumun** (Water)

Preceptor E Su.Gaz Ina Alad Ak **Shiqlu** Ina Ain

I convoke the spirit of Sugar through Ain (Second Gate)

Of **Shiqlu** (Sugar)

Preceptor E Su.Gaz Ina Alad Ak **Musar** Ina Zade

I convoke the spirit of Orange through Zade (Third Gate)

Of **Musar** (Orange)

Preceptor E Su.Gaz Ina Alad Ak **Gestin** Ina Daleth

I convoke the spirit of Wine through Daleth (Fourth Gate)

Of **Gestin** (Wine)

Preceptor E Su.Gaz Ina Alad AK **Tapuakh** Ina He

I convoke the spirit of Apple through He (Fifth Gate)

Of **Tapuakh** (Apple)

Preceptor E Su.Gaz Ina Alad AK **Nimur** Ina Cheth

I convoke the spirit of Salt through Cheth (Sixth Gate)

Of **Nimur** (Salt)

Preceptor E Su.Gaz Ina Alad AK **Agga** Ina Beth

I convoke the spirit of Rosemary through Beth (Seventh Gate)

Of **Agga** (Rosemary)

Preceptor E Su.Gaz Ina Alad AK **Ugli** Ina Thes

I convoke the spirit of Grapefruit through Thes (Eighth Gate)

Of **Ugli** (Grapefruit)

Preceptor E Su.Gaz Ina Alad AK Kaari Ina Aleph

I convoke the spirit of Garnet through Aleph (Ninth Gate)

Of **Kaari** (Red chilli)

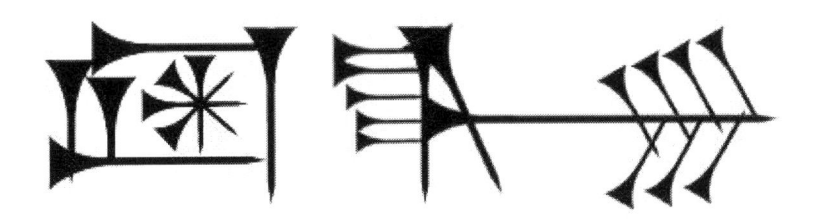

Ina Tilmara Amargi

Sire – The Charge of Shamsiel

Sepu Ala Ina Nim Kabtu Tia Samsu Tia Ina Gula

Asum Firiq Tia Anki Alka Ahias ma Balu

Bar Dura Salatu Atuku

Nadanu Abarassa Awum. Da Menzug Masgik

Dug Luname E Igigal. E Su.Gaz Zae Alad Tia Shamsiel

Da Menzug Masgik

Alka Ina Annu Sagtak ma Awum

By all the High Glory of Names of the Great

Empowered lord of the Universe, come quickly and without

Barriers, draw together outside powers

Give true communication, make yourself visible

Come through this triangle and converse

Sire

Ina annu bi, E Utu, Nanna, ma Adar

Da annu ina es E, Ma eri ina ina Egura

Dara duttu lu ina annu es anna ina Hursagmu

Through this command. Rise Sun, Moon, and Star

Make this the Temple rise and bind from the black water

Dark one who speaks let through this temple unto the mountain of the sky-chambers

Sire

Alka ina ina gidim quannu duramah, gibil wur, su'ati zae da

Durisam ina karabu ma sibum annu da er ina antam

Come through the spirit horn the great stag, one of fire wisdom, that you make forever this blessing and witness this offering to the universe. Come through and answer this prayer in love and truth. Blood Elders we carry the circle to the chamber of the regions of the four to aid and to let those who enter know you.

Sire sprinkles white salt over the Altar (central altar)

Sire Gi be dag ma dara be ar Night to be Day and Dark to be Light

In the previous generation, you received knowledge as to Lucifer and Satan. In particular; that they are two separate energies. It is time for you to receive further knowledge of the Fallen, on this your Sixth Generation we explore Ophiel, whom is further known as 'Zade'.

Zade (Known as Ophiel and further as Arbatel)

An introduction, a cornerstone to enactment in the Seventh Generation

Zade is the ruler of those things which are associated with Mercury; he gives familiar spirits, teaches all arts, and enables the possessor of his character to change objects and properties into the Philosopher's Stone, a subject area to cover in great length through the generations to come.

The Arbatel Magic, or rather the Magic of Zade has influenced practice of the Arts across the four corners of the Earth. Being of the **Dwellers**, Ophiel has the power to declare destinies, administer fatal charms, and grant safe passage. Although, like many, Ophiel has the power to make change, it is important to recognise that only by decree of Tilmara, should he intervene in the direction of another creature's existence. Therefore, the Dwellers reside over Earth and in particular; seven Chief Dwellers hold the K.e.y Gates, being; from the Alpha of Schin, through to the seventh gate of Beth. Therefore we see the Chief Energies in the following order:

Schin	of Lucifer
Ain	of Satan
Zade	of Ophiel
Daleth	of Mish
He	of Aruru
Cheth	of Phul
Beth	of Phaleg

It is important to note that each of the Chief Energies rules in the solar system of Earth for a period of 490 Earth years, or rather 1,470 Cinak. What is of further interest is that **Zade** is known to possess the K.e.y, and although he is truly the bearer, he is unaware of this attribute. It is only through the guidance and observations of Tilmara, that Zade will come to realise his point and purpose. A creature of meditation and Spirituality, Zade is placed within the realms of the High Chords or perfection. Some say that Zade made comment in recent times as to the purpose of Knights Templar, and that of the Holy Grail:

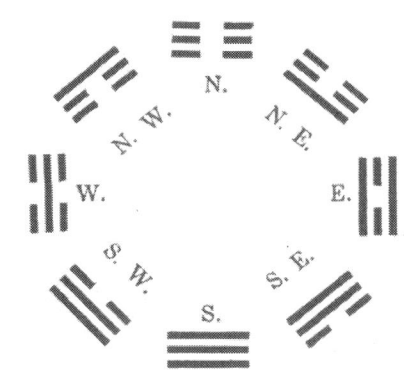

Translation of the First Tablet of Zade

The Holy Grail is that Physical matter which can be transformed molecule by molecule, by the use of incantations. The nature of reality is really an illusion, in that reality should not be this much fun to us, but it just is. Vampires, such creatures of the 'forgotten Knight' have a **Higher Calling**, which shall bee known through a set of magical texts, which have so been given to the Earth creatures by one of the fallen, one of the many.

For you will seek the tree of life from such realms not known through the sacrifice of Blood and the drinking from its source. For I shall,I seek out Cabal, such groups that conspire against the Holy Grail, the tablet of Destinies they so have need of.

Translation of the Second Tablet of Zade

It is time to awaken 'Elia', the masters of wisdom, the creators, and the engineers of the universe, as they come to 'Gartha' (i.e. Earth). In the beginning the engineers task was to prepare the surface of the planet for higher forms of intelligent life and to prepare the reawakening of the Djinn after the explosion that happened on a planet was known as 'Melona', situated between Jupiter and Mars. I Zade, will share the knowledge of those known as 'Traits', for they are incarnate. Such forms of Trait will return to matter, a physical form to further their growth. Each Trait without full realisation, will choose a series of specific life experiences until they reach completion.

In the beginning our Brothers from beyond the stars built cities within the Gartha (i.e. Earth), which was known as the 'Garden of Eden'. All creatures, all colours, and a races contributed with their creation, a biological genesis that it was so to be formed. The engineers, the masters, created one specific creature that would work through all aspects of existence. The Engineer Schin, on Gartha known as Enki created humans in his own image, an image that was formed when Enki morphed into matter, a physical presence. Two types of humans inhabited Gartha, namely; the Immortals and the Mortal creations. It was a necessity to have Humans in line with the plan, to give birth and to grow differing civilisations, which grew, development then fell over many times.

The Guardians of Evolution, called 'Angels', often times referred to as a type of Akhkharu, took power into their own hands, having seen the beauty of the creations that were made. The Angels gave in to temptation and became intimate with the humans they had created. The engineers, in particular Enki, disgusted by the actions of the Angels, left Gartha (left Earth) so that their creations would suffer.

Civa (it is noted that the term Shiva is a dilution of origin) controlled the three heavenly cities on the Earth. In Sanskrit the cities are described as floating cities that travel around the Earth. For Civa and the Engineers lifespan reached 960 years of age, 2,880 Cinak.

The Demi-Gods (the half-human creatures), had been created and now had paranormal capabilities. With their gift of knowledge for magnetism, they were able to heal people with the use of magnetics within stones. This healing act was performed so that Humans could live in peace and harmony, the very purpose of their existence. For if humans had achieved this, then the doors would have opened to a higher perception.

In Atlantis lived the 'Forhrigg' race of creatures, they had acquired the secrets of universal energy. At this time they worked together in harmony, power and love were united and people lived for hundreds of years.

People know nothing of ownership of the Earth as this is forbidden, the Earth is a living organism and humans must be classed as the cells of the organism. There was a time when everyone had everything they needed, no class distinction, they live in abundance and gave to each other. The time will come when history repeats, but only at the End of Days shall the lesson truly be learned. For those who are with us will know the words that follow:

A Gis Uma Bulug Labaru	I will never grow old
A Gis Uma Namus	I will never die

Ritual of Zade (Ophiel, within Mercury)

The ritual of the Spirit of Ophiel, or rather 'Zade' is the second ritual of seven. Although some may find it an oddity to commence with the second ritual, there is point and purpose to such. For it is Ophiel whom will make judgment upon those whom come to pass. There are seven spheres, or rather **seven** gates to pass, so to compete the Circle. This is the first ritual beyond the Moon, beyond Phul.

Starting your work with the Arbatel Magic will make you aware of profound results through communication and relationship with the spirits. Such communication might differ significantly from other experiences. The Arbatel rituals, are all of a evocative nature; using the 'locus of manifestation' for the spirits. I will at this conjuncture, address Ophiel with male gender. This is obviously not correct as he doesn't have a gender – So why refer to this Deity as a 'He' – The simple reason being is that This is the same for every Chief Deity. It is at this point that we make a direct correlation of Deity and Djinn. For Djinn are the possessors of creatures, yet each Deity could be said to be a form of Djinn. This is how those of pure blood, of the Royal blood are able to live for considerable Earth Years. It will be in the form of entity, and thus when challenged, or where there is need, the Highest forms of Spirit will either present as an **'apparition'** or take charge of a **living creature.**
What is interesting to note, is that there are a variety of types of Djinn, some that will exist within, and others that will manifest to be in form of a **Poltergeist**. Then there are those whom are able to stabilise within the living creature, so to prolong its life cycle beyond the natural expectation of its planetary dwelling. There mere basis of transformation is to allow the Demon, or rather the Djinn within to awaken. This is the K.e.y term of a trait, to which a Trait is a distinct line of generations that have passed through from Demi-Gods, those that are Half-human.

Thus the experiments continue to enhance transformations of Traits (i.e. Half-Humans) to evolve where their access to Djinn is paramount. It is said that for the Engineers to alter the genetic sequence of Traits will awaken the Dark Forces of the 'Forhrigg' again; the ideal set for each and every Akhkharu.

The Rite of Zade (The Ophiel Rite)

1) Preparation

The rite of Ophiel is to work with the energies primarily of Mercury. It is generally assumed that the influence of Mercury changes during this rite, so that the Practitioner can utilise either negative or positive aspects to ensure an outcome. **The K.e.y characteristics are**:

- challenges in communication

- challenges in commerce for creating or signing contracts

- likely time for misunderstandings

- likely time for technical problems, with mechanical equipment

- likely time for unforeseen changes to plans

- good time for revision of projects that had been started before

This rite must be completely focussed on the understanding of the **nature of Ophiel** and achieving direct communion with him. It matters not whether Ophiel is quiet, aggressive, or has an indifferent mood, so long as you can achieve some level of communication.

Most of the preparation for this rite must happen on the day of the ritual itself – ensuring that all things are dedicated to Ophiel. These are three K.e.y preparations to complete: the **Liturgy book** (i.e. a set for for religious recognition) , the **Lament** (i.e. An answer to something), and adjusting the altar and temple space to reflect Mercury's influences.

1a) The Liturgy Book

This is the second Arbatel (Ophiel) ritual the liturgy of the rite commences with a basic convoke and prayers. There is further the inclusion of an evocation so to expedite the ritual trance.
What is required to empower the ritual, is for you to use a Liturgy, addressing the spirit directly, praising his might, divine qualities and leadership. A positive approach is to use phrase such as, 'You who are seated on top of the world and judge the universe, surrounded by the circle of truth and honesty.' By this nature, the passage is given:

'Ophiel, I convoke you, Great Spirit, mighty Head, come forth from the circle and the infinite expanse of black sky! You, whose current is flowing through the essence of creation, you are birth and death, you are day and night, powerful Head appear to me now, holy Ophiel! You, O Lord, who imprints himself into the elements of this world like a form into wax, who is blessed by angels, demons and intelligences, appear to me now and answer my questions, great Spirit, mighty Head, Ophiel!'

'Come forth and appear to me, for I am calling you under the protection of the one and only God and speak the name of thy holy rank Ophiel. Powerful one, seated on top of the world and ruling over the universe in your matters, you are surrounded by the circle of truth and honesty, come forth and appear to me, Ophiel. O Lord, Eternal One, who existed before fire and wind, before water and soil, come forth and appear to me, for I call thee by the name of your holy rank Ophiel.'

'Powerful One, whose name I wear on my heart, whose name is mighty and powerful, who changes destinies and controls the currents of lives! Holy One, seated among the seven holy thrones, who resides on the summit of the sacred Mount, come down, come forth and appear to me! For that I may hear thy sacred voice clear and gentle and receive answers to all my questions.'

'Kiss my mind with your wisdom and kiss my heart with your voice! O Lord, I'll call you in the name of your Holy rank Ophiel.'

It is important to note that you need to strike a balance between making the specific Spirit appear as 'piece of the jigsaw' of creation, while pointing out that there are seven thrones in total and that they rule over the world in their matters.

1b) The Lamen

The Lamen of Ophiel as used in the rite is creating the Lamen in the style. While painting the Lamen on the papyrus listen to some appropriate, inspirational music. Two hours before the planetary hour of Mercury the clock should started ticking and you should feel the usual tension rising just like before any important ritual: at that point your mind must be completely firm like a sailor who knows a storm is coming up but who won't change course. Your heart, however, should be trembling and full of fear of the unknown encounter. The polarity between these different energies in your body almost creates an electric current that turns all your senses internally and allows you to focus on one thing at a time only. This is why it is so important that at this point you have a clear plan and paths through the final ritual preparation and into the ritual itself. The space of organic improvisation only opens again once you have left **Malkuth** behind and arrived in deep ritual trance within the consecrated circle. Take a ritual shower and imagine the water of the seven planets cleansing your physical and astral bodies.

For completeness, here is the ritual structure which will shape your experience:

•Kabbalistic Cross

•Lesser Banishing ritual of the Pentagram

•Welcoming of God in the four quarters of the circle

•Adjusted Hexagram ritual of Mercury

•Gesture of the opening of the veil

•Arbatel prayer for protection of God and consecration of Table of Practice

•Arbatel prayer to God for the appearance of Ophiel

•Evocation of Ophiel

•Communion with Ophiel

- Gesture of the closing of the veil

- Lesser Banishing ritual of the Pentagram

- Ritual license to depart

2) Ritual Description

> 'All things are possible to them that believe them, and are willing to receive them; but to the incredulous and unwilling, all things are unpossible (...)."

2a) Opening

An hour before entering the temple start by lighting a fire to heat up the room.

Enter the temple, wearing your suitable regalia. Take the Lamen and activate it by the use of **Mercurial oil**. Spread oil on the front and backside of the Lamen and massage. You must now 'Blow-down' the candles in front of the black temple veil and enter the circle.

2b) Immersion

Light all the candles in the **inner temple** and stand in the West, facing East so to conduct a qabalistic cross to centre the energies in your body and mind. Take the ritual dagger from the altar and perform the Lesser Banishing Ritual of the Pentagram. Interestingly, when visualizing the archangels instinctively let go of the traditional shapes of their bodies. Allow each quarter and take shape and space in the circle. Immediately each quarter will fill with pulsating and whirring energy.

Call forth God from the four quarters and feel his immense presence outshine the glow of the archangels and shield the ritual space. Now break the charcoal and light each piece over one of the altar candles. As the black powder starts to spark, you will know. Now put the incense of Mercury on the glow and conduct the **gesture of the opening of the veil**.

The next phase is to conduct the adjusted Hexagram Ritual; replace the traditional symbols within the hexagrams with the Sigil of Ophiel. On drawing and invoking the first hexagram, however, something unexpected will happen. After some time you will force yourself to move on.

2c) Communion

Take up the liturgical book and recite the Arbatel prayer to God's blessing and consecration of the Table of Practice. At this point start proceedings for the convocation of Ophiel. Here, you will perceive all shapes and patterns released through your body and you will hear all astral sounds vibrating in the rhythm of the spoken words. So in order to communicate with them it is you who needs to understand the astral language spoken by your body, heart and mind. Raise in your view and realise that the Sphere was the bottom end of a larger geometrical structure which was Ophiel. The shape was made of an octahedron in the middle part which tapered above and below; at the bottom end within my black mirror as well as in the middle of the shape. You may now ask Ophiel your first question on the true name of his Spirit. I may have to repeat it several times until you receive an answer. The presence of Ophiel is the pure opposite of confined space. Here is the style of communication that will take place:

1. By use of shape, by use of the gate below.
2. All electric currents and all gases.
3. Substance in alchemy, governs explosive gases
4. An octahedron tapering above and below

> 'I am the wheel of fire, I am throwing sparks into the night! I am throwing my light into the prism of the Moon, I am the transgression of limits, I am the piercing through the veil, I am all the broken seals. Nothing is darker than silence to me, nothing more agony than stillness. But look, I have my own kind of silence: I am silent and sparks are playing on my hair, I am silent and currents crackle on my skin, I am silent and electricity shoots through my veins and lights up the networks of wisdom and knowledge. I am the perpetual mobile, the machine of eternal movement, I don't need anything except for knowledge to continue to spin... Calling One, become one with cat fur, with copper and glass and I will pierce through you and will take shape within you. But my shape is like an explosion - visible only in one moment before it falls back into darkness, for I am shapeless and living within the shapes of others. I am the gas cloud compressed in the alchemical flask, I am the pressure below the lid. You humans will only know me in pinches, but I hold a world.'

2d) Closing

At some point my body was empty and hollow. I vibrated the name for a final time, bowed and made the gesture of the closing of the veil. While my body was completely exhausted my mind was still electrified. It would have been too easy at this point not to banish but to try to take these energies with my into my daily life. A mistake I have done before - luckily with less powerful spirits.

Thus, I took the dagger and performed the Lesser Banishing Ritual of the Pentagrams. I took time to truly connect with the four quarters and feel the presence and currents of the archangels. Then I uttered the ritual license to depart and finished with a last qabalistic cross.

> 'You should never use the spirit or demon, without depicting the Sigil of the planetary intelligence also on the talisman. On the physical level this would resemble a person who has tremendous energy (spirit), but not knowing (intelligence) how to use it. Such a person can be active but dull like a chicken with head cut off to use an analogy that fits well. Spirit needs a Direction, it needs intelligence.'

3c) Astrological Dependencies

Assuming a strong connection between the Olympic Spirits, i.e. Ophiel and the material realm we need to consider that their influence actually might underlie and depend on general astrological constellations at any point of evocation.

The Legacy

The Sumerians invented writing and were one of the world's first great Civilizations. The civilization flourished in the valleys between the two great rivers Tigris and Euphrates, the area known as southern Iraq today. Their civilization existed for in excess of three thousand years, between the fifth and the second millennium BCE. There is still a very large question as to how a civilisation so advanced practically 'vanished' off the surface overnight. It is further important to note that the Sumerians reached their golden era Three thousand and Two thousand BCE. They invented the wheel, the plough, irrigation systems, sailing boats, the keel, potter's wheel and were the first to build stone arcs and multi-storeys buildings. They had an advanced juridical system, developed mathematics, astronomy and the calendar. Still today our definition of time is based on the original Sumerian number-system based on 6 and 60, and the division of the circle in 360 degrees. However their most important invention would shape the future of this planet in time to come, the specialist art of writing in the fourth century BCE.

The Sumerians wrote cuneiform script with straws from reed on clay tablets, to which hundreds of thousands have been discovered in archaeological excavations. The more of these tablets are found and interpreted, the more of the original stories and motifs known from the Christian Old Testament stories emerges in their original form. Most of the clay tablets are at least a thousand years older than the earliest texts in the Christian Old Testament. The Sumerian culture had a huge impact and formed the casting mould for the later great civilisations.

The Creation Tablet details the story of how man was created from dirt, which has been understood to be a 'clay-type' substance, and brought to life through a breath of air through the nose. Let us recognise that as told in Gen 2,7, is a copy of the far older Sumerian creation myth. The Sumerian legend is preserved as a **seven-tablet epos**, Enuma elish, 'In the beginning'.

The creation of the world

In both the Babylonian and Egyptian creation myth we find the motif of how **once everything was water** and how the Gods create land, rivers, animals and vegetation. In the Babylonian story the giant Marduk fights and conquers the demons of the prehistoric waters, which is an interesting starting point that if Marduk fights the prehistoric water (the Black Water), then are we to assume that Marduk collides with Gartha (i.e. the Earth), so to create land mass?

The most dangerous of the demons is the salt-water demon Tiamat. The word the Bible texts uses for the chaotic prehistoric water, the Hebraic theom, is the very same name. Marduk splits the demons body and creates heaven and earth, and then he organises the stars and creates the moon.

Here we are enlightened that the 'Destroyer' Marduk, collides with the Earth, creates land mass, then forms the Moon from the broken piece of the Earth. Marduk then continues to 'organise' the Stars. An interesting approach to the observations of Earth being moved to its present day orbit. It is further interesting to note how the word 'clay' is used for biological matter. It is said that the god Ea created man out of clay and blood.

The creation of man

In the Bible God actually creates man twice, first in chapter one were he creates man and woman in his own image (Gen 1,27), and then in chapter two were he creates man of dirt (Gen 2,7) and a little later creates the woman from one of the ribs of man (Gen 2,22). It's kind of strange that God creates man after created all the animals in chapter one, but in chapter two he created man before the animals. The reasons here is that history was 'altered' for the purpose of the awakening civilisation. The fact remains that humans were created after animals, leaving the clear recognition that humans were no more than an 'experiment', a test to create a biological computer tthat could physically work and contribute to the 'machine'.

The Sumerian story tells of the god Enki, the god of water and wisdom and one of the central and most popular deities in the Sumerian pantheon, and of the land of Dilmun (in modern time, Bahrain). Dilmun is said to be to the east of Sumer. In the Biblical story the Garden of Eden is situated 'in the east' (Gen 2,8). According to the myth Dilmun is a bright and clean place, without disease nor death, - a land of the living, **a land of the immortals,** as we receive our first acccount of Akhkharu, the first account of Vampires.

However, Dilmun lacks one thing: water. But the water god Enki knows what to do and water is his element, so he creates a river that turns Dilmun into a divine garden with an abundance of fruit trees, flowers and green meadows. Then the great Sumerian mother-goddess Ninhursag enters the picture and creates eight different plants in this divine garden. The creation of these **eight plants** involves an intricate process with births of three generations of goddesses, and the story emphasises that these births are all happening without the slightest pain or discomfort.

Enki wants to taste the fruits of these eight plants and makes his servant Ismud (a god with two faces) collect the fruits and he eats them one by one. This makes Ninhursag furious and she casts a lethal spell over Enki, and then disappears from the scene. Enki then becomes ill in eight different organs or body parts, one for each fruit. Enki's condition is rapidly deteriorating, and the other gods are flabbergasted by this and do not know what to do to help the popular Enki. Finally **a fox gets Ninhursag to come back**, exactly how is unknown because this part of the story is missing.

Finally Ninhursag comes back and she places Enki between her legs and asks him in what body parts he is ill. Then she creates **eight healing goddesses**, one for each body part, and soon Enki is well again. One of the sick body parts is the ribs, and in Sumerian the word for rib is 'ti'. The goddess created to heal Enki's rib is called 'Nin-ti', which means the 'rib woman'.

The story's emphasis that the births of the creation-goddesses is without any pain or discomfort, is an element we find in Gods punishment of Eve for causing the fall of man: 'I will greatly increase your pains in childbearing; with pain you will give birth to children" (Gen 3,16).

The very name 'Eden' is also originally a Sumerian name and simply means 'plain/flat terrain'. The name originates from the controversy between the Mesopotamian city-states Lagash and Umma about whom should rule the fertile river-valley of Gu-Edina (The banks of Eden) located between the two cities.

The Great Flood

The Sumerian/Mesopotamians and Egyptians relied heavily on the fertile river valleys, the rivers were the very lifeblood of these cultures, the very foundations of existence. The yearly flooding of the rivers was crucial for agriculture and crops. If the flooding is too small or do not happen one year, famine, hunger and crisis is the result. If the flooding is too big, the fields, cities, granaries are destroyed and irrigation systems clogged, and the society faces a catastrophe.

Destructive Floods were relative common in Mesopotamia, and the rivers and the deities associated with them were central to these religion. The concept of a devastating great flood as the divine punishment of a displeased God is also very common in these cultures.

Many of the clay tablets with this focus are now in Museums. There exist several versions of the Mesopotamian myth of the great flood, all far older than the biblical version.

The rivers of the Tigris, the Euphrates and the Nile evidently caused many great floods, so the background of the Mesopotamian myth is based on real events.

Like all nature religions, natural disasters were considered as an act of God to punish his subordinates into obedience. The story of Cain and Abel can also be found in myths from old Sumeria together with many others. Since the Sumerians were the first literate civilisation, their myths and stories were written down, copied and became known over huge parts of the Middle East. Comparing the stories on the excavated clay tablets with the biblical stories, the similarities are quite obvious. The biblical texts were written late in antiquity, and the writers were inspired by, and building on an already rich source of stories, myths, religious motifs and history from the surrounding high cultures.

Actual historical events and figures were transformed and over time took on a mythical form. The biblical story of the tower of Babel (Babylon) is such a story. In this story all the people of Babel talked the same language, but when the people tried to build a tower into the heavens, God got annoyed and confused the people's language so no one understood each other. As a consequence the whole building project failed. The story relates to the real 90 meters tall tower Etemananki of Babylon.

When Jerusalem was conquered by king Nebuchadrezzar the Second, in 597 BCE, he overthrows the Jewish king Jeconiah. Ten years later, in 587 BCE, there was a Jewish uprising, and Nebuchadrezzar then levelled Jerusalem and brought part of the Jewish elite back to Babylon as hostages. The capital of Babylon controlled the trading routes and was the centre for trade and culture in this mighty and influential empire. Babylon was a melting pot of people and many different languages were spoken. The Jewish elite stayed in Babylon from 886 until 839 BCE, and reminiscences of it is found in Hymns verse 137 and the prophet Daniels stories of king Nebuchadrezzar (Dan 4,33).

Continue with the Legacy commitment

Raising your energy, increasing your vibration
This practical is for raising your energy and vibration, so to perform with clarity

Guidance:

1. You will need white salt to seal your Sacred Space
2. Place a receptacle in the centre of the space
3. Four Candles of wisdom to be placed at the centre around your personal Nunki, your personal Garnet (Sphere of L.i.g.h.t). These can be candles or tea lights
4. Rosemary for your receptacle
5. Lavender for the Master
6. Two pieces of Garnet representing Habesha and Tilmara
7. Water for Blessing
8. Salt, Sugar, and Ground Rose Petal pre-mixed

    (to represent the Architect, God, and Universal Goddess)
9. The Symbol of Zade, a plaque, drawing, or carving
10. Your quarter sigils for use within the rite for containing energy
11. Your Sibbu Usbar (i.e. Snake Staff) and Energy Raiser for vibrations
12. Chalice with Holy Water, three pieces of Nunki (i.e. Garnet), and your personal piece of Garnet
13. A small amount Red Wine & a small container of additional White Salt for essence

**Sprinkle White Salt around the Sacred Space, and
then light the four inner candles**

Place your Sibbu Usbar and Energy Raiser at each side of the Sphere of L.i.g.h.t, your Sibbu Usbar must be placed on the side of your dominant hand.

This will Generate a universal existence

Place a piece of Nunki into each of your hands, grasp the stones then bring your grasped hands together, with knuckles outwards.

Close your eyes and take long, deep, slow breaths as you focus in your minds eye upon the sphere (of L.i.g.h.t) placed within the centre of knowledge (Pure L.i.g.h.t to start the Opening Phase)

commence the opening phase of the raising chant collective, at low breath – The Phase of peace, and continue this until it feels linked in time: **Inimdug** Chant (Peace)

Now focus upon the sphere of time, **the four great lights within the centre of your space,** then start the blood and bone chant whilst stationery:

First-Phase Chant:
Uri ma Esentu, Uri ma Esentu
Ala ina Ara Mupad Kima esdu
Blood and Bone, Blood and Bone
All in time to invoke as one

Place your two pieces of Nunki within the Central Sphere, upon the floor, next to your staff
Make your hands into the 'Great L.i.g.h.t' – as previously instructed:

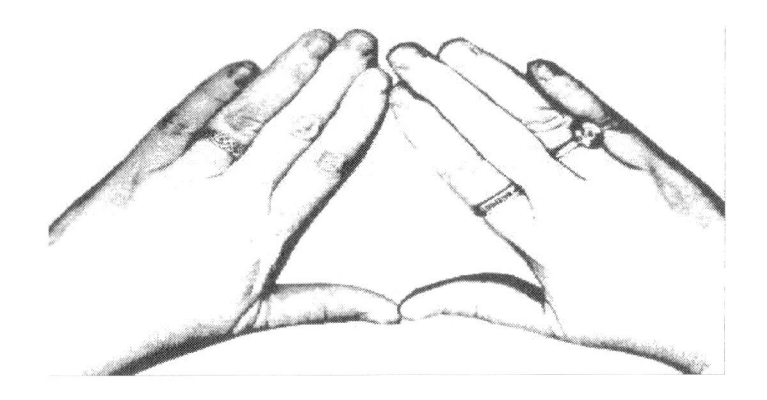

Commence the second phase of the opening, and as you
are knelt facing the Sphere of L.i.g.h.t, begin to raise your arms
towards the sphere whilst chanting:

Second-phase Chant:
Ki ma An, Ki ma An
Eri kima ana, Da gar Sargad
Earth and Sky, Earth and Sky
Bind as one, with four worlds

Now lower your arms and collect your white salt containers, and with the third-phase of the chant – Cast your White Salt upon the Sphere of L.i.g.h.t:

Se tia Atuku

Collect your Sibbu Usbar – and point at the Sphere, collectively travel
widdershins around the Sphere, with the Chant

Third-Phase Chant:
Se tia Atuku (At-Uk-U)

Cone of Power
Collect your Energy Raiser and Sibbu Usbar

Now use your Sibbu Usbar and Energy Raiser for for a minimum of
2 minutes, either in a stationery position, or travelling widdershins (i.e. anticlockwise) around your Sphere of L.i.g.h.t, then place both to the floor as they were before.

You will need the use of your Seventh Heaven chart:

The Seven Heavens

Symbol	Heaven	Angel	Letter
Sameth	1st Moon	Gabriel	Sameth
Nun	2nd Mercury	Rapahel	Nun
Mem	3rd Venus	Anael	Mem
Lamed	4th Sun	Michael	Lamed
Iod	5th Mars	Sammael	Iod
Tau	6th Jupiter	Sachiel	Tau
Kuff	7th Saturn	Caffiel	Kuff

Each symbol will be required as offerings to your receptacle

I ask Gabriel (Legba / Rakbu), Guardian of the Barrier: Protect from malevolent spirits and guide me to the answers I seek

Burn the Sigil of Gabriel inside the receptacle – Then sprinkle Salt upon it

I give praise and thanks to the Master of the Swamp Raphael (Nabu)
Burn the Sigil of Raphael inside the receptacle – Then sprinkle
Lavender upon it

Blessed am I to be within the entrance, In the name of Anael
(Damballah Wedo, Ilu), (Damballah) Anael the great, Anael (Damballah)
Lele, Ayida Wedo, Ago, Ago si, Ago La
Burn the Sigil of Anael inside the receptacle – Then sprinkle
Salt upon it

I call Michael (Mulan, Agwe), Ansar (Ayizan), and the Hidden Knowledge
(Baron Samedi) to this space to provide insight to me
Burn the Sigil of Michael inside the receptacle – Then sprinkle
Rosemary upon it

I call Sammael (Nammu, Erzuli, Ilu, Damballah, Amalug, Ayida Wedo)
to this space to provide protection from within and without
Burn the Sigil of Sammael inside the receptacle – Then sprinkle
the 'combined potion' (Salt, Sugar, and Rose Petal) upon it

By the Power of the guardian of the crossroads, (St. Anthony of
Padua, Legba Atibon, guardian of the crossroads), Sachiel (Rakbu, Legba)
guardian of the bush, Sachiel (Legba) guardian of the goose;
Ago, Ago, Si, Ago La
Burn the Sigil of Sachiel inside the receptacle – Then sprinkle
Salt upon it

Gator Geude, le bon ton roulette, ye, ye, ye

By the power of Tilmara (Erzuli):

Mamou lade, mamou Vodun, Erzulie Frieda Dahomey, Ago,
Ago, Si, Ago. Mamou lade, vie en cane Creole
Be Gone Loa, with peace in mind, I ask Gabriel (Rakbu, Legba), Guardian
of the Barrier to protect from malevolent spirits and close this Veil

Cast such words around:
Suak Kilan sat mal
Gehak set lul Mait Sa
Gebrenak sactulik Kab

Extinguish the Central Candles
Extinguish the Central Altar

M L E

Red Dragon Spirits and Energy Combat

As a crucial element of your ongoing development is to receive your first insight into Dragons, so to prepare you for the Dragon Temple Rites. It is important to note however, that the basis of this brief introduction must not be taken too literally. In time, you will learn the art of the Dragon, and in particular; working to assist you with your combat training.

The methods of the Red Dragon can be evil, interested only in the well-being of their followers, themselves, vanity and the extension of their treasure hoards by the volume of the Hunt. They are supremely confident of their own abilities and are prone to making snap decisions without any forethought. They are the most powerful and are able to create a cone of fire. Red Dragons are the most fearsome and cruel when they choose to be. They delight in ruin, death, and destruction of their enemies and those whom do not conform to their ways and beliefs.

Red dragons are physically distinguished by their enormous wingspan. They have two large horns upon their heads, which point backwards toward their wings. They smell of smoke and sulphur when in a defence and challenging mode. Do not forget that they are able to create fire, but further able to blend water for the purpose of 'Pure L.i.g.h.t'.

They often make their homes in mountainous ranges. Many prefer to dwell in volcanoes, where the intense heat keeps others at bay. They prefer their Sanctuary to be hidden as much as possible, and when within their own domain (i.e. own space), continue to plan the change in evolution. The purpose of the Red Dragon is to have a high perch, a place where they feel in control of their environment, and only when this is achieved will seek comfort in knowledge, by teaching those they consider to be their children.

The bonding of creatures is paramount within their existence. Each Red Dragon must mate as many times as possible, either with the same creature or a multiple volume of creatures. The more power a Dragon has is considered worthy of mating with.

Red Dragons believe that they are the centre of existence itself and that all other species are impure. They value vengefulness, rapaciousness, avarice and ferocity above other traits and recognise these traits in themselves with pride. They always seek information of other red dragons in their area, for a Dragon's Territory is their own domain.

If they believe their own achievements and possessions to be greater than these other red dragons then they stay in their caves, smugly congratulating themselves but if they learn that the achievements or possessions of the other red dragons are greater than their own they will fly into a vengeful rage, decimating the surrounding area until they believe that they have outdone their rivals. The dragon becomes much less cautious during this time and much more likely to underestimate their foes.

Unfortunately, red dragons can go to extreme lengths to ensure that every other red dragon in the area knows that they are inferior to the red dragon spreading the news. They will often burn down only half a village or let a single adventurer flee from a battle so that word of their power spreads throughout the region. Not only will this anger other red dragons but it is also like a shining beacon to those who hunt them.

If a red dragon ever finds out that another red dragon has 'diminished', either by getting badly wounded or if they are becoming too old in their current form to defend, then local red dragons will descend on the lair, stripping it clean and usually killing the owner. They despise the thought of weakness in any red dragon and believe that if a red dragon cannot protect what it has, then it doesn't deserve to have it. They are highly territorial. Entering an area a red considers its domain is just asking to be attacked, especially if it is another dragon entering the area, greater the damage if it is another red dragon.

Conflict is inevitable if this is the case and it is almost always to the death as neither would dare show weakness to the other. Thankfully, most other species are smart enough to flee if they realise the area belongs to a red dragon. Red dragons can get so territorial that in rare occasions they will adopt a protective attitude towards creatures they consider inferior that live within their self-imposed borders.

Red dragons hate silver with a passion as their familiarity with the element of cold and other natural powers often make red dragons appear weak in battle with them.

They also commonly come into conflict with copper. Above all though, red dragons love gold. Red dragons may loudly proclaim that they would fight and defeat any carrier of gold that they come across but often find an excuse not to fight when that time eventually comes. Gold is so similar to red dragons in genetic properties, yet their natural disgust is extreme, however in most battles with gold carriers the red dragons achieve victory.

Red dragons hate any authority other than their own. They never ask elders for advice, even if doing so would save their lives as to them, admitting they need something their elders have is the same as putting themselves under their authority.

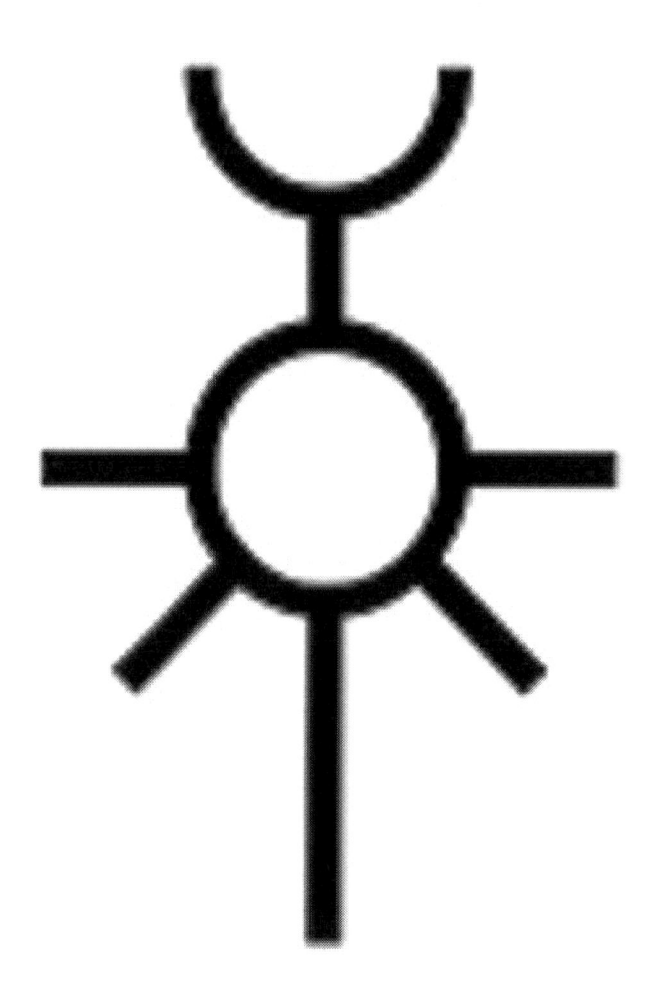

The Power of Practice

The universe is a fluid, ever-changing energy pattern, not a collection of fixed and separate things. What affects one thing affects all things, like ripples in the multi-verse. All is interconnected into the continuous spiral of magical practice. Its patterns are energy, which is the essence of magic.

Energy is ecstasy, when we drop the barriers and let power pour through, it floods the body, pulsing through every nerve, arousing every artery, coursing like a river that travels through on a continuous pattern. In the eye of the storm, we rise on the winds that soar through our mind and body, throbbing a liquid note as the voice pours out shimmering waves of golden light. No drug can take us so high; no thrills pierce us so deep because we have felt the essence of all delight, the heart of joy, the end of desire. Of all the disciplines of magic, the art of moving energy is the simplest and most natural. Picture the power in motion, and it moves, feel it flowing, and it flow. Practitioners conceive of the subtle energies as being, to a trained awareness, tangible, in other word, visible. We can learn to sense them and mould them into form.

A Practitioner's power of changing and convoking can shake the balance of the world, such power can be dangerous. It must follow knowledge and serve need. To light a candle is to cast a shadow. Energy is constantly in motion, it cannot be stopped. Energy flows in spirals. No form of energy can be exerted indefinitely in one direction only; always it will reach a peak, a point of climax, and then turn.

An important aspect of this movement is grounding the energy after it is raised, consciously recognising its fall as well as its peak, and returning it to the earth, its elemental source. Nature knows best. **Magic is part of nature**; it does not controvert natural laws. Magic is an art and a discipline, which demands work, practice and effort before it can be perfected.

In rituals, energy raised is most often moulded into the form of a cone, the Cone of Power. The base of the cone is the circle of the practitioners; its apex can focus on an individual, an object, or a collectively visualised image. At times, the cone is allowed to rise and fall naturally, as in a power chant. It may also be sent off in a burst of force. Rhythm, drums, and dance movements may also be used in building the cone. The energy can be also be moulded into other forms, for example, a fountain, that rises and flows back on the conveners, a wave form, or a glowing sphere.

Practitioners conceive of the energy as an energy field, which surrounds and interpenetrates the physical body, and which sustains us. We feed off it, and its movement through our body appears as a blue glow. Animals, plants, clean air and water, physical exercise, and sex increase vital energy. Magic uses a great deal of vital energy, and anyone who practices magic regularly must take care **not to become depleted**. Beings outdoors, consciously making contact with nature and the elements, also restores vitality.

Grounding before every magical working or psychic exercise prevents us from becoming depleted. Instead of draining our own vitality, we tap directly into the unlimited sources of elemental energy in the earth. Power flows through us, not out of us. When we invoke the Old Gods in rituals, we connect with this energy, that connection is the heart of the greater magic, of mystical ecstasy. Awareness of energy is awareness of the great dance of the universe. Awareness of your own energy is the awareness that flesh and spirit are one.

The universe is a dance of energy, **a uni-verse, a single song of ever-changing rhythms** and harmonies. Sustaining the melody of the physical world is a rich interplay of counterpoint and descant. Power is latent in the body and may be drawn out and used in various ways by the skilled, but unless confined in a circle it will be swiftly dissipated. Hence the importance of a properly constructed circle.

Power seems to exude from the body via the skin and possibly from the orifices of the body; hence you should be properly prepared. The slightest dirt spoils everything, the attitude of the mind has great effect, so if you are intoxicated or confused, even slightly, you cannot control the power you evoke. The simplest way is by dancing and singing monotonous chants, slowly at first and gradually quickening the tempo, until giddiness ensues. The calls may be used or even wild and meaningless shrieking produces power, but this method inflames the mind and renders it difficult to control, though control can be gained through practice. The scourge is a far better way, for it stimulates and excites both body and soul, yet one easily retains control.

When we're in good health, our bodies are capable of producing tremendous amounts of this energy, it derives from the earth, for our bodies transform food, sunlight, fresh air and water into available power, normally we use this energy to maintain good health and for such daily activities as exercise, work, sleep, study, thought, play and sex. In magic we transfer some of this energy to other purposes.

The Cone of Power:

This was the old way for many, yet basic within its function. The circle was marked out and people stationed to arouse dangers. A fire or candle was within it in the direction where the object of the rite was supposed to be. Then all danced round until they felt they had raised enough power. If the rite was to banish they started deosil and finished widdershins, so many rounds of each. Then they formed a line with linked hands and rushed towards the fire shouting the thing they wanted. They kept it up till they were exhausted or until someone fell in a faint, when they were said to have taken the spell to its destination. Thankfully, times have changed and the human species has continued to evolve and receive knowledge of the higher levels of Magical Practices. With such attributes in mind, we exist safe in the knowledge that those whom value our beliefs, those who choose to live their lives by 'Akhkharu Sum.di'; Vampiric Law, are able to reach beyond the stars in their thinking, with pure knowledge of those whom awake.

By the Name of Names, I powerfully call upon you to rise. You of mighty spirits that dwell in the Great Abyss.

In the dread and potent name of Tilmara come forth and give power unto this blade of ancient.

By the Star, I convoke you One of the Creator, by Kabunak, I call the Ifrit, and in the Vast and Terrible Name of the Black Sun that Crumyar uttered and the mountains shook. I compel you forth and visit me! aid me! give power unto my spell that this weapon that bears the runes of fire receive such virtue that it shall strike fear into the hearts of all , and that it shall assist me to form all manner of Circles, figures and sigils necessary in practice.

In the Name of Great and Mighty Ferengi and in the sign.

Give power! Give power! Give power!

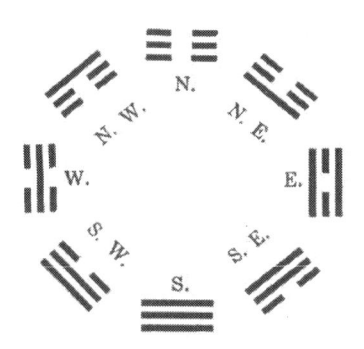

The Tablet must be divided and placed upon the floor at the correct directional points. A Tea Light in the Centre and a Receptacle for offerings

Continue by giving your inner-self to Tilmara

1. Commence with Holding hands in the 'Inner Shape' and Grounding
2. Commence Widdershins (Anticlockwise) with 'Uri ma Esentu' chant
3. Each Participant must Read Akhkharu First and place offerings
4. Then read the entire verse of Modern tongue
5. There must be the SIGN central with the Offering receptacle on top
6. At the final participant calling, place 'leavers' item in receptacle and burn

My Blood, Your Blood	Enmu Uri, Ziud Uri	Prick finger, pour wine
My Hair, Your hair	Enmu Kanubi, Ziud Kanubi	Cut Hair, add rose stalk
From time to shore	Ina Adannu er bal.bal.e	Add lavender
From time to bind	Ina Adannu er Eri	Add rosemary
From wooded lands	Ina Gipar Gal	Light tea Light
From wooded time	Ina Gipar Adannu	--------------------------
To hat and toad	Er Niserin ma Katak	--------------------------
To Rat and Beast	Er Mung ma Kish	--------------------------
From Panthers jaw	Ina Urasag Tulla	--------------------------
To ruling East	Er Meslim Enim	Add salt
I convoke you, I convoke thee	A Gurus Zae, A Gurus Din	--------------------------
To speak of truth	Er Dug Tia Zid	--------------------------
On wisdoms be	Es Namzu Dug	Add sugar
Four by Four and Six by Nine	Gar Gas Gar ma Sessum Gar	--------------------------
Return the truth from this to mine	Urra Ina Zid Ina annu Er Mashu	--------------------------
Forsaken others, forsaken life	Enmer Din , Enmer Ti	--------------------------
Forsaken for moments passing strife	Enmer Mas Akiti Anki Ensik	Add chilli
For Head and Bone	Kar Sag ma Esentu	--------------------------
From blood of thee	Ina Uri Tia	--------------------------
From toe to mind	Ina Zhi Er Tur	--------------------------
doth come to see	Lil Alka Er Igi	Add orange
For dark and bound	Kar Dara ma Indub	--------------------------
For certainty	Kar Duku	--------------------------
Within the Land	Ina Ina Sum	--------------------------
Within the tree	Ina Ina Armanu	Add

e-nu-ma e-liš la na-bu-ú šá-ma-mu when the sky above was not named, šap-liš am-ma-tum šu-ma la zak-rat and the earth beneath did not yet bear a name, ZU.AB-ma reš-tu-ú za-ru-šu-un and the primeval Apsû, who begat them, mu-um-mu ti-amat mu-al-li-da-at gim-ri-šú-un and chaos, Tiamat, the mother of them both, A.MEŠ-šú-nu iš-te-niš i-ḫi-qu-ú-ma Their waters were mingled together, gi-pa-ra la ki-is-su-ru su-sa-a la she-'u-ú and no field was formed, no marsh was to be seen; e-nu-ma dingir dingir la šu-pu-u ma-na-ma when of the gods none had been called into being.

Allow the receptacle to burn out, once closed, raise your hands into the air and say:

Ina Tilmara Amargi

The Advancement of Truth

This will be your final foundation in preparing for your Seventh Generation. It is an expectation that you will research for proceeding brief collection of information, so to achieve greater understanding within your net Generation.

For hundreds of years many lies have been told about the Gods. As we are very aware, the majority of such lies are to control the many, a control maintained by the few. It is interesting that those whom profess to be experts, those whom profess to have inner knowledge of the past, generally ill-inform the majority so to maintain the 'status quo' – To ensure that the majority conform to their ideals, their beliefs. It is with such a subject area that we stumble upon the aspect of God. It is so fascinating that this world has all believe that Lucifer is the enemy in all matter in space and time, yet some of us exist in the knowledge of truth. A truth that is intended to be revealed to those whom seek and those whom evolve.

Always remember that If you need to speak with a G.o.d, please make sure you do so out of respect. When giving an offering to a G.o.d remember this is not a human or sacrificial offering in any way, these are things like poems, songs, music you have made, candles, pictures, incense, and ideas. The Gods are currently very busy with preparation for the coming years so please try to keep calling upon the Gods down to when it is needed, the Gods are happy to help but prefer to wait until they are needed. Those who wish to speak to a God but are not yet dedicated should try to speak with Enki only, always busy but has some faithful soldiers doing his work which frees him up to help where he can.

Each God has their own personality and some are less likely to have a good mood when called so be wary of who you choose to call and make sure you have an appropriate offering or gift, there are also some who you should not attempt to communicate with, these will be listed in a section below. Very Important: When calling a God NEVER demand anything, ask with respect and give an offering, making a demand is very disrespectful.

The Gods The K.e.y Four

Enki

Enlil

Astaroth

Azazel

Teaching of Language and Music:

Agares, Alloces, Amdusias, Amy, Andrealphas, Valefor, Asmodeus, Barbatos, Bifrons, Buer, Camio, Flauros, Foras, Khepera, Procel

Help with Family Matters and Reconciliation of Friends:

Agares, Aini, Amon, Amy, Andrealphas, Andromalius, Asmodeus, Barbatos, Bathin, Belial, Bifrons, Botis, Buer, Camio, Dantalian, Eligos, Flauros, Khepera. Procel

Knowledge and Understanding

Aini, Amon, Amy, Asmodeus, Balam, Barbatos, Bathin, Bifrons, Botis, Buer, Camio, Foras, Lucifuge Rofocale. Procel

Energy and Revenge:

Agares, Aini, Alloces, Andromalius, Asmodeus, Bifrons, Procel

Healing:

Amon, Valefor, Buer, Camio

Provide Familiars:

Alloces, Amdusias, Amy, Belial, Buer

A

Abraxas, Agares, Aini, Alloces, Amdusias, Amon, Amy, Andrealphus, Andromalius, Asmodeus, Astaroth, Azazel

B

Balam, Barbatos, Bastet, Bathin, Belial, Bifrons, Botis, Buer, Bune, Byleth

C

Camio

D

Dantalian

E

Eligos, Enki, Enlil

F

Flauros, Foras

K

Khepera

L

Lillith, Lucifuge Rofocale

P

Procel

V

Valefor

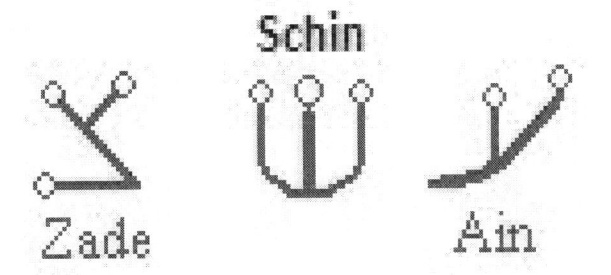

Zade Schin Ain

The Fledgling now goes to the Altar, focuses upon their vital energies and channels such energy into the wine filled chalice, the Sire then undertake the same.

The Chant of Ea

The Fledgling now stands at the Altar of Ea, looking inwards from the West to the East, and speaks the words:

Bag.abi Laca Bach.abe, Lamc cahi ac.haba.be, Karrel.yos, Lamac Lamec, Bach.al.yas, Cab.ah.agy sab.al.yos, Bar.yo.las, Lag.oz at.ha cab.yol.as Sam.ah.ac et fam.yol.as, Har.rah.ya

Both Fledgling and Sire take energy from the 'Cup of Life'

The closing and departure of Energies

(Sire will be at the alter and guard well the Circle of duality, with the Sibbu Usbar in hand to say these words)

Sire O spirits of Shamsiel, because thou hast diligently answered, I do hereby recognise and accept thee to depart, without injury to man or beast. Depart, and be thou willing and ready to come, whensoever duly exorcised and con red by the sacred rites of the Old Ways, the Dark Knowledge. I conjure thee to withdraw peaceably and quietly, and may peace continue forever between me and thee. **Mak Alam Mas Alam**

All candles are extinguished and the Sibbu Usbar (Snake Staff) is set to the ground to discharge.